CULTURALLY RESPONSIVE LEADERSHIP IN HIGHER EDUCATION

Rapidly changing global demographics demand visionary, collaborative, and culturally appropriate leadership practices on university campuses. In the face of widening gaps in academic achievement and socio-economic roadblocks, *Culturally Responsive Leadership in Higher Education* offers a new vision of leadership, where diversity is transformed from challenge into opportunity. This book offers a range of perspectives from culturally, racially, linguistically, ability-, and gender-diverse contributors who demonstrate that effective leadership springs from those who engage, link theory to practice, and promote access, equity, and educational improvement for underserved students. Each chapter explores a critical higher educational leadership issue with feasible strategies and solutions. In this exciting book, theory and research-based chapters unpack culturally responsive leadership, revealing how higher education leaders in the U.S. and international contexts can improve their practice for social equity and educational change.

Lorri J. Santamaría is Associate Professor of Educational Leadership and Head of the School of Learning, Development, and Professional Practice at the University of Auckland, New Zealand.

Andrés P. Santamaría is Lecturer in Educational Leadership for the School of Education at Auckland University of Technology, New Zealand.

CULTURALLY RESPONSIVE LEADERSHIP IN HIGHER EDUCATION

Promoting Access, Equity, and Improvement

Edited by Lorri J. Santamaría
and Andrés P. Santamaría

NEW YORK AND LONDON

First published 2016
by Routledge
711 Third Avenue, New York, NY 10017

and by Routledge
2 Park Square, Milton Park, Abingdon, Oxon, OX14 4RN

Routledge is an imprint of the Taylor & Francis Group, an informa business

© 2016 Taylor & Francis

Library of Congress Cataloging-in-Publication Data
A catalog record for this book has been requested

ISBN: 978-1-138-85479-6 (hbk)
ISBN: 978-1-138-85480-2 (pbk)
ISBN: 978-1-315-72077-7 (ebk)

Typeset in Bembo
by Apex CoVantage, LLC

In loving memory of Kelle Rae Johnson LeDuff. My dear sister, our friend, loving mother, dedicated wife, awesome auntie, respected teacher, and applied critical leader in her own right. May her legacy continue to inspire the next generation as we move forward in this life.

L.J.S. & A.P.S.

CONTENTS

ACKNOWLEDGMENTS

We pay special tribute to each and every one who unconditionally contributed their heart, wisdom, and experience toward the writing throughout this project. The contributing authors represent different facets of our personal and professional journey in academe, from former secondary school students we have mentored who are now postgraduate students at research-intensive universities; to colleagues who completed their doctoral studies in the U.S. as they transcended barriers within higher education contexts; and to our peers spanning international contexts to Canada, South Africa, Australia, and Aotearoa New Zealand, where they engage in and advocate change for social justice and equity. Through relationship, trust, *aroha* (love), and hope, we have joined hands to strengthen our own and others' voices to reshape the lived experiences of those who are impacted by systems of priviiege, tradition, and ignorance. May our collaborations and partnerships further be fortified as we continue to answer the call of change for the greater good.

We would also like to give thanks to Heather Jarrow (our Routledge editor), Lincoln I. Dam, and Deirdre Coleman for their time and support throughout the editing process to help shape and refine this contribution to the field of education.

To our family, especially our children, Kenya and Andrés, we are deeply grateful for your love and inspiration. You provide the purpose within our work.

FOREWORD

When sharing thoughts about education systems of institutions of higher learning, it seems appropriate to first set the contextual relationship with the PreK–12 (pre-school to high school) system. One might consider the relationship to be a natural progression of learning events, which is most often the case. National figures in the U.S. suggest that millions of students are at risk of dropping out of school. Data further reveal that many of these students come from groups that are underserved and underrepresented: students of color, high-mobility students (including foster, migrant, and homeless), English-language learners, students with disabilities, and low-income students (Espósito & Normore, 2015). Although progress has been made in advancing equity agendas of access, participation, and academic achievement for individuals with disabilities and/or those from culturally, linguistically diverse, and economically poor backgrounds, significant work remains. This is particularly true in urban settings, which overwhelmingly serve students who are economically poor and culturally and linguistically diverse, and who lag significantly behind their peers in academic achievement. For example, more than ever, schools are enforcing stricter discipline policies (e.g., zero tolerance), which in turn have contributed to the delinquency of minority youth, especially Latino and African American youth, and increased rates of minority incarceration. Minority youth comprise more than 60% of children detained by juvenile justice systems across the U.S. (Espósito & Normore, 2015). These students are more than eight times as likely as their White peers to be housed in juvenile detention facilities. In all but a few cases, these juveniles passed through traditional educational organizations on their way to incarceration. This path is commonly referred to as the *school-to-prison pipeline* and represents a failure of our educational institutions, and our communities, to serve all students in their care. Surely, a moral and ethical imperative, rooted within a social justice framework, exists to ameliorate such failures.

In the field of PreK–HE (pre-school to higher education), we have been struggling under the aegis of education initiative and reform efforts (e.g., Race to the Top), whose signatories and proponents remain buried in abiding and deep-seated assumptions about education and society. McLaren (2015) stated it best: "in the cognitive framework of many of their supporters, if there is a problem with these policies, these problems are simply anomalies; within their cognitive framework, federal educational policies are generally in the best interests of the country and in no way connected to an institutionally based set of power relationships protecting a dominant racial and class hierarchy where exploitation, racism, and inequality are legitimated and encouraged" (p. xiii). This is where *Culturally Responsive Leadership in Higher Education: Promoting Access, Equity, and Improvement* responds effectively. Editors Lorri and Andrés Santamaría break from the compliance of tranquil minds and courageously examine issues that deal with a plethora of challenges to our educational system and its relation to higher education (HE) systems. The editors push us to tackle issues found in HE institutions, their impact on those institutions, and how they feed each other. Chapter authors—who themselves are culturally, racially, linguistically, and/or gender-diverse educational leaders in a variety of positions in HE settings in the U.S., Pacific Islands, South Africa, Canada, Australia, and New Zealand— have framed scholarly arguments around the Applied Critical Leadership (ACL) model, which includes a theoretical framework and research-identified characteristics. The theoretical framework stems from the work of transformational leadership and critical pedagogy through transformative leadership, in addition to critical theory (including critical race, LatCrit, Queer, feminist, and other critical-based frames) through critical multiculturalism.

Recognition that the role of leaders in any organization—particularly in institutions of higher education—is at least in part to advocate on behalf of traditionally marginalized and poorly served citizens implies that traditional hierarchies and power structures must be deconstructed and reconfigured. In this way, they create a new paradigm that subverts a long-standing system that has privileged certain citizens while oppressing or neglecting others. This would mean that HE leaders must increase their awareness of various explicit and implicit forms of oppression. They need to develop intent to subvert the dominant paradigm, act as a committed advocate for educational change that makes a meaningful and positive impact in the education and lives of systemically marginalized and oppressed students, and extend their scope of influence well beyond the walls of their institutions. Given this perspective, educators are potentially the architects and builders of a new social order wherein traditionally disadvantaged peoples have the same educational opportunities, and, by extension, social opportunities as traditionally advantaged peoples (Giroux, 1998).

The achievement of all PreK–HE students must be viewed both as an economic and moral imperative. For example, the majority of the extant educational literature uses the term *Inclusion* to reference the practice of educating students with *identified* disabilities in the general education setting. However, inclusion as we know it today is rooted in a philosophy that emphasizes the uniqueness of all learners, not just students with disabilities. An emphasis on high-quality classrooms and schools that are welcoming and affirming to all students, especially those most at risk for failure, is both a moral and ethical obligation for society and school systems alike.

In this edited volume, readers are encouraged to reflect on critical issues in their higher educational leadership contexts, to develop working action plans to interrogate organizational inequities and their own leadership practices, cultivating courage to interrupt organizational inequities, and tap wisdom to repair inequities in their professional environments. As they engage with and embrace the content of each chapter, they will note the presence of certain characteristics of "willingness" in the voices and leadership approaches of the contributing authors. These include ageism, institutional racism, affirmative action, LGBTQ-ism; dispelling negative stereotypes for groups with whom they identify; adding authentic research-based information to academic discourse regarding underserved groups; a need to honor all members of their constituencies; giving back to the marginalized community with which they identified and that also served to support their own academic journeys; the need to build trust when working with mainstream constituents or partners, or others who do not share an affinity toward issues related to educational equity; leading by what they call "spirit" or practicing a variation of servant leadership; and providing servant leadership for those who work ultimately to serve the greater good. The contributing authors challenge us to consider the changes we need to make, to personally examine how we teach, learn, educate teachers, focus on the strengths of our students and teachers, and ask ourselves difficult questions about why we teach. Often their scholarly voices reveal nuances and attitudes that embody the theory underlying ACL, as well as providing further evidence of the characteristics reflected in their leadership practice and choice of research agenda. Most important, each chapter features a particular critical higher educational leadership issue with feasible strategies, solutions, outlines, and plans that address the myriad challenges associated with diversity, access, educational equity, difference, and power differentials. The contributors make direct and explicit links bridging theory to practice and educational change, thereby resulting in improved understanding of the ACL's application within HE contexts.

The structural crisis of the capitalist system as a whole only exacerbates the challenges articulated and analyzed so meticulously in this important volume by authors who are uniquely adept and positioned in exposing the exploitative privileges at work in institutions of higher education. Education's social and metabolic control over the lives of our students in postsecondary institutions reflects the policies and practices of the capitalist elite who target the most vulnerable populations in the poorest countries by means of austerity programs (McLaren, 2015). We need a sustainable ecology of educational practices that fosters solutions to the crisis of public PreK–HE education today—policies and practices that refuse to squander the lives of our most marginalized.

The editors and authors of *Culturally Responsive Leadership in Higher Education: Promoting Access, Equity, and Improvement* are united in their refusal to let the voices of dissent remain marginalized in our discussion of education in the 21st century. They tackle issues found in both PreK–12 schools in the original volume (L. J. Santamaría & Santamaría, 2012), and postsecondary institutions in the current volume, their impact on both institutions, and how they feed each other. Further, they present ideas for how to change or modify these issues and refuse to disregard the context of the external world when planning and plotting educational reform. The upshot of this work compels us to examine not only how educational policies are produced for the least advantaged in our education systems, but also how educators and students are themselves produced in the wider institutional, cultural, and economic arrangements of society. This book will prove invaluable to all who choose to call themselves educators. It is crafted from the professional experiences, intellectual engagements, and moral commitments of the contributors. It is a work based on the foundation of equity, access, and social justice, via a multitude of lenses used to view and attempt to understand the need for a vested interest in programs and support structures that promote and foster collaboration among those leading and working in education at all levels.

Anthony H. Normore
California State University Dominguez Hills,
California

References

Espósito, M. C., & Normore, A. H. (Eds.). (2015). *Inclusive practices and social justice leadership for special populations in urban settings: A moral imperative.* Chapel Hill, NC: Information Age.

Giroux, H. A. (1998). *Channel surfing: Racism, the media, and the destruction of today's youth.* New York, NY: St. Martin's Press.

McLaren, P. (2015). Foreword. In M. C. Espósito & A. H. Normore (Eds.), *Inclusive practices and social justice leadership for special populations in urban settings: A moral imperative* (pp. xiii–xx). Chapel Hill, NC: Information Age.

Santamaría, L. J., & Santamaría, A. P. (2012). *Applied critical leadership in education: Choosing change.* New York, NY: Routledge.

1

INTRODUCTION

The Urgent Call for Culturally Responsive Leadership in Higher Education

Lorri J. Santamaría and Andrés P. Santamaría

We begin, as we have in the past, with this premise: "It is an undeniable conclusion that the educational system and its partners have failed to produce citizens who can contribute to and benefit from a world that offers enormous opportunity" (Fullan, 2001, cited in Santamaría & Santamaría, 2012, p. 152). As a result, the U.S. and similar nations are plagued by widening gaps in academic achievement, and social and economic opportunity that separate economically disadvantaged, culturally and linguistically diverse learners (e.g., those of African, Latino/a, Indigenous, or Pacific Island descent) in schools from their mainstream, middle-class and often White or European-descent peers (Akiba, LeTendre, & Scribner, 2007). Educational inequities, disparities, uneven access, and exclusion have become the focus of educational leadership attention, energy and fiscal resources (California Department of Education [CDE], 2007; Darling-Hammond, 1999, 2007; Vanneman, Hamilton, Baldwin Anderson, & Rahman, 2009).

Over the last 20 years, much time has been spent identifying and discussing various gaps (e.g., academic, social, economic) that impact systemically underserved students. These disparities have been confirmed by empirical research (e.g., Darling-Hammond, 2007; Vanneman et al., 2009). Yet, within the context of these academic conversations, there have been few scholarly contributions addressing ways in which achievement gaps affect students on college and university campuses, trickling into the national equity agenda designed to protect educational inequities (Nevarez & Wood, 2010, 2014). Although equity and access issues are carried through early childhood education, primary, intermediate, and secondary schools, the educational leadership needs in tertiary settings are specific to the complexities present at that particular level (Middlehurst &

Elton, 1992). These differences may be compounded depending on the type of institution (e.g., community college, polytechnic, research-intensive) under consideration.

Differentiating Educational Leadership in Higher Education

Educational leadership in the academy is conceptualized by Blaschke, Frost, and Hattke (2014) as consisting of "conflictory institutional" ways of supporting organizations encompassing elements of leadership, governance, and management (LGM) (p. 711). These scholars describe ways in which university leadership is shifting from engaging relational and, consequently, more collegial governance patterns to more neo-liberal, business-like ways of management in complementary micro patterns. These micro ways of leading involve leading the scholarship of academic work as well as coordination of courses, people (students and colleagues), and resources in a somewhat contrived and often diverse community within a larger geopolitical community. Equity and access toward improvement are issues that necessitate micro patterns of leadership in order to enact change (Santamaría, 2012, 2014a).

Unfortunately, micro patterns of leadership practice do not feature in research on educational leadership in higher education (HE). This has resulted in a theory-to-practice vacuum in the field regarding what one might consider effective leadership practices in academe (Bryman, 2007; Kezar, 2002). In fact, Blaschke et al. (2014) argue that "there is little explanation of how universities perform their everyday practices of LGM on the micro-level of (inter)actions, let alone face organizational change" (p. 713). In direct response to the lack of information and research on understanding the micro-levels of leadership, governance, and management in tertiary settings, this book provides experiential and often empirical examples of complementary ways of leading. The practices presented here promote equity and access to benefit systemically underserved and, as a result, underperforming students through change in a variety of culturally and linguistically diverse tertiary settings in the U.S., New Zealand, and Australia.

More specifically, this edited book introduces the perspectives of 29 culturally, linguistically, racially, ability-, and gender-diverse scholars and educational leaders from the U.S., Australia, South Africa, Tonga, Samoa, and New Zealand, who each work toward equity, access, and improvement, while serving academic and professional staff leadership roles. Drawing on each author's bird's-eye view and micro-level leadership experience, this volume takes readers from the base of common knowledge about what we know, what we can feasibly do in terms of organizational improvement on an institutional level with our knowledge, and a deeper understanding of racial and cultural inequities. It also aims to communicate actions that we, as critical leaders, can employ to transformatively facilitate authentic change and progress toward re-visioning a strengths-based and improvement-focused equity agenda in HE contexts.

A Question of Power

Currently, educational researchers, leaders, and practitioners in the U.S. and other Western predominantly English-speaking countries are increasingly understanding the need for practical transformative models, frameworks, and theories to address educational disparities resulting in academic chasms (Capps, Fix, Murray, Passel, & Herwantoro, 2005; CDE, 2007; Darling-Hammond, 2007; May & Sleeter, 2010). Research findings indicate that educators are also beginning to understand that unequal distribution of power and cultural capital at institutional levels may very well result in some gaps, particularly at college and university levels (Anyon, 2009; Bailey & Morest, 2006; Capps et al., 2005; Goldenberg, 2008; Lum, 2009; Nevarez & Wood, 2010).

The Evolution of Equity and Access Concerns in Educational Leadership

Over time, educational leadership has evolved as a discipline and come to a 'place' where scholars and practitioners can discuss racial inequality and how it manifests itself in academic achievement and other critical, educationally based gaps with certainty, as a micro-level of leadership. Educators from kindergarten level through higher education (K–HE) in general have come a long way from academic conversations about multicultural education as supplemental curriculum to diversity as something to consider; to education for social justice and equity as necessary for student access to learning; and, more currently, to the common understanding of the need for an equity agenda in order to institute access for student learning and equal outcomes for all students.

Similarly, educational inequality as an issue has moved from a concern, since *Brown vs. the Board of Education*, to take the center of the educational stage with the advent of transparent, accountability-driven data, and, as a result, a growing institutional platform. Preliminary changes are taking place in K–12 education and there are current conversations with regard to graduation initiatives, freshman and transfer success programs, and the like in higher education. However, there are quantifiably fewer critical conversations and leadership initiatives designed to reach and impact learners at the college and university level.

Culturally Responsive Leadership in the Academy

Rather than waiting to hear about best practices from K–12 education efforts or reports on the outcomes from newly instituted graduation initiatives, which will be a long time coming, this book informs educational leaders committed to higher education today about ways to move their institutions and organizations from common knowledge regarding equity agendas and pervasive tertiary achievement gaps, to a place of practical action with immediate applicability, resulting in educational change. This book unpacks and clarifies culturally responsive leadership by building and expanding Gay's (2000; 2010) seminal work on cultural responsivity and Santamaría and Santamaría's (2012) Applied Critical Leadership (ACL) theoretical framework approach, along with related research (Santamaría, 2014b; Santamaría & Jean-Marie, 2014; Santamaría, Santamaría, & Dam, 2014; Santamaría, Santamaría, Webber, & Pearson, 2014). Authors of this volume concur with Johnson and Fuller's (2014) assertion that culturally responsive leadership is "derived from the concept of culturally responsive pedagogy, [and] involves those leadership philosophies, practices, and policies that create inclusive schooling environments for students and families from ethnically and culturally diverse backgrounds" (p. 1). These and other scholars further define culturally responsive leadership as theory and educational leadership practices (e.g., influence, management, administrative) that take into consideration race, ethnicity, language, culture, and gender. These include the emphasis on high expectations for academic achievement; pedagogical and social inclusion of students' history, core values, community, and cultural knowledge; work toward "develop[ing] a critical consciousness among both students and faculty to challenge inequities in the larger society" (Johnson & Fuller, 2014, p. 1); and the institutionalization of organizational structures to empower systemically underserved students, families, and communities (e.g., Agosto, Dias, Kaiza, Alvarez McHatton, & Elam, 2013; Beachum, 2011; Brown, Benkovitz, Muttillo, & Urban, 2011; Riehl, 2000; Santamaría & Santamaría, 2012; Theoharis, 2008). Few scholars have taken a look at what it means to define, unpack, and understand culturally responsive leadership with regard to access, equity, and improvement in academe (e.g., Kezar, 2002).

To this end, chapters in this volume provide further evidence linking culturally responsive leadership to ACL applications and characteristics of educational leaders in HE. This work is substantiated by empirical research and examples provided by those practicing ACL at individual leader levels, micro-levels, and working toward macro-institutional levels. This contribution provides educational leaders, scholars, and practitioners at institutes of higher learning with guidelines and key facilitation processes to re-conceptualize an equity agenda through meaningful structured exemplars and action plans envisaged to fire their communities' perceptions around how racial and cultural inequities contribute to achievement and related gaps. Utilizing the principles of ACL as cultural responsivity and informed purposeful facilitation, these kinds of strategies have the potential to result in the creation of feasible context-specific equity agendas as a response to the kinds of complex inequities that constitute achievement and other gaps in colleges and universities nationwide and worldwide.

Applied Critical Leadership Research in Education: An Overview

Applied Critical Leadership is—*a strengths-based model of leadership practice where educational leaders consider the social context of their educational communities and empower individual members of these communities based on the educational leaders' identities (i.e., subjectivity, biases, assumptions, race, class, gender, and traditions) as perceived through a critical race theory (CRT) or other critical lens (e.g., LatCrit, Queer, Feminist, TribalCrit).*

(Santamaría & Santamaría, 2012, p. 5)

There is scant literature available identifying and celebrating the positive attributes of educational leaders from historically oppressed, underrepresented groups and those who identify with them, and further ways in which these individuals acquire mainstream institutional access to create real change (Jean-Marie, 2006; Jean-Marie, James, & Bynum, 2006). Understanding how principles of transformative leadership, critical multiculturalism, and critical race theory (CRT) interface and intersect is in the nature of how transformative leadership in HE, as a part of powerful equity agendas to address academic and other gaps separating learners, can be re-conceptualized as an innovative idea worthy of exploration.

ACL research was originally conceived as a means to explore and explain culturally responsive leadership practices of historically oppressed individuals who express multiple intersecting self-identities and characteristics ranging from the obvious (e.g., race, ethnicity, linguistic, physical) to the subtle or hidden (e.g., gender identity, HIV-positive, post-traumatic stress syndrome). What we noticed and subsequently documented was that the identity and experiences of diverse educational leaders impacted their leadership practice. Often, this impact was positive and appeared to address the very issues of social justice and educational equity that were being linked to increased academic achievement in K–HE education. Of particular interest was our nascent observation that some individuals who were not from these historically underserved populations (e.g., African, Latino/a, Native American, English-language learner, Lesbian, Bisexual, Gay, Transgender, Queer) sometimes chose to race themselves outside of 'Whiteness' reaching beyond the descriptions of being 'White allies' found in related literature, and choosing to practice leadership through a CRT lens (Brown, 2002; Haney Lopez, 1998; Stalvey, 1989). We maintained that it was easier, and in some cases more natural, for a person of color to adopt this lens. In fact, some White educational leaders, who could also be considered allies, chose to take education for social justice and equity further by actually joining 'us others' in our active interruption of educational inequities, access issues, and various 'gaps.' This resulted in a reversal of some of the institutionalized inequities and access issues in our organizations.

Following our instincts, we sought empirical proof of this phenomenon and thus created a working hypothesis based on previous research, our own professional experiences in educational leadership, and consideration of related literature. The hypothesis was and remains that when leaders of color, otherwise marginalized individuals, or those who may choose to practice leadership through a CRT lens, make leadership decisions, they reflect and draw upon positive attributes of their identities and life experiences within their societal locality, asking themselves questions such as: In what ways does my identity (i.e., subjectivity, biases, assumptions, race, class, gender, and traditions) *enhance* my ability to see other perspectives and therefore provide effective leadership? Hence, what are the affirmative attributes that render me different and unique that might be explored and developed in order to build and improve my leadership practice (Santamaría & Santamaría, 2012, p. xii)? Lived answers to these questions provide the foundation for a different leadership expression or approach more responsive to social justice, educational equity, and educational change for the greater good of all learners, teachers, and educational stakeholders involved (Santamaría, 2014b).

The original ACL research study followed 11 critical leaders for one year. These culturally responsive individuals served in diverse PreK–HE professional leadership roles ranging from Preschool Director to University AVP or Undergraduate Research, and included an elementary school principal, a K–12 district psychologist, and a Pride Center Director. Culturally, racially, linguistically, and gender-diverse participants included two Chicanas (one a Lesbian), one Native American woman, two Latinos, one Jamaican American man, a Japanese Okinawan male, an Arab American woman, and four White women, three of whom, during the course of the study, opted to 'race themselves out of Whiteness'—one claiming her Italian roots, one her stronger identification with the LGBTQ community, and the other with her Jewish heritage. Interviews, observations, and organization documents were analyzed in order to determine whether the 11 leaders exhibited salient characteristics. Since that time, we have engaged self-described applied critical leaders in Aotearoa New Zealand, working in primary, intermediate, and secondary schools and in one university working toward Māori success as Māori (Santamaría et al., 2014).

Findings from these research endeavors provide the framework for this book and indicate that applied critical leaders led in ways that were transformative, counter status quo, and pro social justice, including the promotion of educational equity. The leadership traits and characteristics captured were also markedly and qualitatively different from styles, types, or models described in mainstream educational leadership literature. In Figure 1.1, key transformative leadership principles realized through the application of critical multiculturalism were viewed through the theoretical lens of critical race theory, resulting in ACL (Santamaría & Santamaría, 2012).

What we are finding in expanded iterations of ACL research is that the educational leaders queried are in the process of pushing their professional *thinking about leadership* for social justice toward *thinking about changing leadership practice* resulting in social justice and educational equity (e.g., Santamaría et al., 2014; Santamaría, Santamaría, & Santamaría, 2015). This way of thinking, leading, and acting moves the leader from participating in an intellectual exercise to applying concrete and possibly measureable action. The approach directly links educational leadership theory and critical theory to practice and, therefore, as the authors demonstrate, could very well result in substantive educational change.

The empirical aspect of this edited book aims to further identify culturally responsive characteristics and underscore principles to evidence an alternative dynamic leadership model relevant for higher educational contexts. This dimension builds on models such as transformative leadership (Shields, 2010) and critical multiculturalism (May & Sleeter, 2010) to better understand the leadership practices of individuals of color who also actively lead for social justice and educational equity in the academy.

Chapter authors will frame scholarly arguments concerning culturally responsive leadership around the ACL model, which includes the theoretical framework illustrated (Figure 1.1) and research-identified characteristics.

The chapters in this book are valuable and substantive because each empirically captures and reflects the micro-levels regarding the *how to* or *applied* aspects of critical leadership, which are, as Blaschke et al. (2014) assert, all but absent from mainstream leadership literature focused on higher education.

The ACL model features research findings that identify salient common culturally responsive leadership characteristics present in each of the study's participants at varying levels, which impact their leadership practices and result in more socially just and equitable PreK–HE educational settings (Johnson & Fuller, 2014). More current work has been done in Aotearoa New Zealand, with emergent ACL research being undertaken in Australia. Different contexts where ACL has been found include early childhood education (Santamaría & Santamaría, 2014); special education (Santamaría et al., 2015); health and physical education (Fitzpatrick & Santamaría, 2015); and Māori HE (Santamaría, Lee, & Harker, 2014). Additional research is needed to ascertain whether culturally responsive leadership empirically serves to increase academic achievement, as findings suggest.

Regardless of the educational level or leadership position held, or the country in which leadership was practiced, applied critical leaders each reported:

1. Willingness to *initiate and engage in critical conversations* with individuals and groups even when the topic was not popular for the greater good of the whole group (e.g., ageism, institutional racism, affirmative action, LGBTQ-ism);

2. Willingness to *choose to assume a CRT or critical lens* in order to consider multiple perspectives of critical issues;

3. Use of *consensus building as the preferred strategy for decision-making*; consciousness of "stereotype threat" or fulfilling negative stereotypes associated with their group, working hard to dispel negative stereotypes for groups with whom they identify;

4. Feeling for the *need to make empirical contributions* and, thus, add authentic research-based information to academic discourse regarding underserved groups;

5. Feeling for the *need to honor all members of their constituencies* (e.g., staff, parents, community members);

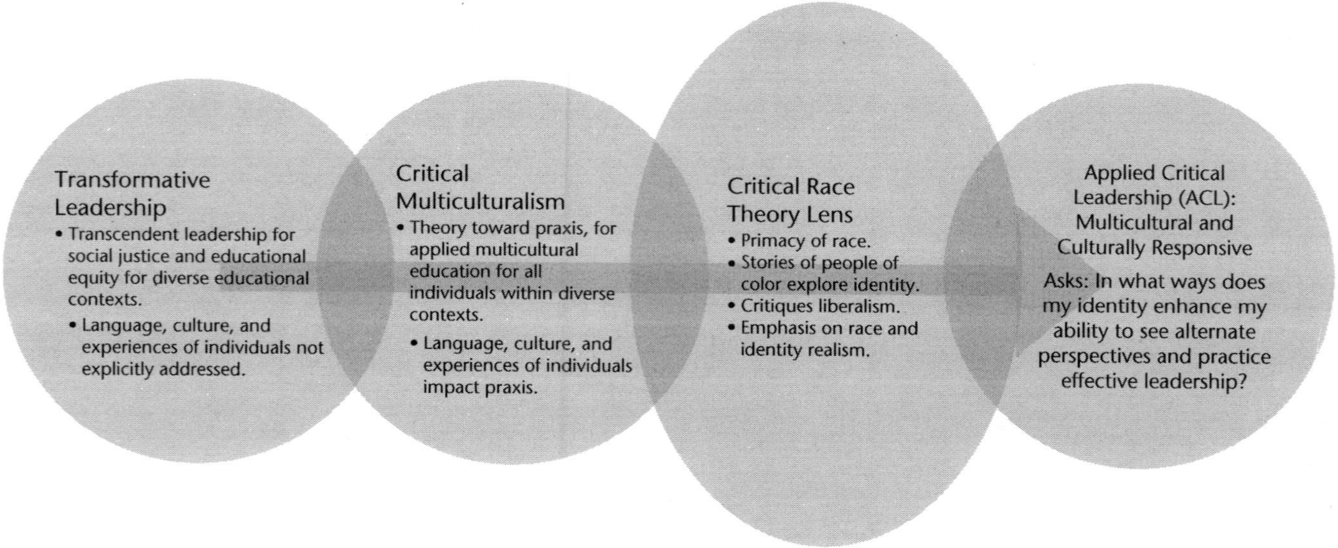

Transformative Leadership
- Transcendent leadership for social justice and educational equity for diverse educational contexts.
- Language, culture, and experiences of individuals not explicitly addressed.

Critical Multiculturalism
- Theory toward praxis, for applied multicultural education for all individuals within diverse contexts.
- Language, culture, and experiences of individuals impact praxis.

Critical Race Theory Lens
- Primacy of race.
- Stories of people of color explore identity.
- Critiques liberalism.
- Emphasis on race and identity realism.

Applied Critical Leadership (ACL): Multicultural and Culturally Responsive
Asks: In what ways does my identity enhance my ability to see alternate perspectives and practice effective leadership?

FIGURE 1.1 ACL Theoretical Framework (adapted from Santamaría & Santamaría, 2012, p. 8)

6. Tendency to *lead by example to meet an unresolved educational need* or challenge *for the purpose of giving back* to the marginalized community with which they identified and that also served to support their own academic journeys;

7. Feeling that it was *their responsibility to bring critical issues* with regard to race, ethnicity, gender, and class *to their constituents for resolution.* If they didn't address issues around race, language, gender, and power, critical issues would not be brought to surface;

8. Feeling for the *need to build trust when working with mainstream constituents* or partners, or others who do not share an affinity for issues related to educational equity;

9. Led by what they call "spirit" or practice a variation of servant leadership, where *expression of leadership practices may be classified as transformative*, servant leadership for those who work ultimately to serve the greater good.

Certainly, as scholars, students, and practitioners delve into chapters in this book, they will note the presence of these characteristics in the voices and leadership approaches of contributing authors. Often their scholarly voices reveal nuances and attitudes that embody the theory underlying ACL as well as providing further evidence of culturally responsive characteristics reflected above in their leadership practice and choice of research agenda. Most important, each chapter will feature a particular critical higher educational leadership issue with feasible strategies, solutions, outlines, and plans addressing challenges associated with diversity, access, educational equity, difference, power differentials, and the like. The authors make direct and explicit links bridging theory to practice and educational change. We are honored to have them with us as we continue our journey to better understand, further develop, and apply the original theory.

Culturally Responsive Leadership in Higher Education: A Blueprint for Promoting Access, Equity, and Improvement

This book further expands the nature of culturally responsive leadership within ACL to HE contexts in particular, where much has been written on leadership practices but little has been written about critical leadership issues with regard to disparities between groups based upon race, class, gender, or other difference of historical and systemic consequence. Further, where there has been much written about leadership theory, there has been little linking those theories to actual practice, particularly in the academy (e.g., Kezar, 2002). Here we intentionally explore culturally responsive aspects of ACL through the higher educational perspectives of (1) interrupting inequities and -isms inherent to higher education, (2) identifying and addressing barriers for historically underserved graduate students seeking leadership careers through doctorate programs, (3) advancing avenues toward higher educational leadership roles, and (4) highlighting instances of institutionalized ACL in a variety of distinct HE settings.

These perspectives provide organization and function as sections with which to divide 15 substantive chapters informing readers about culturally responsive ACL applications in HE. A rarefied consortium of 29 culturally, racially, linguistically, ability- and gender-diverse authors, and practicing educational leaders in higher education contributed chapters that employ a wide variety of research approaches. These range from case study and qualitative research to mixed methods and quantitative methodology complemented by detailed research practice to inform readers about authentic applications of culturally responsive ACL in HE contexts. Previously, these topics have not been adequately addressed nor solutions presented for educational leadership in HE contexts either in the U.S. or in the global arena.

Culturally Responsive Leadership as a Means for Educational Change

The book is presented in four sections featuring text boxes with "Ideas in Brief" (summaries) and "Culturally Responsive Leadership in Practice" (strategies), both for easy access and immediate applicability of ideas conveyed. The first section is *Interrupting Inequities for Improving Access in Higher Education*. The second is *Adapting Culturally Responsive Leadership to Benefit Those Who Are Systemically Underserved*. The third section is *Ways of Leading toward Increased Equity and Improved Student Achievement*, with the last, *Institutionalized Culturally Responsive Leadership: Implementation for Social Justice and Equity*. Individually, each chapter offers context-specific situational ACL guidelines. However, taken together, the chapters provide a hopeful outlook for ways in which equity issues might be approached in the academy. The chapters reveal salient core strategies that are thematic in nature, rendering them at the ready for leaders in HE to adapt and use to guide their leadership practice. This example of scholarly research to practice provides an invaluable professional resource to educational leaders in HE. This volume gives readers food for thought with regard to challenges and roadblocks, as well as solutions and new ways of thinking about leadership pathways and access for a more diverse leadership pool to address the needs of an increasingly diverse society in the U.S. and to increasing cultural, linguistic, and economic diversity globally.

Thinking about ways in which racism and other social prejudices can be interrupted with strategies to do so is a powerful application of culturally responsive leadership as a way of professional practice—moving the professional conversation from theory to action. Mentoring, recruiting, selecting, and supporting nontraditional leaders who represent historically underserved backgrounds is necessary if new ways of thinking about old issues is a priority for real organizational change. As a result of underrepresentation of women of color and other systemically underrepresented individuals in educational leadership in HE, those of us in leadership positions must be, and remain, diligent in the advancement of increased avenues enabling access. Finally, if we can work to institutionalize such innovative approaches as ACL, we will be moving toward greater progress in higher and all education.

It is our hope that you find *Culturally Responsive Leadership in Higher Education* a book that captures and reveals prime examples of the kinds of leadership practices by educational leaders who aim to meet the challenges of equity and access for systemically underserved students head-on and improve their organizations from the inside out. This edited contribution serves as a means to nurture and mentor scholars, practitioners, and aspiring, as well as practicing, educational leaders in diverse contexts by scaffolding authentic substantive change in leadership practices for social equity and educational change in higher education.

References

Agosto, V., Dias, L., Kaiza, L., Alvarez McHatton, P., & Elam, D. (2013). Culture-based leadership and preparation: A qualitative meta-synthesis of the literature. In L. C. Tillman & J. S. Scheurich (Eds.), *Handbook of research on educational leadership for equity and diversity* (pp. 625–650). New York, NY: Routledge.

Akiba, M., LeTendre, G. K., & Scribner, J. P. (2007). Teacher quality, opportunity gap, and national achievement in 46 countries. *Educational Researcher, 36*(7), 369–387.

Anyon, Y. (2009). Sociological theories of learning disabilities: Understanding racial disproportionality in special education. *Journal of Human Behavior in the Social Environment, 19*(1), 44–57.

Bailey, T., & Morest, V. S. (2006). *Defending the community college equity agenda.* Baltimore, MD: Johns Hopkins University Press.

Beachum, F. (2011). Culturally relevant leadership for complex 21st-century school contexts. In F. W. English (Ed.), *The SAGE handbook of educational leadership: Advances in theory, research, and practice* (2nd ed., pp. 27–35). Thousand Oaks, CA: Sage.

Blaschke, S., Frost, J., & Hattke, F. (2014). Towards a micro foundation of leadership, governance, and management in universities. *Higher Education, 68*(5), 711–732.

Brown, C. S. (2002). *Refusing racism: White allies and the struggle for civil rights.* New York, NY: Teachers College Press.

Brown, K., Benkovitz, J., Muttillo, A. J., & Urban, T. (2011). Leading schools of excellence and equity: Documenting effective strategies in closing achievement gaps. *Teachers College Record, 113*(1), 57–96.

Bryman, A. (2007). Effective leadership in higher education: A literature review. *Studies in Higher Education, 32*(6), 693–710.

California Department of Education (CDE). (2007). *State of education address.* Retrieved from http://www.cde.ca.gov/eo/in/se/yr07soe.asp

Capps, R., Fix, M., Murray, L., Passel, J. S., & Herwantoro, S. (2005). *The new demography of American schools: Immigration and the No Child Left Behind Act.* Washington, DC: Urban Institute.

Darling-Hammond, L. (1999). *Teacher quality and student achievement: A review of state policy evidence.* Seattle, WA: Center for the Study of Teaching and Policy.

Darling-Hammond, L. (2007). Educational quality and equality: What it will take to leave no child behind. In B. D. Smedley & A. Jenkins (Eds.), *All things being equal: Instigating opportunity at an inequitable time* (pp. 39–78). New York, NY: New Press.

Fitzpatrick, K., & Santamaría, L. J. (2015). Disrupting racialisation: Considering critical leadership in the field of PE. *Association Internationale des Ecoles Superieures d'Education Physique/International Association for Physical Education in Higher Education, Special Issue* (pp. 1–15). doi:10.1080/17408989.2014.990372

Fullan, M. G. (2001). *The new meaning of educational change* (3rd ed.). New York, NY: Teachers College Press.

Gay, G. (2000). *Culturally responsive teaching: Theory, research, and practice.* New York, NY: Teachers College Press.

Gay, G. (2010). *Culturally responsive teaching: Theory, research, and practice* (2nd ed.). New York, NY: Teachers College Press.

Goldenberg, C. (2008). Teaching English language learners: What the research does and does not say. *American Educator, 32*(2), 8–44.

Haney Lopez, I. (1998). *White by law: The legal construction of race.* New York, NY: New York University Press.

Jean-Marie, G. (2006). Welcoming the unwelcomed: A social justice imperative of African-American female leaders. *Educational Foundations, 20*(1–2), 83–102.

Jean-Marie, G., James, C., & Bynum, S. (2006). Black women activists, leaders, and educators: Transforming urban educational practice. In J. L. Kincheloe, K. Hayes, K. Rose, & P. M. Anderson (Eds.), *The Praeger handbook of urban education* (pp. 59–69). Westport, CT: Greenwood Press.

Johnson, L., & Fuller, C. (2014). Culturally responsive leadership (pp. 1–10). Oxford Bibliographies. New York, NY: Oxford University Press. Retrieved from oxfordbibliographies.com. doi:10.1093/OBO/9780199756810-0067

Kezar, A. (2002). Overcoming obstacles to change within urban institutions: The mobile framework and engaging institutional culture. *Metropolitan Universities Journal, 13*(2), 68–80.

Lum, L. (2009). The Obama era: A post-racial society? *Diverse: Issues in Higher Education, 25*(26), 14–16.

May, S., & Sleeter, C. E. (2010). *Critical multiculturalism: Theory and praxis.* New York, NY: Routledge.

Middlehurst, R., & Elton, L. (1992). Leadership and management in higher education. *Studies in Higher Education, 17*(3), 251–264.

Nevarez, C., & Wood, J. L. (2010). *Community college leadership and administration: Theory, practice and change.* New York, NY: Peter Lang.

Nevarez, C., & Wood, L. (Eds.). (2014). *Ethical leadership and the community college: Paradigms, decision-making, and praxis.* Charlotte, NC: Information Age.

Riehl, C. J. (2000). The principal's role in creating inclusive schools for diverse students: A review of normative, empirical, and critical literature on the practice of educational administration. *Review of Educational Research, 70*(1), 55–81.

Santamaría, C. G., Santamaría, A. P., & Santamaría, L. J. (2015, April). *Applied critical leadership fostering school-family-community relations: Innovation for Latino immigrant parents of students with disabilities.* Paper presented at the meeting of American Educational Research Association (AERA), Chicago, IL.

Santamaría, L. J. (2012). Applied critical leadership in action: Re-visioning an equity agenda to address the community college achievement gap. *Journal of Transformative Leadership and Policy Studies, 2*(1), 15–21.

Santamaría, L. J. (2014a). Interrupting educational campus inequities. In C. Nevarez & L. Wood (Eds.), *Ethical leadership and the community college: Paradigms, decision-making, and praxis* (pp. 103–110). Charlotte, NC: Information Age.

Santamaría, L. J. (2014b). Critical change for the greater good: Multicultural dimensions of educational leadership toward social justice and educational equity. *Education Administration Quarterly (EAQ), 50*(3), 347–391. doi:10.1177/0013161X13505287

Santamaría, L. J., & Jean-Marie, G. (2014). Cross-cultural dimensions of applied, critical, and transformational leadership: Women principals advancing social justice and educational equity. *Cambridge Educational Journal, 44*(3), 333–360.

Santamaría, L. J., Lee, J., & Harker, N. (2014). Optimising Māori academic achievement (OMAA): An Indigenous led, international, inter-institutional higher education initiative. In F. Cram, H. Phillips, P. Sauni, & C. Tuagalu (Eds.), *Māori and Pasifika higher education horizons* (pp. 201–220). Bingley, UK: Emerald Books.

Santamaría, L. J., & Santamaría, A. P. (2012). *Applied critical leadership in education: Choosing change.* New York, NY: Routledge.

Santamaría, L. J., & Santamaría, A. P. (2014). Culturally responsive leadership in early childhood education settings: A critical comparative consideration. In H. Hedges & V. Podmore (Eds.), *Early childhood education: Pedagogy, professionalism, and policy* (pp. 97–113). University of Auckland Faculty of Education Research Monograph. Melbourne, Australia: Pearson Books.

Santamaría, L. J., Santamaría, A. P., & Dam, L. I. (2014). Applied critical leadership through Latino/a lenses: An alternative approach to educational leadership. *Revista Internacional de Educación para la Justicia Social/International Journal of Education for Social Justice, 3*(2), 161–180.

Santamaría, L. J., Santamaría, A. P., Webber, M., & Pearson, H. (2014). Indigenous urban school leadership (IUSL): A critical cross-cultural comparative analysis of educational leaders in New Zealand and the United States. *Canadian and International Education (CIE), 43*(1), 1–21.

Shields, C. M. (2010). Transformative leadership: Working toward equity in diverse contexts. *Education Administration Quarterly, 46*(4), 558–589.

Stalvey, L. (1989). *The education of a WASP.* Madison: University of Wisconsin Press.

Theoharis, G. (2008). Woven in deeply: Identity and leadership of urban social justice principals. *Education and Urban Society, 41*(1), 3–25.

Vanneman, A., Hamilton, L., Baldwin Anderson, J., & Rahman, T. (2009). Achievement gaps: How Black and White students in public schools perform in mathematics and reading on the national assessment of educational progress (NCES 2009–455). National Center for Education Statistics, Institute of Education Sciences, U.S. Department of Education. Washington, DC.

PART I

Interrupting Inequities for Improving Access in Higher Education

2

UNPACKING INSTITUTIONAL CULTURE TO DIVERSIFY THE LEADERSHIP PIPELINE

Lorri J. Santamaría, Jennifer Jeffries, and Andrés P. Santamaría

IDEA IN BRIEF

This chapter affords aspiring and practicing educational leaders with a blueprint to guide and assist their engagement in focused, courageous, and fearless leadership action, examining assumptions around the implicit and explicit pathways to leadership opportunities in their particular tertiary organizations. The chapter invites educational leaders to participate in a range of reflexive activities wherein they learn about characteristics of Applied Critical Leadership (ACL) as a research-based theory-to-practice approach toward culturally responsive, socially just, and equitable leadership practice (Santamaría & Santamaría, 2012). Additionally, the authors invite and encourage readers to reflect on critical issues in their educational leadership contexts, to develop action plans to interrogate organizational inequities and leadership practices that may encourage or inhibit access for others to enter higher education and serve as educational leaders in the academy.

Keywords: leadership development, equity, inequity, organizational change

To be fair, it depends on who you query, but according to the Council of State Governments, the top five issues in education are school readiness, experiential and work-base learning, academic success for systemically underserved populations, innovative state accountability systems, and academic work associated with the advanced attainment of degrees (Goins, 2015). Educational inequity is a theme spiraling through each one of these issues as underscored by Chief Justice Sonia Sotomayor in her speech to the Philadelphia Bar Association in March 2011. In this address she added diversity to the list of priorities by stating: "Inequality in education is the most pressing issue in diversity in the U.S." This and related issues are of as much concern in higher education as they are at every other level and sector pertaining to education in our country and others with similar historical and societal conditions. One way to address educational inequities is to ensure there are qualified individuals who understand complex education issues at the table.

Leithwood and Riehl (2003) have contributed a considerable amount of research in the field of educational leadership. Their research findings tell us that successful educational leaders set direction for their organizations, actively develop people and the organization, respond to opportunities and challenges that arise from accountability measures, and respond effectively to opportunities and challenges that come as a result of educating diverse groups of students. With regard to diversity, the scholars note gaps in the research identifying "ways in which diversity in educational leadership can be fostered, so that individuals with appropriately rich backgrounds, values, and community connections are placed in positions to lead our schools" (p. 5). These researchers affirm that leaders are needed to "develop visions that embody the best thinking about teaching and learning that are effective for the populations they serve" (p. 5). They also assert that "school leaders can promote equity and justice for all students by establishing school climates where patterns of discrimination are challenged and negated" (p. 6).

The call for diversity in educational leadership underscores the persistent lack of culturally and linguistically diverse leaders over time documented by researchers like McGee Banks (2007) and Santamaría and Santamaría (2012), even while schools and universities in the U.S. and in similar countries become more diverse (Akiba, LeTendre, & Scribner, 2007). The claims posed cause those in leadership positions to wonder how one knows when a candidate's background is sufficiently rich for their values and community connections to ensure the potential leaders are worthy to lead African American, Latino, or American Indian teaching and learning communities. What about the other core leadership practices involving influence and outcomes? Don't educational leaders need to be able to do these things as well? This chapter considers ways in which leaders in tertiary settings can change their everyday practice to create conditions to attract, nurture, develop, and encourage appropriate leaders promoting diversity in higher education.

We begin this chapter by asking who are the educational leaders attaining academic and professional staff positions in higher education where leaders might be expected to address educational inequities? Who are the individuals helping to identify and implement andragogy (adult teaching and learning) appropriate and effective for culturally and linguistically diverse populations? Which individuals promote equity and justice for students in academe while establishing an environment where patterns of discrimination are called out, challenged, and undone? Who is equipped and able to push progressive alternatives to educational leadership practices in tertiary settings? Who are the individuals typically invited into the higher education leadership-preparation pipeline? What is the nature of this leadership pipeline? How does it function? Are there misalignments in what tertiary policies or guidelines 'say' and what they 'do' with regard to pathways toward educational leadership?

In this chapter we further consider whether the academy has embedded cultural practices, habits, or norms that support or prohibit aspiring academic and professional staff who are educational leaders to realize their professional goals to work in the field of educational leadership and administration. Using findings from research on Applied Critical Leadership (ACL) as a theoretical framework (Santamaría & Santamaría, 2012), supporting literature on leadership as a moral imperative (Fullan, 2003), and an interactive iterative process toward leader vulnerability and humility (Robertson, 2011; Yancy, 2015), this contribution examines and sheds light on organizational culture in higher education. The aim is to bring readers and practicing leaders in the academy to contemplate conditions in their own institutions that prevent individuals from having a nondiscriminatory shot at success in accessing pathways toward academic and professional educational leadership roles. The chapter ends with a participatory action plan inviting readers and practicing leaders to change their practice with regard to the educational leadership pipeline, providing pathways for systemically underserved individuals in higher education to gain access.

The following research questions serve to more precisely frame this work: In what ways does ACL inform educational leadership practice in tertiary contexts? Are there norms in the culture of the educational organization that impede leadership pathways that should be interrupted in order to increase equitable opportunities to academic and professional leadership roles and positions? What can individuals occupying formal leadership roles do to illuminate the hidden culture or curriculum associated with these pathways in academe?

Literature Frames

Applied Critical Leadership

Applied Critical Leadership (ACL) is an approach or way of thinking about culturally responsive leadership for social justice and educational equity, based on the theoretical underpinnings of transformative leadership (Shields, 2010), critical multiculturalism (May & Sleeter, 2010), and critical race theory (Ladson-Billings, 2009). In this approach, educational leaders ultimately choose to practice leadership by leading through a critical race theory lens while employing elements of transformative leadership and critical multiculturalism grounded in the most positive aspects of the leaders' own identity (Santamaría & Santamaría, 2012). Transformative leadership, in this case, is leadership that considers the complexity of positioning educational organizations within greater socio-political and socio-historical realities with strong considerations for the practice of social justice and equity, and a vision of reconciled injustices (Quantz, Rogers, & Dantley, 1991). These authors contend that "conversations around issues of emancipation and domination" are indicative of those who practice transformative leadership (Quantz et al., 1991, p. 112). Thus, transformative leadership lends itself to action-oriented practice, pushing the boundaries between power, authority, justice, democracy, and the individual vs. the collective (Weiner, 2003).

Critical multiculturalism complements transformative leadership in that it incorporates critical race theory and critical pedagogy for the purposes of "interrogating and advancing various critical theoretical threads" (May & Sleeter, 2010, p. 10). This theory demonstrates the need to build solidarity across diverse communities, argues the need to embrace struggles against oppression that others face, and challenges educators to locate their own individual and collective histories, critically and reflectively, including associated power relations (May & Sleeter, 2010). Further, and not unlike transformative leadership, critical multiculturalism gives priority to structural analysis of unequal power relationships. It analyzes the role of institutionalized inequities, and names and challenges racism and other forms of injustice. Critical multiculturalism and transformative leadership provide a natural theoretical springboard for ACL.

In their studies of practices of culturally responsive educational leaders who practice ACL, Santamaría & Santamaría (2012) and Santamaría, Santamaría, Webber, & Pearson (2014) found salient features of ACL to be present in nine culturally, linguistically, and gender-diverse educational leaders working in PreK–12 and higher educational contexts in the U.S. and more than 40 educational leaders working in Indigenous Māori school contexts in New Zealand (NZ). From multi–case study research, the researchers found that critical leaders drew on positive attributes of their identities associated with race, culture, or gender; employed a critical race theory (CRT) lens to consider multiple perspectives; used consensus building as the preferred strategy for decision-making; and felt a need to honor all members of their constituencies. Critical leaders also led by example to meet unresolved educational needs or challenges; felt the need to build trust when working with mainstream constituents or partners or others who did not share an affinity for issues related to educational equity; could be classified as transformative, servant leaders who worked ultimately to serve the greater good; made empirical contributions and, thus, added authentic research-based information to academic discourse regarding underserved groups. Finally, and most relevant to this present contribution, findings indicated critical leaders responding to a visceral moral imperative were willing to initiate and engage in critical conversations with constituents in order to enact change via improved practice.

Two significant notions beyond the nine characteristics of ACL found in the inquiries cited also emerged and serve to further shape this chapter. The first was non-White participants' suggestions of the existence of a 'hidden curriculum or culture' associated with attaining leadership positions. Iglesias (2009) also found this 'naming' of 'hidden curriculum' in his study of Latino superintendents. The second was the finding that all of the leaders, including upward of seven White women and four White men were able to, *by intentional choice*, assume a critical race theory lens while practicing leadership in their particular contexts (Santamaría & Jean-Marie, 2014; Santamaría & Santamaría, 2012). These two findings, coupled with participants' initiation and engagement in critical conversations within their educational communities, further provide the premise for this chapter, which takes a closer look at ways in which the most influential educational leaders think about and create equitable pathways to careers in educational leadership.

Moral Imperative

Social justice and educational equity are moral imperatives for educational leaders and practitioners enacted by individuals who feel compelled to act morally in educational contexts (Fullan, 2003; Fullan, Cuttress, & Kilcher, 2005). Moral imperatives are not routinely institutionalized. Policies are the closest concept, and some may argue that all policies are not moral. We argue a moral purpose for leadership enacted within educational contexts must be able to morph, adjust, and shift with the change inherent to the complexities present in dynamic and ever-changing contexts. Applied critical leaders in ACL research demonstrated characteristics that are aligned with a consideration of moral imperative as illustrated in Table 2.1 (Santamaría & Santamaría, 2012). Each characteristic lends itself to a moral action in an ideal institute of higher education as imagined by Fullan (1993).

Leaders with a moral imperative like the ones described in Table 2.1 would be highly desired in any tertiary institution. Hiring practices and succession planning in these organizations would include rubrics reflecting the knowledge, skills, and dispositions required of an educational leader beyond requisite leadership and management skills to lead the institution into the future. However, when we look closely, there appear to be misalignments in what university policies and guidelines 'say' and what is 'done' in routine practice. Some of these policies are written while others are part of the culture of the place or the 'hidden curriculum' alluded to earlier (Iglesias, 2009). Some of these misalignments impact individual pathways toward educational leadership. These alignments are referred to in the literature as theories of action.

TABLE 2.1 ACL and a Moral Leadership Imperative

ACL Characteristics (Santamaría & Santamaría, 2012, p. 82)	Best Faculty of Education (Fullan, 1993, p. 7)
Draw on positive attributes of identities associated with race, culture, or gender	Respected and engaged as a vital part of the university as a whole, valuing and practicing exemplary teaching
Employ a critical lens to consider multiple perspectives	Engage in constant inquiry
Use consensus building as the preferred strategy for decision-making. Feel the need to honor all members of constituencies (inviting silenced voices to table)	Visible and valued internationally in a way that contributes locally and globally
Lead by example to meet unresolved educational needs or challenges	Form partnerships with schools and other agencies
Describe the need to build trust when working with mainstream constituents, partners, or others who do not share an affinity for issues related to educational equity	Working collaboratively to build regional, national, and international networks
Can be classified as transformative, servant leaders who work ultimately to serve the greater good	Commit to producing agents of educational and social improvement
Make empirical contributions adding research-based information to academic discourse regarding underserved groups	Commit to continuous improvement through program innovation and evaluation
Willing to initiate and engage in critical conversations with constituents to enact change and improved practice	Model and develop collaboration among staff and students and developing lifelong learning

Theories of Action

Argyris and Schön (1974) conceptualize educational leader and practitioner mismatches as the distinction between 'espoused theories' and 'theories-in-use,' otherwise understood as a conflict between 'walking the talk.' Often, as indicated, organizations' espoused theories regarding diversity show up in their policies, which are frequently politically correct or aligned with legal compliance regulations. Organizations' theories-in-use, however, indicate contrasting actions that are often institutionalized resulting in educational inequities. Examples of some of these inequities include acceptance criteria for systemically underserved students, difficulties for faculty of color to attain tenure and promotion, and low numbers of faculty members or leaders of color. If institutions of higher education with sound espoused theories and lax theories-in-use are to increase the number of the most appropriate people to serve in a variety of leadership roles, current leaders need to unlearn behaviors that result in ignored, and thus unintentionally enabled, status quo patterns of institutionalized discrimination. We deliberately state 'unintentionally enabled' because we surmise, as does Argyris (1976), that the business of unlearning is a tall order for individuals in educational leadership positions for a variety of reasons.

Changing one's theoretical approach to leadership is difficult because of the atmosphere of deception and trust associated with administration as the 'dark side,' working for 'big brother,' and top-down mandates. It is also difficult because when leaders' practice appears to be overly distributed or trusting, it can also be perceived to deviate from the norm. This could backfire on a leader promoting change. Finally, in order to change, one must explore and reflect on personal values, beliefs, and feelings. Becoming conscious of one's own espoused theories and theories-in-use causes one to challenge or question foundational ways of thinking, acting, and decision-making that have formed over one's professional career or even lifetime. Changing one's theories of action is arduous work requiring support, sometimes resources, and time.

From this perspective, we wonder about the role learning processes play in problem solving and decision-making. Can individuals change the ways in which they learn and process information? Essentially, in this context, we are asking leaders in higher education contexts if they can adjust their approach to solving equity and access issues. We also want to know whether or not they are able to make decisions resulting in the promotion of equity and access with increased educational outcomes for systemically underserved students. Ultimately, we want to know if these leaders can unlearn biases, assumptions, and ways of thinking about hiring, promoting, and bringing to the table the most appropriate people to add to the organizational capital of the institution. It is these new leaders who will usher in change to shift organizational culture until deficit thinking and patterns are reversed and replaced with equitable and just practices. This would be the ideal.

Changing Theories of Action

But is it possible to interrupt one's espoused theory and/or theory-in-use? We have already established that it is difficult, to say the least. Argyris (1976) would say we may be able to if we could somehow isolate and analyze leaders' actions to the degree the actions can be repeated with fidelity "so decision makers can learn from their actions and adapt their decision-making and behavior accordingly" within feasible environmental, professional, psychological, and emotional constraints (p. 365). In Argyris and Schön's (1974) seminal research, there are two types of learning associated with one's theoretical approach to leadership practice. In single-loop learning, leaders operate from a locus of control over themselves and others. They lead in order to achieve a purpose as defined by an outside agency. They succeed by being and doing the best, suppressing negative feelings, and emphasizing rationality. For most educational leaders these ways of leading are foundational and they give rise to deception and mistrust of administration as the norm.

Double-loop learning, on the other hand, relies on the provision or seeking of valid information, free and informed choice for those involved, internal organizational commitment, high trust amongst constituents, and sharing power with competent and relevant individuals (Argyris and Schön, 1974). Santamaría and Santamaría (2012) state that leaders can change if they *choose* to change. Are the culturally responsive leaders identified in ACL research more prone to double-loop learning? Does double-loop learning indicate a moral imperative? The characteristics outlined in Table 2.1 demonstrate leaders who seek out information, embrace choice, are committed to their institutions, practice in high trust spaces, and practice high levels of distributed leadership. Applied critical leaders have a moral imperative toward change and improving education for all. Is it any wonder that those accustomed to single-loop learning find it difficult to change?

Therefore, with regard to reshaping pathways to academic and professional educational leadership positions in higher education, and the manner in which leadership is expressed in these contexts, we contend that any leader can *choose* change. Engaging in change or double-loop learning is a choice. We also assert that any leader can *apply* an alternative lens or alter his or her own espoused theory to inform leadership practice in response to the needs of the organization. This may not be popular, but it is possible. Likewise, anyone in a leadership role can *invite* others to join the effort. There is a collaborative, community-building aspect to this kind of practice and it begins with being inclusive when looking for colleagues and fellow leaders to take up the cause. It takes courage and vulnerability to change one's practice. For that reason, we ask leaders in tertiary settings to engage willingly in double-loop learning and to enter a place of vulnerability to honestly challenge and change assumptions (e.g., hidden culture or curriculum) and ways of being and thinking in education (Robertson, 2011).

Vulnerability and Humility

In her research complementing that of Argyris (1976), Santamaría & Santamaría (2012), and Fullan (1993), Robertson (2011) calls educational leaders into a space where they might consider becoming vulnerable enough to push their assumptions about education aside long enough to see where they might require growth. The notion of educational leaders reflecting on their practice long enough to change, adjust, or modify it almost seems absurd in the current climate within the context of the issues presented at the beginning of this contribution. Robertson and these researchers, however, suggest self-reflection as being necessary in order to process educational change and the associated challenges.

In Yancy's (2015) contribution, humility is offered as being necessary for educational leaders to realize that change, or at the very least adjustment of privileged disposition, is needed for the most influential and often most mainstream leaders (e.g., European-descent males in the U.S.) to think deeply about how to change cultural norms or organizational ways of being in higher educational settings. Yancy goes on to suggest educational leaders engage a type of Socratic questioning in order to test and adjust their ways of thinking and acting. Forming new ways of being or habits, he suggests, gradually results in leaders' examination of the principles that give rise to their habitual ways of thinking and doing. The process of engaging in the choosing to change results in educational leaders' ability to respect all students, families, and communities in their constituency as members of a shared humanity and experience. This then can develop into a moral, organizational principle where inequity becomes intolerable and is thus challenged, interrupted, and negated as normal practice. And so how do we begin the work?

Reflexive Considerations Challenging Norms

Norms, as defined in this chapter, are the conditions in your institute of higher learning that prevent individuals from fairly and successfully accessing pathways to educational leadership roles. These conditions can be rooted in attitudes, procedures, traditions, policies, and other formal or informal cultural norms. In this chapter we consider organizational culture as comprising a pattern of shared assumptions invented, discovered, or developed and reinforced by a given group that have worked well enough to be considered valid and therefore are taught to new members (Schein, 2004). Organizational norms, we suggest, are the formal and informal agreements, based on patterns of shared assumptions, acted out by individuals in the organization.

If this is the case, and you are able to arrive at an understanding or place of vulnerability and humility, you might be able to look closely enough at yourself and your organization to engage in double-loop learning to align to a theory-in-use that results in wider and more inclusive leadership and succession planning pathways for your institution. You can engage this work alone or with a supportive group of colleagues with similar aspirations. Argyris and Schön (1974) suggest the support of a group is necessary for double-loop change-of-action theory.

A Closer Look at Self

Being as vulnerable and humble as possible, ask yourself the following questions based on Santamaría and Santamaría's (2012) research: In what ways does my identity (e.g., race, gender, ethnicity) or biases enhance and/or inhibit my ability and willingness to see alternative perspectives in my leadership practice? What privilege or unearned advantage do I have that might create blind spots in my leadership lens? How can I use my privilege to enact equity and access for systemically underserved groups in my practice of ACL? It might help if you wrote down, documented, audiotaped, or videotaped your responses, dating them for future reference to check for changes in your response.

A Closer Look at Your Organization

After reflectively considering the questions of self, further challenge yourself with the following questions in terms of your educational context: What is the theory-in-use and the theory in practice in my organization around assigning or recruiting for leadership roles? Are our words and actions aligned so that they match and we have integrity? Where are the 'spaces' in which words and actions are 'misaligned'? We suggest that in the gap caused by the misalignment between word and action, educational leaders who are willing to take an honest look often find the 'hidden culture or curriculum' described by the participants in Santamaría & Santamaría's (2012) and Iglesias's (2009) studies, as well as the organizational inequities that need your attention at your institution of higher learning.

Interruption of the 'norms' in how you think about your identity and your role as a leader with regard to 'walking the talk,' coupled with the way in which you think about misalignment in your organization, is necessary for the kind of educational change involved with increasing equity in systems where inequities are a natural part of the culture. Like Argyris (1976), we suggest to educational leaders who are ready for this kind of action, to engage others who are committed to the cause, enlist allies and fellow 'warriors' willing to understand, and take steps to break inequitable habits of mind, heart, and body.

Toward a Plan of Action for Culturally Responsive Leadership

So now what? you might ask. We suggest habits of inequity can be broken with intentional actions resulting in double-loop learning. If you are leading a professional development effort, you can engage staff to join you using a less threatening issue than reversing racist hiring practices for leadership roles! Make it a moral imperative that is less threatening at first to appeal to many. Better yet, let your staff determine what institutional behavior they would like to change. If you are working on your own, you can get started right away. Just remember, you will be challenging and questioning core assumptions, beliefs, and values that you may hold near and dear to what makes you, well, *you*. Change is not for the fainthearted.

Breaking the kinds of habits we have presented in this chapter is not impossible but it does require a reason and rationale for change. Change for the sake of change is not being suggested. We are asking you to think about the state of equity and access impacting leadership pathways in your institution. It might be that in your organization all leadership roles are from within, where a 'grow your own' leadership culture is prevalent. In these cases, there is no Equal Opportunity Officer appointed on the search committee, as is standard for an academic or professional staff role. As a result, leaders and managers are shoulder tapped by those in current roles. If an aspiring leader is not in the circle of influence of the current leadership regime, they won't be given the opportunity. The problem in this example is clear. The leadership selection process is not open, transparent, or accessible to all potential or aspiring leaders. Beyond this chapter, this may be thought of as the **recognition** of inequities. Just because a person is in a leadership role, it does not mean they are able to discern or even recognize inequities. Argyris (1976) might have considered this stage the isolation of actions that have been repeated enough to be able to recognize that the actions are not positive. Applied critical leaders in previous studies relied on group consensus in situations where silenced constituents were present in order to determine which inequities to address. For your context, we suggest you bring the best allies to the table to help you identify and understand what change is warranted and why. Next, ask yourself the following questions: What will happen if the change isn't realized? What will happen if it is? What will be the disparity or improvement as a result? Capture your thoughts for this exercise independently or in a group. This realization will set the course for the rest of your journey.

After you have recognized and sufficiently named and identified inequities needing attention, you will need to identify different leadership behaviors to replace the previous and now unwanted or rejected behavior. We call this the **interruption** of inequities. With regard to transitioning from single- to double-loop learning for change, this activity concerns analysis of detrimental behavior to the degree that alternative behaviors may be posed (Argyris, 1976). We argue that it is not difficult to disrupt dysfunction, but it can be shocking to members of your constituency who are accustomed to business as usual. Naming and acknowledging inequities is one thing, but bringing in and implementing replacement behaviors is altogether different. Regarding the issue presented in this chapter, the leader looking to invite culturally and linguistically diverse prospects into the leadership pool would depart from the practice of shoulder tapping her cronies. Instead, like applied critical leaders in previous research considered, the leader would carry out a search in fundamentally different ways.

For example, the leader may put out a call for aspiring leaders, launch a leadership development initiative, invite those seeking leadership positions to contact her directly, seek nominations from faculty and staff, or actively and openly recruit in different locations on campus. Replacement behaviors of this nature are more transparent and indicative of an atmosphere rich in trust, and will take considerable time for the changes to become institutionalized normative behaviors. While replacing old practices, it is important to periodically revisit the rationale for change. Again, individual or group documentation of the changed behaviors against the original premise for shifting can help to identify sign posts, key catalysts, as well as challenges that emerge during the change process. Some questions to ask at this point include: Are the replacement practices a match for the issue identified? Who are other allies needed to identify core replacement behaviors? What are some other options for replacement behaviors that haven't been considered? Is this approach working? What challenges or opportunities have arisen as a result of this work?

To move organizational behavior into a preferred theory-in-use, coaching and correction of the targeted habit are necessary until the new behavior takes root or until the **reparation** of inequities is completed. In this stage of change, leaders demonstrate the ability to learn from previous mistakes and adapt their behaviors accordingly (Argyris, 1976). In our estimation, reparation takes more time than interrupting, replacing, and transforming theories of action. This is the most profound level of change and moves the change from the individual out to the greater organization. Applied critical leaders are in a constant state of reparation. Revisit the characteristics in Table 2.1. You will see negotiation after negotiation involving community members as well as constituents. Culturally responsive leaders tap into the depths of the most positive aspects of their identities to find novel ways to read and interact with their contexts. Trust is built, lost, and rebuilt in efforts to lead by example in a way that benefits the most underserved as well as all students. The examples found in Applied Critical Leadership research reveal that, in order to repair inequities, individual or group exploration of values, beliefs, worldviews, and emotions are necessary. For example, the leader who changed her practices and strategy for selecting future leaders will attract attention from those in the organization who subscribe to the crony shoulder-tap way of selecting incoming leadership. When new leaders are known entities, core and long-standing values and beliefs of the organization remain intact and untested. When those in the wings are people known to the leaders in the organization, they are more easily trusted. The old boys' network was never a myth.

When you are in the stages of reparation, ask yourself and your constituents the following questions: Will the actions we have taken sustain my tenure in this position? In what ways have I worked collaboratively to meet the need identified at the onset of this endeavor to change my leadership practice? What steps do I need to take in order to institutionalize this way of leading? What measureable improvement outcomes are associated with this change? What overall impact toward positive change can be attributed to this shift in thinking and leadership practice?

Conclusion: Changing the 'Game'

In this chapter we identified equity and access issues in the academy that impact the educational leadership practitioner pipeline. We also identified, with the help of Leithwood and Riehl (2003), the kinds of leadership activities undertaken by successful educational leaders. Through this work, the need for culturally responsive leaders who promote equity and justice in culturally and linguistically diverse contexts was established, as was the need to foster organizational culture where patterns of discrimination are identified, challenged, and reversed. By way of a literature review, we took issue with misalignments between institutional policy and organizational norms regarding diversity best practices while also considering research on Applied Critical Leadership (Santamaría & Santamaría, 2012), the role of a moral imperative in leadership practices (Fullan, 2003), and theories of action (Argyris & Schön, 1974). Based on this work, we proposed strategies for leaders in academe to align organizational espoused theories with equitable theories-in-action. It is our hope that this work can be used as a practical guide for emerging and practicing leaders looking to establish clarity and purpose around identifying, recruiting, hiring, and supporting 'appropriate' culturally responsive leaders in higher education settings, while being able to address issues involving equity and access toward improvement for systemically underserved students and their communities in tertiary settings. Our answers depend on our willingness to enter spaces of change and become vulnerable enough to enact equity where it is lacking in academe.

References

Akiba, M., LeTendre, G. K., & Scribner, J. P. (2007). Teacher quality, opportunity gap, and national achievement in 46 countries. *Educational Researcher, 36*(7), 369–387.

Argyris, C. (1976). Single-loop and double-loop models in research on decision making. *Administrative Science Quarterly, 21*, 363–375.

Argyris, C., & Schön, D. A. (1974). *Theory into practice: Increasing professional effectiveness.* San Francisco, CA: Jossey-Bass.

Fullan, M. G. (1993). Why teachers must become change agents. *Educational Leadership, 50*(6), 1–13.

Fullan, M. (Ed.). (2003). *The moral imperative of school leadership.* Thousand Oaks, CA: Corwin Press.

Fullan, M., Cuttress, C., & Kilcher, A. (2005). Eight forces for leaders of change. *National Staff Development Council, 26*(4), 54–64.

Goins, P. (2015). *Top 5 issues in education report.* Council of State Governments. Retrieved from http://knowledgecenter.csg.org/kc/content/top-five-issues-2015-education

Iglesias, N. (2009). *Latino superintendents' identities: A critical study of cultural, personal, and professional worlds* (Unpublished doctoral dissertation). California State University San Marcos, San Marcos, CA.

Ladson-Billings, G. (2009). "Who you callin' nappy-headed?" A critical race theory look at the construction of Black women. *Race, Ethnicity and Education, 12*, 87–99.

Leithwood, K. A., & Riehl, C. (2003). *What we know about successful school leadership.* Philadelphia, PA: Laboratory for Student Success, Temple University. Retrieved from http://dcbsimpson.com/randd-leithwood-successful-leadership.pdf

May, S., & Sleeter, C. E. (Eds.). (2010). *Critical multiculturalism: Theory and praxis.* New York, NY: Routledge.

McGee Banks, C. A. (2007). Gender and race as factors in educational leadership and administration. In *The Jossey-Bass reader on educational leadership* (2nd ed., pp. 299–338). San Francisco, CA: Jossey-Bass.

McKown, C., & Weinstein, R. S. (2008). Teacher expectations, classroom context, and the achievement gap. *Journal of School Psychology, 46*(3), 235–261.

Quantz, R., Rogers, J., & Dantley, M. (1991). Rethinking transformative leadership toward democratic reform of schools. *Journal of Education, 173*(3), 96–118.

Robertson, J. (2011, January). *Leadership true to moral purpose: Schools as social service centres to improve learning opportunities for all.* Paper presented at the 24th International Congress for School Effectiveness and Improvement, Le Meridien Hotel, Limassol, Cyprus (Vol. 4).

Santamaría, L. J., & Jean-Marie, G. (2014). Cross-cultural dimensions of applied, critical, and transformational leadership: Women principals advancing social justice and educational equity. *Cambridge Journal of Education, 44*(3), 333–360.

Santamaría, L. J., & Santamaría, A. P. (2012). *Applied critical leadership in education: Choosing change.* New York, NY: Routledge.

Santamaría, L. J., Santamaría, A. P., Webber, M., & Pearson, H. (2014). Indigenous urban school leadership (IUSL): A critical cross-cultural comparative analysis of educational leaders in New Zealand and the United States. *Canadian and International Education/Education canadienne et internationale, 43*(1), Article 5. Retrieved from http://ir.lib.uwo.ca/cie-eci/vol43/iss1/5

Schein, E. H. (2004). The learning culture and the learning leader. *Organizational culture and leadership* (3rd ed., pp. 365–383). San Francisco, CA: Jossey-Bass.

Shields, C. M. (2010). Transformative leadership: Working toward equity in diverse contexts. *Education Administration Quarterly, 46*, 558–589.

Sotomayor, S. (2011, March 11). Philadelphia Bar Association address. Retrieved from http://philadelphia.cbslocal.com/2011/03/11/supreme-court-justice-sotomayor-honored-by-philadelphia-bar-association/

Weiner, E. J. (2003). Secretary Paulo Freire and the democratization of power: Toward a theory of transformative leadership. *Educational Philosophy and Theory, 35*, 89–106.

Yancy, G. (2015). Tarrying together. *Educational Philosophy and Theory, 47*(1), 26–35.

3

APPLIED CRITICAL LEADERSHIP AND SENSE OF BELONGING

Lessons Learned from Cultural Center Staff and Lesbian, Gay, and Bisexual Latino/a Students

Sonia Rosado and Gregory J. Toya

IDEA IN BRIEF

This chapter addresses critical leadership as a foundation to develop students and staff through Distributed Relational Leadership (DRL). Higher education leaders will be introduced to strategies, approaches, and procedures to apply critical leadership to their practice. Through the infusion of two doctoral dissertations (Rosado, 2011; Toya, 2011), readers will know how to create a transformational atmosphere to develop students and staff as critical leaders.

Applying DRL is an integral approach to creating the space, relationships, identity development, and resources necessary to develop critical leaders. Resources such as cultural centers create safe space, community, social networks, and other options for underserved students, such as Lesbian, Gay, and Bisexual (LGB) students of color. Safe space, community, and resources enhance identity development, sense of belonging, mattering, and retention for underserved students. Underserved students such as LGB students of color, struggling with their sexual and cultural identity, utilize resources such as cultural centers, lesbian gay bisexual transgender (LGBT) centers, and academic support centers to receive support, validation, and acceptance of their identities.

In this chapter, readers will learn how to create a cycle of critical leadership that contributes to closing the educational achievement gap and serves as a pathway to graduate education for underserved students.

Keywords: cultural centers, sense of belonging, lesbian, gay, and bisexual, underserved students, applied critical leadership, distributed relational leadership, transformational educational leadership, multiple dimensions of identity, academic persistence

Higher education staff members have the opportunity to utilize Applied Critical Leadership (ACL) to create an environment that empowers underserved and LGB students of color to succeed in a college environment (Santamaría & Santamaría, 2012). In *Applied Critical Leadership in Education: Choosing Change*, Santamaría & Santamaría (2012) define ACL as a strengths-based model of leadership practice that reconceptualizes Transformational Educational Leadership (TEL) (p. 5). Transformational Educational Leadership engages the full person, suggests redistribution of power, and inspires others to transcend interests for the good of the group (p. 8). ACL adds to TEL through the interface and intersection of transformational leadership, critical pedagogy, and critical race theory (p. 5). Critical pedagogy considers social contexts and views education as a means of empowerment and a way to allow individuals to make choices that influence their world (McLaren, 2003). Critical race theory recognizes that racism is normal to society and storytelling as an important form of exploring racial identity (Ladson-Billings & Tate, 1995). This chapter calls on higher education staff to implement ACL to increase the retention, persistence, and safety of underserved and LGB students of color.

To practice ACL, staff should apply fluid leadership practices to empower underserved and LGB students of color. Underserved students are defined as "financially disadvantaged, racial/minorities, and first generation individuals who are not represented in colleges and universities in proportion to their representation in the K–12 educational system or in society at large" (Bragg, Kim, & Rubin, 2005, p. 6). To successfully integrate Applied Critical Leadership into their work, critical leaders need to infuse critical race theory, critical pedagogy, and transformation leadership into their leadership practice. Moreover, ACL entails infusion of an individual's personal identities and empathy for student perspectives to serve students with multiple dimensions of identities (MDIs). "Scholars who consider leadership for social justice explore ways in which leaders in education can shift their perspectives by deliberately attempting to see situations through the eyes of others with alternative points of views" (Santamaría & Santamaría, 2012, p. 10). Furthermore, critical university staff leaders use their personal experiences to relate to the experiences of underserved and LGB students of color.

The critical issue for this chapter is the retention, academic persistence, and safety of underserved and LGB students of color. Through the synthesis of two doctoral dissertations (Rosado, 2011; Toya, 2011), the authors explain the need for ACL with underserved and LGB students of color. Moreover, the authors provide practical strategies on how to facilitate the retention, persistence, and safety of underserved and LGB students of color.

Educational Context for LGB Students of Color

The educational achievement gap for a rising underserved collegiate population is currently manifested in the disparity of student outcomes between White and Asian students with Black, Latinos, Native/Indigenous, Southeast Asian, and their Pacific Islander peers (Singleton & Linton, 2006). Valencia (2002) further defined the disparity of student outcomes as the "persistent, pervasive, and disproportionate low rates of student test scores, retention, and college-enrollment" (p. 4). Swail (2003) indicated that the six-year graduation rate of students enrolling in four-year institutions for the 1995–96 academic year were as follows: 46% African American, 47% Latino, 67% White, and 72% Asian, confirming that the achievement gap continues. Additionally, LGB students of color are at risk for their lives since they may be faced with dual-identity distresses that may focus on both their sexual and racial identities. Dealing with identity crises can contribute to LGB students of color not fully concentrating on their academics. Identity issues may cause LGB students of color to drop out and/or not graduate from the university.

It is imperative to highlight why LGB youth need mentors, role models, resources, and education to assist with the development of their sexual identity. In the recent past, there have been a number of suicides within the young LGB population in the United States. During the month of September 2010, there were five suicides involving LGB students. These teenagers experienced some form of harassment and/or assault, social exclusion, isolation, bullying, or teasing by their peers. They failed to get support from school administrators since bullying was not seen as a serious problem when the students expressed their concerns to school administrators (Benjamin, 2010; Diaz & Kosciw, 2009; Hensel, 2010; Howorth, 2010; O'Hare, 2010; Spaulding, 2010). These disturbing events send a call to higher education administrators to implement practical leadership strategies that facilitate student success and honor the identities and communities of LGB students of color. Perhaps a critical leadership approach, as Santamaría and Santamaría (2012) identify, is one possible solution for meeting the needs of this systemically underserved community.

Critical Leadership

Critical Leadership is a direct application of critical theory and addresses the action-oriented aspect of critical race theory (Santamaría & Santamaría, 2012). Educational leadership theory, critical feminist theory, leadership for social justice, and perspectives on change offer foundational and alternative theoretical approaches to constructive ways of thinking about educational leadership for the 21st century (Capper, 1993; hooks, 1990; Scheurich & Skrla, 2003; Terrell & Lindsey, 2009; Van Nostrand, 1993). These works capture and reflect important research and critical conversations challenging assumptions about leadership and approaches to educating current and future generations of learners in U.S. schools, and consider race, gender, and oppression as factors affecting students' everyday lives in educational contexts. In Nee-Benham, Cooper, and Almee-Benham's (1998) seminal feminist perspective, the voices of culturally and linguistically diverse educational leaders are captured working hard at *choosing change* to shape their work as opposed to *choosing to change* in response to their work. How, then, do underserved and LGB Latino/a students become critical leaders, and how do underserved and LGB Latino/a students attain academic persistence? It is important to note that once LGB Latino/a students feel comfortable with their multiple identities, they become involved individuals (critical leaders) on their college campus and give back to their communities. In return, this assists underserved and LGB Latino/a students to network with various individuals on campus and become aware of the resources that may benefit their needs. This, in turn, contributes to their academic persistence.

Having the opportunity to research LGB Latino/a students at a four-year institution provided a space to address issues that relate to these students' MDIs, specifically sexuality and cultural identities. The LGB Latino/a students identify their various identities and comprehend how they intersect with one another. Based on their experiences, LGB Latino/a students are able to touch upon the inequalities they encounter as an LGB Latino/a student by finding or developing their own social networks. These help support them as individuals and teach them how to navigate their way through a university setting. LGB Latino/a students are aware of how going to college and the resources offered in college give them the opportunity to explore their sexuality and learn more about themselves.

LGB Latino/a Student Multiple Identities

Before coming to college, these students did not have a space to explore and critically think about their MDIs. Once there, they are exposed to the multiple resources on campus, such as the Lesbian Gay Bisexual Transgender (LGBT) Resource Center, the Cross Cultural Center, Women's Center, outreach programs, tutoring services, student organizations, ethnic studies courses, and wellness resources. These organizations give them a holistic understanding of themselves, as well as the knowledge, language, and support to help them feel comfortable and secure with their identities and learn how to persist academically at the university level, regardless of their family circumstances. It is important to point out that LGB Latino/a students who reach this level of autonomy are able to serve as critical leaders to other students who lack guidance, agency, and self-concept. In this chapter, LGB critical leaders of color are those who assist their peers with their own identity process, since these students may lack support from their families and/or cultural backgrounds and/or do not have role models that relate to their sexual and cultural identities.

In working with LGB Latino/a students, it is critical to recognize as a staff member that one is not dealing with a single identity but with multiple identities. To begin to understand students of color in a more effective manner, the authors will provide the reader with an example of what it is to be an LGB Latino/a student and, more specifically, an LGB Latino/a student on a university campus.

The challenges of dual-subordinated identities (identifying as both Latino/a and LGB) cause frustration, anger, and struggle for students to feel welcomed or accepted since they do not fit into any one community (Harley, Nowak, Gassaway, & Savage, 2002). Being comfortable with having dual/multiple identities allows ethnic and sexual minorities to find satisfaction in life and increase self-esteem (Crawford, Allison, Zamboni, & Soto, 2002). LGB Latino/a students seek allies who enhance their culture and also their sexuality in order to feel complete. Understanding both their sexuality and cultural identities is an initial step toward assisting them in their identity development. Becoming familiar with the culture of LGB students is a key point to consider when serving this student community.

Latino/a Family Values Conflict

The traditional Latino/a family values culture and family relationships. In the Latino/a culture *familismo* is a value that represents loyalty, reciprocity, and solidarity within the family (Galanti, 2003; Raffaelli & Ontai, 2004). *Respeto* means respect for the family and the hierarchy in social relationships (Raffaelli & Ontai, 2004). In addition, *personalismo* (intimate and personal relationships) is an important concept that involves a high degree of intimacy and concern for their families (Galanti, 2003). Both parents are involved in making decisions or it can be left for the mother to decide (Vega, 1990).

The Latino/a culture stresses the idea of family unity that indicates that individuals need to focus on the family desires and/or needs over their own. This may make it hard for LGB Latino/a students to come out to their family because they do not want to disappoint their family members. Personal problems are not shared outside of the family since family is seen as the resource to help solve personal issues (Galanti, 2003; Vega, 1990). LGB Latino/a students struggle with coming out to their immediate family since their sexual identity goes against their religion and the traditional gender expectations of what a woman or man should live up to. Religion plays a significant role in Latino/a families and the problems experienced by the LGB Latino/as are rooted in the overwhelmingly religious aspect that is tightly linked to the Latino/a culture (Garcia, 1998).This may also make it difficult for an LGB Latino/a student to seek confidentiality from extended family members. The Latino/a culture has traditional strong gender roles that females and males are expected to follow (Galanti, 2003; Raffaelli & Ontai, 2004). Gender-typing, a phenomenon in which parents treat their children differently based on gender, occurs more often in ethnic cultures than in nonethnic ones (Lippa & Tan, 2001; Raffaelli & Ontai, 2004). In Latino/a culture children are regulated by their gender and are strongly encouraged to follow certain expectations. These cultural expectations hinder the development of the LGB Latino/a students and make them feel marginalized or not accepted in their culture. Therefore, it is usually left to them to deal with the situation and hope that everything gets better.

LGB Latino/a Sense of Belonging

Having the opportunity to attend a university gives these students a chance to be themselves. Once the LGB Latino/a student leaves their home and attends an academic institution that demonstrates support and provides them with the tools necessary to be successful, the LGB Latino/a student can begin to foster new relationships outside their immediate families. The friendships that are established during the college experience, Summer Bridge, Queer People of Color organization, during courses, and so forth help students remain on campus. LGB Latino/a students create an extended family away from home (Way, Gingold, Rotenberg, & Kuriakose, 2005) and find a sense of belonging at the institution by building trusting and positive relationships that acknowledge and validate their various identities (Duck, 1991; Galupo, 2009; Way & Chen, 2000). The majority of these students do not have support for their sexual orientation from their immediate families back in their hometowns.

In higher education settings, students develop friendships with those that they can connect with through their shared cultural experiences. This provides them with the notion that they are not alone and that others like them are experiencing, or have experienced, the same things. Antonio (2004) states how individuals select friendships based on their identities, personality traits, interests, attitudes, and values. They support and guide one another to feel more comfortable with their sexuality, and work toward accepting their feelings toward their sexual identity. Knowing what we know about the experiences of LGB Latino/a students: How do you, as a higher education administrator/staff/faculty community member, assist in better serving this underrepresented student population?

Applied Critical Leadership and Staff

Student Affairs staff who practice Applied Critical Leadership can create transformational environments that promote underserved student persistence (Santamaría & Santamaría, 2012). Infusing a critical race theory lens that recognizes the existence of race and racism in U.S. society, Student Affairs staff can create safe havens from racism and a home-away-from-home environment that positively contributes to the success of underserved students (Jones, Castellanos, & Cole, 2002; Ladson-Billings & Donnor, 2005; Toya, 2011; Welch, 2009). Campus cultural centers (e.g., LGBT, Women's, Cross Cultural) may reduce the impact of racism by decreasing the sense of isolation, alienation, and lack of belonging experienced by underserved students (June, 1996; Patton, 2006; Rosado, 2011; Welch, 2009). Moreover, cultural centers contribute to narrowing the educational achievement gap by serving as sources of retention, persistence, and a sense of belonging for underserved students (Jones et al., 2002; Patton, 2006; Rosado, 2011; Toya, 2011; Turner; 1994).

Distributed Relational Leadership

Congruent with the tenets of Applied Critical Leadership, higher education staff members can promote underserved student retention, persistence, sense of belonging, and mattering through Distributed Relational Leadership (Toya, 2011). Distributed Relational Leadership (DRL) combines the characteristics of *relational leadership* (Komives, Lucas, & McMahon, 2007) and *distributed leadership* (Spillane, 2006). Komives, Lucas, and McMahon (2007) defined relational leadership as "a relational and ethical process of people together attempting to accomplish positive change" (p. 74). Relationships are the most important element in the leadership process and involve a purposeful intent to create positive change (Komives et al., 2007). In distributed leadership, "the interactions of leaders, followers, and their situation" are key components to implementing this collaborative, shared leadership philosophy (Spillane, 2006, p. 4). In congruence with Applied Critical Leadership and Transformational Leadership, DRL redirects power from positional leadership to multiple members of the organization (Santamaría & Santamaría, 2012; Spillane, 2006). DRL is actualized by implementing shared leadership roles that focus on building positive relationships with students and staff (Toya, 2011).

Staff and student relationships can positively influence the sense of belonging and mattering for both students and staff involved. Beginning with the purposeful process of greeting students by name, staff can intentionally build relationships with students (Toya, 2011). DRL is also characterized by showing continued care and concern for students, serving as mentors, and promoting student ownership in the center space. The staff creates community by fostering friendships and familial-type relationships. Toya (2011) also found that students reported that staff diversity and relationships with staff led to a comfortable, safe, and home-away-from-home environment. A diverse staff that relates to the diverse communities of the institution increases the diversity of students using the center and enhances the safe space and home-away-from-home function of the center (Toya, 2011). The home-away-from-home environment helps students be themselves, spend time with friends, fulfill various academic and co-curricular needs, relax, escape, and feel safe (Jones et al., 2002; June, 1996; Patton, 2006). The home-away-from-home environment promotes retention and a sense of belonging for underserved students (Jones et al., 2002; Toya, 2011).

DRL also enhances student ownership and a sense of belonging to cultural centers (Toya, 2011). Staff members may form relationships with students to promote student ownership in the center. Student ownership may be displayed by the leadership roles of center "residents" who perform staff-like responsibilities such as providing center tours and staffing the center. In Toya's (2011) study, DRL was evident within the center's staffing as student staff served an equally important, or in some cases greater, role when compared to full-time staff in creating student ownership and a sense of belonging.

Developing Critical Leaders

Distributed Relational Leadership also contributes to creating a cycle of developing critical leaders. According to Toya (2011), the cultural center demonstrated distributed relational leadership by integrating activities for students focused on social justice education and identity development. Students who were engaged in such activities showed interest in working for cultural centers and/or entering student affairs and higher education as a profession. Congruent with Applied Critical Leadership, students' promotion to roles of critical leadership is enhanced when higher education student support centers implement practices that develop students' sense of social justice and identity (Santamaría & Santamaría, 2012).

Practical Strategies to Promote Safety and Persistence for Underserved Students

1. *Validate multiple identities.* Critical leaders should validate and recognize LGB Latino/a students as resources with regard to their multiple dimensions of identity (MDIs). Harper, Jernewall, and Zea (2004) and Parks, Hughes, and Matthews (2004) articulated that it is necessary in research to give voice to emerging science and theory for LGB people of color in order to provide proper services to this unique group of individuals.
2. *Campus resources.* Provide resources that focus on the needs of LGB Latino/a students (Evans & Wall, 2000). Resources like Summer Bridge, LGBT Resource Center, Cross Cultural Center, and Ethnic Studies give underserved students a sense of belonging, while providing support, social networks, and a space to explore and understand their multiple identities (Rosado, 2011; Toya, 2011).
3. *Space.* Sufficient space is needed for campus resource centers that enhance the retention, persistence, and safety of LGB students of color. Adequate space for cultural centers may realize the safe-space, home-away-from home, and resource functions of the centers (Toya, 2011).
4. *Social justice programming.* Programming and workshops addressing racism, cultural awareness, oppression, and inequity promote an inclusive campus climate for LGB Latino/a students (Hurtado, Milem, Clayton-Pedersen, & Allen, 1998; Jones et al., 2002; Princes, 1994; Rosado, 2011). Social justice learning outcomes can be realized in various program and workshop formats, such as film and lecture series, cultural musical performances; and dialogue groups (Jones et al., 2002; June, 1996; Princes, 1994).
5. *Inclusive programming.* Critical leaders should provide programs that address the MDIs for LGB Latino/a students (Rosado, 2011; Toya, 2011). Athanases and Larrabee (2003) recommend that future guest panels, literatures, videos, and so forth should include LGB people of color and of various ages to diversify the LGB population for learners.

6. *Developing critical leaders through diversity and equity training.* Campuses need to train staff/students to learn how to become critical leaders to better serve LGB Latino/a students. Moreover, critical leaders should teach colleagues how to serve as advocates/allies for these students. Santamaría & Santamaría (2012) assert the importance of research that would result in the development of critical leaders who are able to act courageously in the face of current and future needs in education based on their own cultural, linguistic, or disadvantaged experiences and backgrounds. Institutions need to ensure that resources cater to the cultural aspects of LGB Latino/a students in order to understand these students' needs for achieving academic success.

7. *Hiring diverse critical leaders.* Universities and colleges need to hire Student Affairs staff that reflect the social identities and understand the needs of undeserved students (June, 1996; Patton, 2006). Campuses need to consider hiring staff members who have the knowledge, skills, and experience to create a home-away-from-home for underserved students (Patton, 2006; Toya, 2011). Hiring LGB Latino/a university educators (Hurtado et al., 1998) to serve in formal or informal capacities can benefit LGB Latino/as by giving them mentors and role models they can relate to in terms of multiple identities, the Latino/a culture, and their academic endeavors.

8. *Distributed Relational Leadership.* Cultural center staff utilizing distributed relational leadership creates community, space, and programs that support LGB Latino/a students (Toya, 2011). DRL promotes multiple leaders to influence affect, knowledge, and practice (Spillane, 2006). Staff positional leaders should consider a distributed leadership style that draws upon the strengths of the entire staff. Building relationships is the most important component to the relational leadership process (Komives et al., 2007). Influencing the staff to establish meaningful relationships with students promotes mattering, sense of belonging, and retention of LGB Latino/a students (Toya, 2011).

9. *Cycle of developing critical leaders.* Critical leaders should provide intentional opportunities for LGB Latino/a students to engage in social justice and identity development practices. Actively encouraging and mentoring LGB Latino/a students to apply for student staff positions may influence them to pursue higher education careers and fill the need for greater numbers of critical leaders in higher education.

CULTURALLY RESPONSIVE LEADERSHIP IN PRACTICE

You have just been hired to work at La Jolla State University (LJSU), pseudonym, as the inaugural Director of the Queer People of Color Resource Center (QPCRC). This is an avant-garde center and a new position at LJSU. The Dean of Students charges you to staff and conceptualize the space of the center. You have been informed that LGB Latino/a students experience mental health distress because LJSU does not support their MDIs. LGB Latino/a students express a dire need for their "own" space. The Dean charges you with increasing the sense of belonging, safety, and academic persistence rate of LGB Latino/a students on campus.

Based on the theoretical and cultural context provided in this chapter, reflect on the following as you place yourself in the new role of LJSU's QPCRC Director:

- What will you include in your vision and mission of the QPCRC to align the strategic objectives of the Center to the needs of LGB Latino/a students?
- What culturally responsive strategies will you use to hire and train the Center staff?
- What resources will you need to tap into to support the Center's vision and mission?
- What will you do to foster LGB Latino/a students' development of their MDIs?
- How will the QPCRC increase the retention, persistence, and safety of LGB Latino/a students?
- How will you integrate practical applications of Distributed Relational Leadership and Applied Critical Leadership within the QPCRC?

Conclusion

Rapid demographic changes, the educational achievement gap, LGB student suicide, and the MDIs experienced by LGB Latino/a students call for higher education staff to implement more equitable ways to support this underserved student population. Staying abreast of current issues and trends will better inform our ability to successfully put into practice Distributed Relational Leadership and Applied Critical Leadership to enhance the success of LGB Latino/a students. "Critical leaders need to provide evidence that Applied Critical leadership will serve to benefit all learners and eventually close the achievement gaps separating our nation's learners" (Santamaría & Santamaría, 2012, p. 6).

Higher education staff implementing DRL and ACL can create an inclusive environment to increase the retention, persistence, and safety of LGB Latino/a students in a university setting, particularly in cultural centers. Staff members being conscious of their privileges, applying critical race theory, and navigating their diverse identities may strengthen staff–student relationships and equity interaction with underserved and LGB Latino/a students. It is imperative for higher education staff to transcend their own self-interests for the good of the group or organization, and engage in creating spaces that allow for transformational change for LGB Latino/a students (Bass, 1985; Santamaría & Santamaría, 2012).

References

Antonio, A. L. (2004). When does race matter in college friendships? Exploring men's diverse and homogeneous friendship groups. *The Review of Higher Education, 27*(4), 553–575.

Athanases, S. Z., & Larrabee, T. G. (2003). Towards a consistent stance in teaching for equity learning to advocate for Lesbian- and Gay-identified youth. *Teaching and Teacher Education, 19*(2), 237–261.

Bass, B. M. (1985). *Leadership and performance beyond expectation.* New York, NY: Free Press.

Benjamin, Y. (2010, November). *Bullied Tehachapi gay teen Seth Walsh dies after suicide attempt.* Retrieved from http://www.sfgate.com/cgibin/blogs/ybenjamin/detail?entry_id=73326

Bragg, D. D., Kim, E., & Rubin, M. B. (2005, November). *Academic pathways: Policies and practices of the fifty states to reach underserved students.* Paper presented at the annual meeting of the Association for the Study of Higher Education, Philadelphia, PA.

Capper, C. (Ed.). (1993). *Educational administration in a pluralistic society.* Albany: State University of New York.

Crawford, I., Allison, K. W., Zamboni, B. D., & Soto, T. (2002). The influence of dual-identity development on the psychosocial functioning of African-American gay and bisexual men. *Journal of Sex Research, 39*(3), 179–189.

Diaz, E. M., & Kosciw, J. W. (2009). *Shared differences: The experiences of lesbian, bisexual, and transgender students of color in our nation's schools.* New York, NY: GLSEN.

Duck, S. (1991). *Understanding relationships.* New York, NY: Guilford Press.

Evans, N. J., & Wall, V. A. (2000). Parting thoughts: An agenda for addressing sexual orientation issues on campus. In V. A. Wall & N. J. Evans (Eds.), *Toward acceptance: Sexual orientation issues on campus* (pp. 389–401). Lanham, MD: University Press of America.

Galanti, G. (2003). The Hispanic family and male-female relationships: An overview. *Journal of Transcultural Nursing, 14*, 180–185.

Galupo, M. P. (2009). Cross-category friendship patterns: Comparison of heterosexual and sexual minority adults. *Journal of Social and Personal Relationships, 26*(6–7), 811–831.

Garcia, B. (1998). *The development of Latino gay identity.* New York, NY: Garland Publishing.

Harley, D. A., Nowak, T. M., Gassaway, L. J., & Savage, T. A. (2002). Lesbian, gay, bisexual, and transgender college students with disabilities: A look at multiple cultural minorities. *Psychology in the Schools, 39*(5), 525–538.

Harper, G. W., Jernewall, N., & Zea, M. C. (2004). Giving voice to emerging science and theory for lesbian, gay, and bisexual people of color. *Cultural Diversity and Ethnic Minority Psychology, 10*(3), 187–199.

Hensel, K. (2010, November). *Teen suicide victim hangs himself from barn rafters.* Retrieved from http://www.wishtv.com/dpp/news/local/east_central/teen-suicide-victim-hangs-himself-from-barn-rafters

hooks, b. (1990). Culture to culture: Ethnography and cultural studies as critical intervention. In b. hooks (Ed.), *Yearning: Race, gender, and cultural politics* (pp. 123–133). Boston, MA: South End Press.

Howorth, C. (2010, November). *Another gay teen suicide.* Retrieved from http://www.thedailybeast.com/blogs-and-stories/2010-10-02/raymond-chase-becomes-fifth-suicide-victim/

Hurtado, S., Milem, J., Clayton-Pedersen, A., & Allen, W. (1998). Enhancing campus climate for racial/ethnic diversity: Educational policy and practice. *The Review of Higher Education, 21*(3), 279–302.

Jones, L., Castellanos, J., & Cole, D. (2002). Examining the ethnic student experience at predominately White institutions: A case study. *Journal of Hispanic Higher Education, 1*(1), 19–39.

June, V. (1996). *Inside a multicultural center: Narratives of identity, cohesion, and racism at a predominately white institution* (Unpublished doctoral dissertation). Washington State University, Pullman, WA.

Komives, S. R., Lucas, N., & McMahon, T. R. (2007). *Exploring leadership: For college students who want to make a difference* (2nd ed.). San Francisco, CA: Jossey-Bass.

Ladson-Billings, G., & Donnor, J. (2005). The moral activist role of critical race theory. In N. Denzin & Y. Lincoln (Eds.), *Handbook of qualitative research* (3rd ed., pp. 279–301). Thousand Oaks, CA: Sage.

Ladson-Billings, G., & Tate, W. F., IV. (1995). Toward a critical race theory of education. *Teachers College Record, 97*, 47–68.

Lippa, R. A., & Tan, F. D. (2001). Does culture moderate the relationship between sexual orientation and gender-related personality traits? *Cross-Cultural Research, 35*, 65–87.

McLaren, P. (2003). *Life in schools: An introduction to critical pedagogy in the foundations of education* (4th ed.). Albany, NY: Allyn & Bacon.

Nee-Benham, M.K.P., Cooper, J. E., & Almee-Benham, M. (1998). *Let my spirit soar: Narratives of diverse women in school leadership.* Thousand Oakes, CA: Corwin Press.

O'Hare, P. (2010, November). *Parents say bullies drove their son to take his life.* Retrieved from http://www.chron.com/disp/story.mpl/metropolitan/7220896.html

Parks, C. A., Hughes, T. L., & Matthews, A. K. (2004). Race/ethnicity and sexual orientation: Intersecting identities giving voice to emerging science and theory for lesbian, gay, and bisexual people of color. *Cultural Diversity and Ethnic Minority Psychology, 10*(3), 241–254.

Patton, L. D. (2006). The voice of reason: A qualitative examination of black student perceptions of black culture centers. *Journal of College Student Development, 47*(6), 628–646.

Princes, C.D.W. (1994, March). *The precarious question of black cultural centers versus multicultural centers.* Paper presented at the annual conference of the Pennsylvania Black Conference on Higher Education, Harrisburg, PA.

Raffaelli, M., & Ontai, L. L. (2004). Gender socialization in Latino/a families: Results from two retrospective studies. *Sex Roles, 50*(5/6), 287–299.

Rosado, S. (2011). *Browning the rainbow: The academic persistence and multiple dimensions of identities of lesbian, gay, bisexual Latino/a students* (Unpublished doctoral dissertation). California State University San Marcos and University of California San Diego, CA.

Santamaría, L. J., & Santamaría, A. P. (2012). *Applied critical leadership in education: Choosing change.* New York, NY: Routledge.

Scheurich, J. J., & Skrla, L. (2003). Continuing the conversation on equity and accountability. In L. Skrla & J. J. Scheurich (Eds.), *Educational equity and accountability: Policies, paradigms, and politics* (pp. 39–49). New York, NY: Routledge.

Singleton, G. E., & Linton, C. (2006). *Courageous conversations about race: A field guide for achieving equity in schools.* Thousand Oaks, CA: Corwin Press.

Spaulding, P. (2010, November). *Why did Tyler Clementi die?* Retrieved from http://articles.cnn.com/2010–09–30/opinion/spaulding.rutgers.suicide_1_tyler-clementi-video-suicide-harassment-gay-students?_s=PM:OPINION

Spillane, J. P. (2006). *Distributed Leadership.* San Francisco, CA: Jossey-Bass.

Swail, W. S. (2003). *Retaining minority students in higher education: A framework for success.* ASHE-ERIC Report. San Francisco, CA: Jossey-Bass Higher Education.

Terrell, R., & Lindsey, R. (2009). *Culturally proficient leadership: The personal journey begins within.* Thousand Oaks CA: Corwin Press.

Toya, G. J. (2011). *Cultural center staff: A grounded theory of distributed relational leadership and retention* (Unpublished doctoral dissertation). California State University San Marcos and University of California San Diego, CA.

Turner, C.S.V. (1994). Guests in someone else's house: Students of color. *The Review of Higher Education, 17*(4), 355–370.

Valencia, R. (2002). The plight of Chicano students: An overview of schooling conditions and outcomes. In R. R. Valencia (Ed.), *Chicano school failure and success past, present and future* (pp. 3–51). New York, NY: Routledge Falmer.

Van Nostrand, C. H. (1993). *Gender responsible leadership: Detecting bias, implementing interventions.* Newbury Park, CA: Sage.

Vega, W. A. (1990). Hispanic families in the 1980s: A decade of research. *Journal of Marriage and Family, 52*(4), 1015–1024.

Way, N., & Chen, L. (2000). Close and general friendships among African American, Latino, and Asian American adolescents from low-income families. *Journal of Adolescent Research, 15*(2), 274–301.

Way, N., Gingold, R., Rotenberg, M., & Kuriakose, G. (2005). Close friendships among urban, ethnic-minority adolescents. *New Directions for Child and Adolescent Development, 107,* 41–59.

Welch, E. (2009). *Havens, harbors, and hope for underrepresented and marginalized student success* (Unpublished doctoral dissertation). California State University San Marcos, San Diego State University, and University of California San Diego, CA.

4

"I AM CULTURALLY AWARE, I AM CULTURALLY BURDENED"

Poetry and Narrative as Critical Practice in Teacher Education

Katie Fitzpatrick and Vanessa Langi

IDEA IN BRIEF

In this chapter, the authors—a critical teacher educator and an undergraduate student—reflect together on how using narrative and poetry enabled them both to engage with issues of diversity and equity. The chapter draws on a poem written by the second author, which was completed for a course assessment. The course, and use of poetry and narrative therein, are discussed as an example of critical practice in higher education. By co-authoring the chapter, the authors also re-imagine students as leaders in education and in the academy who can co-write with and contribute new insights to the academic literature.

Keywords: student voice, critical practice, poetry, narrative, diversity

> *Music speaks truth.*
> *I am other.*
> *"Short hair, don't care." My mother tongue is my first language but it's lost.*
> *I'm making the effort to find it. I like shorts and singlets. I respect my*
> *body. I enjoy watching cultural customs. I acknowledge cultural customs.*
> *But I'm still wearing shorts and singlets. And hanging out with boys.*
> *And drinking. Like a fish. And riding a bike on a Sunday. They tell me*
> *they disapprove. With their face. I must owe them money. Until you can*
> *supply, rather than deny, until you've learnt what I've learnt, I'll keep*
> *my short hair.*

We begin this chapter with an extract from a poem that the second author, Vanessa, wrote for an undergraduate course assignment. We will explain the context of the poem shortly, but Vanessa wrote it as part of a course completed in the final year of her teaching degree that was taught by the first author, Katie. This chapter, then, is the product of conversations between an undergraduate teacher education student (who is now teaching full-time in a school) and a teacher educator. We decided to co-author this discussion in order to undermine the usual authorial voice of education research and leadership; to show that student voice should carry through, not only as a result of research studies, but as students speaking directly back to the academy in research publications and scholarly literature. In this sense, we re-imagine students as leaders in education and in the academy who can co-write with and contribute new insights to the academic literature, even before they are engaged in postgraduate study. During the final year of Vanessa's four-year teacher education degree, we had many conversations about issues of equity, exclusion, racism, and how we each tried to deal with these through our educational practice. But it is important that you also understand who we are and how we got to be here (hooks, 2010).

Vanessa is a Tongan New Zealander who grew up in Auckland, in a working-class family. Katie is a Pākehā (European) New Zealander who grew up in a working-class rural family. Katie has spent much of her career, both as a high school teacher and as an academic, working with culturally and linguistically diverse students. Her work has focused on bringing students' perspectives and experiences to light, and seeking to understand them in relation to wider social issues at the intersection of class, place, ethnicity, culture, and gender/sexuality (K. Fitzpatrick, 2013b). She has also highlighted the importance and potential of critical approaches to education in her discipline (K. Fitzpatrick, 2010; K. Fitzpatrick, 2013a; K. Fitzpatrick, 2013b; K. Fitzpatrick & Tinning, 2014; K. Fitzpatrick & McGlashan, in press) and values poetic and narrative as creative forms of research communication (E. Fitzpatrick & Fitzpatrick, 2015; K. Fitzpatrick, 2012). Vanessa is currently teaching at a diverse and low socioeconomic urban high school in South Auckland, New Zealand (NZ). Her academic interests are in critical and multicultural pedagogies, sociology, culture and curriculum, and indigenous concepts of teaching and learning. She brings these perspectives to her (high school) teaching subjects of health and physical education. In this chapter, the authors discuss notions of access and equity in higher education.

In the extract from the poem we began with, Vanessa is commenting on what it means to be a Tongan woman in New Zealand. Tongans are (first-, second-, and third-generation) immigrants to New Zealand from the island of Tonga in the Pacific. They are often categorized as Pacific Islanders (or Pasifika peoples) and aggregated with those who identify with Samoan, Cook Islands, Fijian, and other ethnicities. While there are connections between these groups, they also have distinct cultures and languages (Anae, Coxon, Mara, Wendt-Samu, & Finau, 2001; Fusitu'a & Coxon, 1998; Tupuola, 2004). The abstract from the poem that we began with is a commentary on social expectations at the intersection of gender, ethnicity, and religion; Vanessa is commenting on her conscious resistance to gendered expectations to have long hair, to gender and cultural expectations around (not) wearing shorts, hanging out with boys and drinking alcohol, and religious and cultural expectations about observing the Sabbath (by not riding a bike on Sundays).

Vanessa feels the disapproval of others and she is aware of her rebellion. She is also aware of what it means to be a Tongan woman in teacher education and at university and she brings a critical perspective to her positioning. In this sense, Vanessa has developed an awareness of social issues and her positioning within them. In this chapter, we consider these issues and share Vanessa's poetry as a form of expression and exploration. Vanessa's poem was a course assignment that required students to reflect, via personal narratives, on issues of equity in their lives. Before sharing and analyzing the poem together, we first consider this kind of work in higher education and how it articulates with critical practice more generally.

Critical Practice in TE

Critical scholars have, for decades, advocated pedagogical approaches in schools and teacher education programs to help teachers and students to become aware of, name, and work against the inequities created by and reinforced in the field of education. A range of theoretical positions is used and these are, of course, complex and differ across social, cultural, and geographical contexts. Nor do inequities only concern culture and ethnicity; they also work across social class, gender, sexuality, locality, and ability. Therefore, strategies in teacher education need to be both context-relevant and varied. Work in this area has been referred to as critical pedagogy (Giroux, 2005; Greene, 2009; McLaren, 2003), critical inquiry (Carr, 1995; Wright, Burrows, & Macdonald, 2004), critical thinking (Brookfield, 2012; hooks, 2010), transformative pedagogy (Ukpokodu, 2009; Wink, 2005), multicultural education (Banks, 1996; 1997a,b; 2001), and critical multiculturalism (May & Sleeter, 2010), among other labels. These ideas have also been taken up in educational leadership (Santamaría & Santamaría, 2012). All of this work is related to notions of education for freedom and social justice, and democratic education (e.g., Ayres, Quinn, & Stovall, 2009; Dewey, 2012; Greene, 1988; Luke & Gore, 1992). While proponents of the above-listed areas of scholarship also have quite different political positions and ontological underpinnings, they are all in some ways influenced by the Frankfurt school and Freirean, critical, and/or feminist theories. These don't necessarily sit comfortably alongside each other, and debates between more structuralist/

Marxist and poststructuralist approaches have ensued (Ellsworth, 1989; Kohli, 1998; Lather, 1998; Luke & Gore, 1992). We will not discuss these here, but will instead share our critical practice in one course, from the perspective of a teacher educator and a recently graduated student and, in so doing, we highlight how aspects of the above-mentioned work were explored in a specific teacher education program.

Thinking about Culture and Diversity in Teacher Education (Katie)

Having worked in teacher education for over 10 years, I have struggled with how best to engage my students in thinking critically and sociologically about issues of ethnicity, racism, gender, sexuality, body size, and ability. I have tried different strategies, many of which connect with the fields of critical practice in education. One of the problems I continually encounter is the narrowness of experience that many students bring to discussions, because of the dominance of White middle-class students in programs. While I have always had a percentage of students from non-White backgrounds in my courses, these students are often the minority, and speak back to and inform the class from the margins. Sometimes they remain silent because it is either unsafe to speak or they are just tired of being 'the voice' of difference every time (May & Sleeter, 2010). I share my own experiences of teaching in diverse communities and of partnering with indigenous and migrant students in high schools (Fitzpatrick, 2013a, 2013b) and I employ a diverse range of strategies including democratic approaches, student-led discussions, inquiry-based approaches, and various content (listed further below) but, as a Pākeha (White) educator, I am limited in my ability to disrupt dominant perceptions, when class members engaged in the discussions are overwhelmingly White. I have sought to understand this phenomenon via the literature in critical education and teacher education.

Students in teacher education, as in other sites, bring with them an array of ideologies, beliefs, values, and dispositions with regard to their place in the education system (Bartolome, 2004; hooks, 2010). Many of these are based on their own experiences and a result of dominant social discourses. Challenging these assumptions is a key task of teacher-education programs but, while many of us teaching in such programs aim to disrupt and widen students' views, these are strongly formed by and within their cultural backgrounds. This is important because, in most Western countries, the teaching workforce does not reflect the growing ethnic and cultural diversity of classrooms (May & Sleeter, 2010). As Bartolome (2004) argues, teacher-education programs are concerned with equipping teachers with the best possible tools. She notes, however, that these tend to focus on practical strategies at the expense of a deeper engagement with "teachers' own assumptions, values, and beliefs" (Bartolome, 2004, p. 97). The latter is crucial because, the day-to-day decisions we make in the classroom, as well as the big-picture programmatic and structural decisions made in schools, are all a function of deeply held beliefs and assumptions about education, about communities and what is 'best' for students. Brookfield (1995) argues that:

> One of the hardest things teachers have to learn is that the sincerity of their intentions does not guarantee the purity of their practice. The cultural, psychological, and political complexities of learning and the ways in which power complicates all human relationships (including those between students and teachers) mean that teaching can never be innocent.
>
> *(p. 2)*

In this sense, teachers, like all other professionals, are caught in a myriad of complex power relations. While many teachers desire social change and greater equity, being able to 'see' how schools and wider social relations contribute to inequalities is the first step.

Teacher educators, however, are also caught up in dominant understandings—even those who purport to be critically orientated and focused on social justice. As a population, teacher educators are a lot less diverse than undergraduate student teachers, and certainly less diverse than many communities and schools. Rather than lamenting the difficulty of shifting the perceptions and values of our teacher education students, we can perhaps partner with those in our classes who are from non-White backgrounds and begin conversations that challenge ourselves, and the assumptions of our courses.

Embedding Narrative in Course Work

To this end, as part of one of my courses, I invite students to write personal narratives of their backgrounds at the intersection of social class, ethnicity, culture, gender, ability, and sexuality. The course is called 'curriculum issues in health and physical education'. The students are all studying to be teachers in secondary schools, and they complete this course in the final year of a four-year program.

hooks (2010) argues that critical approaches to issues of power in education begin with personal experiences. Understanding our own biographies along the lines of social class, ethnicity, gender, and ability can help us to begin to name and expose the norms of cultural practice we live, and which have formed our dispositions. My students are required to read hooks's account of her experiences in her book *Teaching Critical Thinking: Practical Wisdom* (2010). She begins the book with an account of growing up and attending university amid racially segregated communities in the U.S. in the middle of the 20th century, and she talks directly about the racism and sexism she experienced in education contexts. She also highlights the importance of the teachers who humanized and who attended to the experiences and struggles of students. I encourage my students, while writing their personal biographies, to use creative forms of expression: to tell stories, write poems, use narrative. I draw on my own work in this area (Fitzpatrick, 2013a; Fitzpatrick & Fitzpatrick, 2015) by way of example. During this task, we also explore a range of issues in the fields of health and physical education (these two subjects are interwoven in curriculum in NZ), drawing on literature that questions gender sexuality, ability, racialization, body size, health, and so forth (e.g., Burrows & Wright, 2004; Gard & Wright, 2005; Hokowhitu, 2008; Rich, Holroyd, & Evans, 2004; Sykes & McPhail, 2008) as well as literature on critical thinking and narrative writing (e.g., Brookfield, 1995; Brookfield, 2012; Langellier, 1999).

Poetry and narrative are included as part of the course design in the hope of engaging the students emotionally and disrupting normative forms of expression. Joe Kincheloe (2008), reminds us:

> Knowing and learning are not simply intellectual and scholarly activities but also *practical and sensuous activities* infused by the impassioned spirit. Critical pedagogy is dedicated to addressing and embodying these affective, emotional and lived dimensions of everyday life in a way that connects students to people in groups and as individuals.
>
> *(p. 11, emphasis added)*

Barone (2010) argues that poetry has a critical purpose, pointing out "the power of art to challenge and disrupt prevailing regimes of truth by raising new questions without obvious answers." He proceeds to explain that poems "proffer a vision that is an alternative to the conventional, at odds with the commonplace, the usual lens through which we view the world" (p. 331). Further below we share Vanessa's poem, but first background her experiences, which help the frame of context of her creative expression.

Understanding Cultural Background (Vanessa)

> Kole (mu'a) keu hufanga atu he ngaahi tala fakatapu', ka e 'ataa mu'a e faingamalie koeni keu fai atu ha ki'i fakamatala (lea) mei he finemotu'a (fefine) tu'a mo ma'olalo koeni, kiate kimoutolu 'i he potungaue ako. (ke lea atu ki he kainga fanau ako).

I was born in New Zealand to parents who had migrated to Australia from Tonga as young adults before relocating to South Auckland, New Zealand, with very limited English. Prior to primary school, I was fluent in Tongan. As I transitioned into primary school, I became fluent in English but, along with my family, was still highly involved in the Tongan community. At a young age, my family moved to a middle-class/more affluent suburb of Southeast Auckland, and 'assimilated' to the culture of this particular community—Pākehā and Western culture. *"I'd love to go back to when we played as kids, but things changed, and that's the way it is."*

(Tupac). In the course, I reflected on my childhood through my poem. It is at this stage where I feel that I was 'in and out' of my ethnic identity and most annoyed and angry at being what I saw as 'too brown for life.' Throughout high school, it became increasingly evident that there were complexities with the various social relationships that existed all around me. It was made known to me that I should only associate myself with 'brown' people. I also learnt of the derogatory terms 'bunga' and 'chinks.' *"In the famous words of Mr King, why can't we all just get along?"* (Twista). The journey I have experienced so far, and have begun to express through narrative, is one where inner-conflict is constant; 'negotiating' my cultural identities as I experience multiple fields of practice, and feeling like a 'fish out of water.' As Melinda Webber (2012a) has discovered, experiences such as this are important for the racial-ethnic identity development of adolescents, as they learn to "rebel against communally prescribed and socially ascribed racial-ethnic identities, at the same time nurturing a sense of belonging, pride, and positive attachment to one's racial-ethnic identity" (Webber, 2012a, p. 22).

Reflecting and Challenging through Poetry

For the first assignment last year, I (Vanessa) wrote an extended spoken word poem. In so doing, I drew on song lyrics that inspired me and linked to my experiences. These include a range of artists: Bob Marley, Tupac, John Mayer, Adeaze (a New Zealand hip-hop band), and Natasha Bedingfield. For me, *Music speaks truth*. I find comfort in music, I learn through music, and I can identify myself through music. I have always been fascinated by lyrical content. Artists such as Bob Marley and Tupac Shakur—whose lyrics I used in my poem—have a cult following, both as living artists and posthumously, as they speak volumes with their artistry, being able to weave multiple stories or themes and messages within a song. They give true accounts of social issues and their place in society at the time; these are often political, sometimes perceived as controversial but, more important for me, their music is relatable as they reflect on and challenge dominant ideologies of their time, as well as their own worldview.

The first part of the poem we began this chapter with commented on gender. In the sections that follow, we reflect together about the meanings that are evident in other parts of the poem and, where appropriate, offer background on the context. For readability here, we use the third person for this analysis. The second part of the poem comments on religion and racism. Tongan communities in New Zealand have a strong focus on the church as a core of the community. It is also a place where language and cultural protocol are preserved. Although strongly committed to church and to Tongan culture, Vanessa also has a critical view of aspects of religion:

"So what's the go, G O D?" Preach. Did God tell you himself? Who the hell made these rules up? Who are you to tell me yay or nay? Who really gains from

your weekly tithe? Apparently I'm a skeptic. Apparently I need to be saved. I'll respect that that's your view. And my view is that you've got a one-track mind, blinded by one set of rules that you believe to be the one and only, irrespective of others around you. Bigot. And how is it that I was only taught a real Sexuality Education in the third year of my degree? Saved.

The poem comments on how Vanessa's Tongan identity is received by others outside the Pacific Island community, and how she experiences racialized assumptions about ethnicity and about being an immigrant:

"In the famous words of Mr King, why can't we all just get along?" Too brown for life. Speak to me properly; I was educated in this country too. And no, I'm not from South Auckland. Educate yourself before you tell me to go back to where I came from. Of course you feel superior; world is founded on oppression and your 'people' pretty much raped it. In the netball arena, we're equal. But at a regatta, I'm obviously too brown for you to talk to me. No new friends.

There is a sense in the poem here of the insidious racialized assumptions that non-White people experience in general and in the fields of sport and physical education in particular (Azzarito, 2009; Harrison, Azzarito, & Burden, 2004; Hokowhitu, 2004; Palmer, 2007). This is mixed, in this example, with social class assumptions within the sports of netball and 'the regatta' (which is a rowing competition). In New Zealand, netball is a sport that crosses social classes and ethnicities, but the rowing 'regatta' is definitely the reserve of wealthy schools and communities—very few young Pacific Island people row.

The poem then goes on to name the kind of racialized assumptions experienced on a daily basis as people read Vanessa's skin color and embodiment, and make assumptions about where she was born and about her parents:

"In this bright future you can't forget your past." What are you? Tongan. Were you born there? No, here. Is that your car? Yes. Is that your house? Yes. What do your parents do? They've provided for quality living. They mirror morals and values of my grandparents and great grandparents. They tell funny jokes. They know how to throw a party. They sober drive me. They give me my freedom. They let me be. They don't force Tongan culture down my throat. They don't make me eat, breathe and live church. They understand the world I grew up in. They are a testament to sacrifice and love. Oh, but you wanted to hear that they're working-class immigrants with factory jobs.

The poem also critiques messages about health and body size that are a function of obesity discourses (which, in New Zealand, target Pacific Island communities). Vanessa works in a gym part-time and aims to work against the negative and destructive messages in the media about Pacific Islanders, which tend to stereotype these communities as fat, lazy, obese, and unhealthy (K. Fitzpatrick, 2013b; Loto et al., 2006).

> *"We don't have education, we have inspiration; if I was educated I would be a damn fool."*
> *Pacific Island mind-set: prioritise traditions; a healthy lifestyle is boring, silly.*
> *"Damn you're skinny." No way! "Sick of being the fat one. My weight has always held me back." Commit. Persevere. And I will do the same for you. How bad do you want it? "This is so cool. Why are you doing this? Why do you want to?" I don't like what I see. There's no excuse for it.*
> *So here's me pushing for change. What is the use of my education if my hands do not match? Educate. And inspire. High school PE teacher, you were the catalyst. Goal: be better to students than you were to me.*

In the last part of the poem, there is a sense of pedagogical response and how Vanessa aims to respond to issues of discrimination in the classroom:

> *"I'd love to go back to when we played as kids, but things changed, and that's the way it is." Tell the children the truth. Teach the children the world. Times have changed. "Faggot." Cringe. "Gay." Cringe. "Slut." Defensive. Not in my class. Freedom of speech. Freedom to listen. Criticize without ignorance. Peace is a verb. I am other. You are other. Is it feasible?*

The poem ends with a statement about self:

> *"You've come too far, you ain't gon give up. Don't quit cos you ain't a quitter."*
> *I will be the first to graduate. Crap. Instagram spits my truth. My blurb reads: Vanessa Langi—Tongan—Kiwi—Liberal Take—Citizen of the World (peace sign and love heart emoticon to end).*
> *I am of Tongan. I am first generation Aotearoa born. I am a lover of diversity. I am pro democracy.*
> *I am culturally aware. I am culturally burdened. I aspire to exemplify.*
> *I am other.*
> *"The rest is still unwritten."*
> *Peace + Love.*

Vanessa: In reflecting now on the course I completed at university, I think *"You've come too far, you ain't gon give up. Don't quit cos you ain't a quitter."* The previously mentioned course 'curriculum issues in health and physical education' allowed me to draw connections between personal and academic analyses, and to seek a synthesis between the sometimes disparate poles of a Tongan-NZ woman who has lived in two diverse parts of Auckland city. I left appreciative of a lecturer who allowed us to speak, and who genuinely valued honest, student voices. From a student's perspective, I felt a great sense of affirmation in 'voicing' my journey. We analyzed educational ideas and practices and set them within the context of our individual worldviews. Through self-reflection in my personal narrative, and by listening to my peers throughout the course, there were some validated and shared meanings among classmates, infuriating discussions with others, and sensitive topics discussed. However, I would like to think that it enabled us to critically examine long-standing social and curriculum issues, extend social relationships, improve interpersonal communication and intercultural understandings, and develop knowledge of cultural and linguistic diversity. The social world is complex and ever-changing, and as such, the way we write about ourselves may be of the same nature (Langellier, 1999). What is written by students can enlighten teachers about the experience of our 'longa'i fanau' (youth) living in a multi-ethnic society. Personal narratives can be a way for teachers to create a context to help students affirm and strengthen their identities, to help students become aware of the culturally diverse place they live in and the negative stereotypes that exist (which are rife and influential in the lives of our young people). Both of these can lead to favorable educational outcomes (Webber, 2012b).

Final Thoughts

In writing this piece together, we both have a richer understanding of the different cultural contexts informing our practice as teachers and students. In opening up the space to reflect together on course content focused on issues of social justice, and on poetic representations of personal stories and experiences, we have met in the 'in-between spaces' of culture (Bhabha, 1994). We each hail from different cultural backgrounds and we both rail against the injustices we see, feel, and experience in education settings. If teacher education courses can be spaces where not only the assumptions of students are challenged, but also places for teacher educators to deepen their understandings of inequities in the lives of students, then we are more likely to achieve the deeper engagement that Bartolome (2004) calls for. We argue that creative, poetic and narrative reflections can be a small part of this process. We end with another two pieces of poetry, one each, written upon reflection on writing this chapter.

Katie: Discovery

Speaking with you requires me to listen
I quieten my voice to hear your stories

And my internal
*   histories herstories*
*   weave their own way to meet up*

we can't turn them off

Echoing in our words, are reverberations of place,
The long tail of generations lives in ignorance of
other

and we are

both women   our bodies moving through time
carrying the crosses our ancestors gifted to us
with love   with the limits of necessity

and right now, we name those edges
we name them together

Vanessa: Journey

The quest of my heritage on the vaka sailed by my ancestors, across generations,
*   and now through me.*
Cultural pride, cultural yearning, sailed in waves on waves; you see,
The hope is multiculturalism, the struggle is biculturalism, my internal fight is
*   dualism; release me.*
I am not the long haired girl of beauty. I am not the tafe lolo girl of purity.
I am all churched out. I am done with principality.
But cultural history
Is my necessity.
"In this great future you can't forget your past." Ode to Patelisio and Mele
*   Loloahi.*
Epitome.
I imagine her under the sun, clapping twice for that next cup of kava; smiling,
*   singing, dancing, and he*
Ringing the Angelus bell and working til he is under the star of the sea.
Their seeds grew in an abundance of life lessons on love and respect for all, spoilt
*   with constant company,*
Disregard for nobility,
Deep faith in the Father Almighty,
Intercessions to Mother Mary,
To cope in this stratified society.
Clarity.
Label me
As a prodigy
Of an F.O.B.
See me
As a product of suffering hands and feet through double shifts in factories.
Know me
As the investment from sacrifice, courage, motivation. Surrounding me

Their perceptions, loose foundation, this white nation, misinterpretation,
   misconception, mis-education, messing with me.
That empty mentality
Can lead to the beauty of vulnerability
In which we dabble with in poetry,
Or let the trapped silence be the rope for my usos, my tokouas to end in tragedy.
This is our tainted society, negativity, conformity,
You don't get it if you're not angry.
Social responsibility,
You're telling me?
It took me a while to find reality;
My identity
Is widespread. I'm making the most out of a life of a minority.
Legacy,
Will be my story.
I too have a dream, with a fear of inadequacy.
Will the thoughts/feelings/words written, spoken, internally, externally,
This PE degree
Match the actions of these hands? Heilala planted, deeply rooted as I continue this
   hala kuo papa; I'll ride the smooth sails, take the rain and all the battles upstream
For without it where would I be?
For without it who would I be?
The path well trodden carries on with Miss Langi.
You see,
Self discovery,
This has a no-end theory.
Journey.

CULTURALLY RESPONSIVE LEADERSHIP IN PRACTICE

Katie and Vanessa demonstrate ways ACL serves to interrupt inequities in teacher education from the perspectives of women who are White faculty and students of color. The authors both draw on positive aspects of their Pākehā and Tongan identities and reflect using poetry as a means to convey the essence of what it means to be women with particular raced and gendered identities in teacher education in New Zealand. Both authors also assume critical theoretical lenses. Katie to critique power differentials associated with race, gender, and class in the fields of health and physical education within teacher education; Vanessa to add a critical counter-narrative to deficit theories in the literature regarding Pasifika and Tongan women. By deliberately engaging the reader with prose and poetry, and a dually presented counter-story (Solórzano & Yosso, 2002), the chapter serves to disrupt and expand existing critical literature by initiating a more complex critical conversation about truth-telling in teacher education. The authors invite practitioners, aspiring leaders, and students to:

- Work as mentors or co-authors promoting scholarly contributions in mainstream venues to facilitate bringing previously silenced voices into higher education narratives, critical or otherwise (ACL-honoring constituents; reversing negative stereotypes; making empirical contributions adding authentic previously silenced voices to decision-making processes)
- Work in cross-cultural pairs or groups in order to gain understanding of differing worldviews (ACL-leading by example to meet unresolved educational challenge; building trust with those different from oneself)

Further, Katie, in *choosing* to initiate an inclusive critical research platform that serves to consider and critique scholarly discourse regarding race, class, ethnicity, and gender within the context of cultural and linguistic diversity, can be considered a White ally within the context of applied critical leadership. Vanessa, too, *chose* to engage aspects of her own leadership practice as a result of agreeing to co-author with a White academic who was also her former teacher. These decisions were based on a relationship of trust between them. Both women exhibited critical leadership characteristics by abandoning assumptions associated with the cultural memberships each brought into their relationship to work together for a constructive purpose. Their example provides a template for others in uneven power and identity relationships to work in tandem on equity and access issues in the academy.

References

Anae, M., Coxon, E., Mara, D., Wendt-Samu, T., & Finau, C. (2001). *Pasifika education research guidelines.* Wellington, New Zealand: Ministry of Education.

Ayres, W., Quinn, T., & Stovall, D. (Eds.). (2009). *Handbook of social justice in education.* New York, NY: Routledge.

Azzarito, L. (2009). The panopticon of physical education: Pretty, active and ideally white. *Physical Education and Sport Pedagogy, 14*(1), 19–39.

Banks, J. A. (Ed.). (1996). *Multicultural education, transformative knowledge, and action.* New York, NY: Teachers College Press.

Banks, J. A. (1997a). *Teaching strategies for ethnic studies* (6th ed.). Boston, MA: Allyn & Bacon.

Banks, J. A. (1997b). *Educating citizens in a multicultural society.* New York, NY: Teachers College Press.

Banks, J. A. (2001). *Cultural diversity and education: Foundations, curriculum and teaching* (4th ed.). Boston, MA: Allyn & Bacon.

Barone, T. (2010). Educational poetry that shakes, rocks, and rattles. In T. Huber-Warring (Ed.), *Storied inquiries in international landscapes: An anthology of educational research* (pp. 331–335). Charlotte, NC: Information Age.

Bartolome, L. (2004). Critical pedagogy and teacher education: Radicalizing prospective teachers. *Teacher Education Quarterly, 31*(1), 97–122.

Bhabha, H. (1994). *The location of culture*. New York, NY: Routledge.

Brookfield, S. D. (1995). *Becoming a critically reflective teacher.* San Francisco, CA: Jossey-Bass.

Brookfield, S. D. (2012). *Teaching for critical thinking: Tools and techniques to help students question their assumptions.* San Francisco, CA: Jossey-Bass.

Burrows, L., & Wright, J. (2004). The good life: New Zealand children's perspectives on health and self. *Sport, Education and Society, 9*(2), 193–205.

Carr, W. (1995). *For education: Towards critical educational inquiry.* Buckingham, UK: Open University Press.

Dewey, J. (2012). *Democracy and education: An introduction to the philosophy of education.* Los Angeles, CA: Indo-European Publishing.

Ellsworth, E. (1989). Why doesn't this feel empowering? Working through the repressive myths of critical pedagogy. *Harvard Educational Review, 59*(3), 297–325.

Fitzpatrick, E., & Fitzpatrick, K. (2015). Disturbing the divide: Poetry as improvisation to disorder power relationships in research supervision. *Qualitative Inquiry, 1*, 50–58. doi:10.1177/1077800414542692

Fitzpatrick, K. (2010). A critical multicultural approach to physical education: Challenging discourses of physicality and building resistant practices in schools. In S. May & C. Sleeter (Eds.), *Critical multiculturalism: Theory and praxis* (pp. 177–190). New York, NY: Routledge.

Fitzpatrick, K. (2012). 'That's how the light gets in': Poetry, self, and representation in ethnographic research. *Cultural Studies, Critical Methodologies, 12*(1), 8–14. doi:10. 1177/1532708611430479

Fitzpatrick, K. (2013a). Brown bodies, racialisation and physical education. *Sport, Education and Society, 18*(2), 135–153. doi:10.1080/13573322.2011.559221

Fitzpatrick, K. (2013b). *Critical pedagogy, physical education and urban schooling.* New York, NY: Peter Lang.

Fitzpatrick, K., & McGlashan, H. (in press). Rethinking 'straight' pedagogy: Gender, sexuality and PE. In D. Robinson, L. Randall, & W. J. Harvey (Eds.), *Critical pedagogy within physical education: Problematizing sociocultural, political, and institutional practices and assumptions.*

Fitzpatrick, K., & Tinning, R. (Eds.). (2014). *Health education: Critical perspectives.* London, UK: Routledge.

Fusitu'a, L., & Coxon, E. (1998). Ko e 'ulungaanga faka- tonga mo e ako lelei: Tongan culture and academic achievement. *New Zealand Journal of Educational Studies, 33*(1), 23–38.

Gard, M., & Wright, J. (2005). *The obesity epidemic: Science, morality and ideology.* London, UK: Routledge.

Giroux, H. (2005). The terror of neoliberalism: Rethinking the significance of cultural politics. *College Literature, 32*(1), 1–19.

Greene, M. (1988). *The dialectic of freedom.* New York, NY: Teachers College Press.

Greene, M. (2009). In search of a critical pedagogy. In A. Darder, P. Baltodano, & R. D. Torres (Eds.), *The critical pedagogy reader* (2nd ed., pp. 84–96). New York, NY: Routledge.

Harrison, L., Azzarito, L., & Burden, J. (2004). Perceptions of athletic superiority: A view from the other side. *Race, Ethnicity and Education, 7*(2), 149–166.

Hokowhitu, B. (2004). 'Physical beings': Stereotypes, sport and the 'physical education' of New Zealand Māori. In J. A. Mangan & A. Ritchie (Eds.), *Ethnicity, sport, identity: Struggles for status* (pp. 192–218). London, UK: Frank Cass.

Hokowhitu, B. (2008). Understanding the Māori and Pacific body: Towards a critical physical education pedagogy. *Journal of Physical Education New Zealand, 41*(3), 81–91.

hooks, b. (2010). *Teaching critical thinking: Practical wisdom.* New York, NY: Routledge.

Kincheloe, J. L. (2008). *Critical pedagogy primer.* New York, NY: Peter Lang.

Kohli, W. (1998). Critical education and embodied subjects: Making the poststructural turn. *Educational Theory, 48*(4), 511–519.

Langellier, K. (1999). Personal narrative, performance, performativity: Two or three things I know for sure. *Text and Performance Quarterly, 19*(2), 125–144.

Lather, P. (1998). Critical pedagogies and its complicities: A praxis of stuck places. *Educational Theory, 48*(4), 487–497.

Loto, R., Hodgetts, D., Chamberlain, K., Nikora, L. W., Karapu, R., & Barnett, A. (2006). Pasifika in the news: The portrayal of Pacific peoples in the New Zealand press. *Journal of Community and Applied Social Psychology, 16*(2), 100–118.

Luke, C., & Gore, J. M. (Eds.). (1992). *Feminisms and critical pedagogy.* New York, NY: Routledge.

May, S., & Sleeter, C. (2010). Introduction: Critical multiculturalism: Theory and praxis. In S. May & C. Sleeter (Eds.), *Critical multiculturalism: Theory and praxis* (pp. 1–16). New York, NY: Routledge.

McLaren, P. (2003). *Life in schools: An introduction to critical pedagogy in the foundations of education.* Boston, MA: Allyn & Bacon.

Palmer, F. (2007). Treaty principles and Māori sport: Contemporary issues. In C. Collins & S. Jackson (Eds.), *Sport in Aotearoa/New Zealand society* (2nd ed., pp. 307–334). Melbourne, Australia: Thomson.

Rich, E., Holroyd, R., & Evans, J. (2004). 'Hungry to be noticed': Young women, anorexia and schooling. In J. Evans, B. Davies, & J. Wright (Eds.), *Body knowledge and control: Studies in the sociology of physical education and health* (pp. 173–190). London, UK: Routledge.

Santamaría, L. J., & Santamaría, A. P. 2012. *Applied critical leadership in education: Choosing change.* New York, NY: Routledge.

Solórzano, D. G., & Yosso, T. J. (2002). Critical race methodology: Counter-storytelling as an analytical framework for education research. *Qualitative Inquiry, 8*(1), 23–44.

Sykes, H., & McPhail, D. (2008). Unbearable lessons: Contesting fat phobia in physical education. *Sociology of Sport Journal, 25*(1), 66–96.

Tupuola, A. (2004). Pasifika edgewalkers: Complicating the achieved identity status in youth research. *Journal of Intercultural Studies, 25*(1), 87–100.

Ukpokodu, O. (2009). The practice of transformative pedagogy. *Journal on Excellence in College Teaching, 20*(2), 43–67.

Webber, M. (2012a). Identity matters: The role of racial-ethnic identity for Māori students in multiethnic secondary schools. *SET: Research Information for Teachers, 2,* 20–25.

Webber, M. (2012b). Adolescent racial-ethnic identity: Behaviors, perceptions, and challenges in urban multiethnic school contexts. In M. N. Agee, T. McIntosh, P. Culbertson, & C. O. Makasiale (Eds.), *Pacific identities and well-being: Cross-cultural perspectives* (pp. 5–26). New York, NY: Routledge.

Wink, J. (2005). *Critical pedagogy: Notes from the real world.* Boston, MA: Pearson.

Wright, J., Burrows, L., & Macdonald, D. (Eds.). (2004). *Critical inquiry and problem-solving in physical education.* London, UK: Routledge.

PART II

Adapting Culturally Responsive Leadership to Benefit Those Who Are Systemically Underserved

5

WOMEN OF COLOR AND APPLIED CRITICAL LEADERSHIP

Individual, Professional, and Institutional Strategies for Advancement

Brenda Lloyd-Jones*

IDEA IN BRIEF

Women of color continue to be underrepresented in upper-level leadership positions at predominantly White institutions (PWIs) of higher education in the U.S. PWIs have been unsuccessful in diversifying their own senior systems of governance to reflect the changing face of a globalized era. This chapter responds to a call for the advancement of theories and practice relevant to women of color in leadership positions and faculty appointments by advancing Applied Critical Leadership (ACL) Theory as a culturally responsive approach for transcending barriers and other challenges in the academy. Drawing on the findings from a review of extant literature on the pertinent issues, the author provides individual, professional, and institutional strategies for practicing culturally responsive leadership and career support for women of color who aspire to or currently serve in senior leadership roles in academia. The conclusion offers a call to action for both women of color and their potential allies who seek an inclusive and constructive academic environment.

Keywords: women of color, senior leadership positions, strategies, predominantly White institutions (PWIs)

Academe is a "system that is unwelcoming to women and people of color" according to a Benchmarking Women's Leadership in the United States report (Gangone, 2013, p. 4). Although deeply alarming, this research finding merely confirms what is documented in much of the literature on the experiences of women of color scholars at American universities and colleges. This scholarship corroborates empirical evidence that substantiates the persistent systemic barriers to advancement in the academy that women and, in particular, women of color continue to confront. Although women of color have made substantial gains with respect to academic achievements since the United States (U.S.) Supreme Court ruling of *Brown v. Board of Education* in 1954, they continue to be underrepresented in high-ranking governance roles at predominantly White institutions (PWIs) of higher education in the U.S. Presumed to promote equal access to education and democratic ideals, PWIs have been unsuccessful at diversifying their own senior-level system of governance to reflect the changing face of a globalized era. This problem merits critical examination, given changing demographics indicating that by 2042 racial minority groups will make up the majority of the U.S. population (U.S. Census Bureau, 2014). Moreover, research suggests that the lack of upward trajectories of women of color as senior administrators in academe "stems not from a lack of preparation or the requisite knowledge and skills but rather the resistant and persistent presence of discriminatory practices and the biases that sustain them" (Welch, 2011, p. 3).

A growing body of research describes the lived experiences of women of color in the professoriate (e.g., Baez, 2011; Hune, 2011; Lloyd-Jones, 2009; Turner, 2002). However, sightings of women of color at senior leadership positions in academe are few, and research that focuses on them and the ways in which they access and sustain these roles is scant (Blackwood & Brown-Welty, 2011; Chen & Hune, 2011; Grant, this volume). Though scholarly and practical approaches providing support for women of color in upper-echelon leadership in the academy are essential, few theoretical frameworks offer specific strategies of career support for women of color who aspire to achieve leadership roles or persist in them. Given the paucity of leadership theory and practices specifically concerned with race and gender disparities and the barriers and challenges unique to women of color in higher education leadership, this chapter responds to a call for the advancement of theories and practice relevant to women of color in leadership roles in the academy by differentiating Applied Critical Leadership (ACL) Theory as a culturally responsive approach and discussing how women of color can integrate critical leadership practices into their academic careers in an effort to strategically move up to the top ranks of the faculty and the administration. The significance of this chapter lies in its contribution to the literature on the general topic of women of color in higher education and its promise of practical steps developed to support women of color who aspire to senior-level leadership roles or who currently serve in upper-level leadership positions in the academy. Lastly, the chapter concludes with a call to action for both women of color in the academy and potential allies.

The term "women of color" is used throughout this chapter to describe women who share membership in groups marginalized by their race, ethnicity, and gender. They include African Americans, Asian/Pacific Americans, Hispanics/

Latinas, and American Indians. Specific racial and ethnic groups have experienced a legacy of oppression, slavery, colonization, and/or conquest (Bernal, Trimble, Burlew, & Leong, 2003), which are threads that bind many women of color in their efforts to fully and equally participate in U.S. culture and to access opportunities, resources, and positions within the ivory tower (Lloyd-Jones, 2011).

When examining the progress of women of color in higher education, institutional research is generally categorized by gender or race, but rarely both. Gender data that combines women of color with White women, however, obscures the impact of race on the progress of women of color (Hune, 2011). Racial and/or ethnic data are also problematic in that they tend to reflect all racial and ethnic groups jointly, which distorts the understanding of groups that tend to be distinct in their histories, cultures, and access to opportunity. As a way to address the presumption that the experiences of women of color are monolithic, the chapter will include data for each group. Additionally, this level of analysis may point the way toward strategies for increasing the population of underrepresented groups in areas of authority in higher education.

The Status of Women of Color in Academe

Gender and race/ethnicity have been the focus of much discussion on college and university campuses. The academic conversation has included a concentration on the inclusion of historically marginalized and currently underrepresented faculty and administrators. An emphasis on inclusion and diversity creates a welcoming, affirming, supportive environment in which women of color could feel empowered and a genuine sense of belonging. However, women of color remain conspicuously absent from senior-level administrative and high-ranking leadership positions at PWIs of higher education in the U.S. They represent 10.6% of professors who are full-time administrators (Jackson & O'Callaghan, 2009). Although women of color outnumber men of color (7.4%) in higher education administration, women of color often face the double jeopardy of racism/ethnic discrimination and sexism. Further, stereotypes, beliefs, and historical views about women of color as leaders are often rooted in leadership theories, such as the "Great Man" theory, which is described as the earliest theory of leadership and can be traced back to the early 1900s. As its name implies, this concept posited leadership a male quality, particularly in terms of military leadership (Stogdill, 1974). Moreover, in the U.S., leadership has been identified with men, since they have historically held positions of greatest authority and power. Most traits associated with leaders have been masculine-agentic (i.e., forceful, aggressive, authoritative). Despite the fact that the Great Man theory has been proven inaccurate, it still often influences who is seen as capable of leadership. Such perspectives have generated stereotypes that have frequently been shown to be fallacious; yet they negatively influence access to leadership positions by women of color (Lloyd-Jones, 2011).

The path to the most senior ranks of the faculty and administrative leadership positions is typically that of academic affairs. Senior leadership positions in higher education are presidents/chancellors, provosts, and academic deans, which are primarily male-dominated positions. Individuals who engage the path to high-ranking leadership roles tend to enter academia as assistant professors, earn tenured positions, and eventually are promoted to the rank of full professor. Among women professors in the U.S., 6.6% of women associate professors and 4.8% of full professors are Black; 6.2% of women associate professors and 4.9% of full professors are Asian; 3.4% of associate professors and 2.8% of full professors are Latina; and 82% of women associate professors and 86.6% of women full professors are White (Chronicle of Higher Education, 2012). Full-time American Indian faculty constitute a mere 0.5% of faculty members in the U.S., "making this an elusive demographic to capture" (Mackey, 2014, p. 37). These data illustrate the underrepresentation of women of color associate and full professors.

The lack of gender and racial/ethnic diversity in decision-making roles at PWIs is particularly problematic in view of the ever-changing nature of the demographics in academe. The student populations of universities and colleges are becoming increasingly diverse (Jackson & O'Callaghan, 2009), and the absence or presence of racially/ethnically diverse administrators communicates a message to students, faculty, and other administrators of color that can influence their sense of being welcomed and sense of belonging (Grant, this volume). In fact, researchers who monitor higher education have identified access, retention, and advancement for administrators of color as an area of concern, particularly in senior-level positions at PWIs. Additionally, the experience of administrators of color as determined by their progress in academe is an indicator of institutional commitment to diversity (Jackson & O'Callaghan, 2011). Changing demographics, retention of students, and advancement of faculty and administrators of color provide sound rationales for PWIs to engage in practices that eliminate institutional, social, and internal impediments, thereby diversifying the upper-level administrative ranks of higher education in terms of gender, race, and ethnicity.

Despite these incentives, some researchers have identified reasons for the persistence of low numbers of women of color in academia, and Ford (2011) has synthesized the literature on the experiences of women of color at PWIs:

- The "Chilly Climate" Problem: Universities and colleges are isolating environments for Women of Color (WOC) faculty members, including a lack of relationships, promotion, and tenure (Antonio, 2002; Olsen, Maple, & Stage, 1995; Turner, 2002).
- Issues of Legitimacy: WOC report difficulty gaining respect and credibility as qualified teachers and scholars from students and faculty (Harlow, 2003).
- Tokenization and Cultural Taxation: WOC are expected to teach about issues of race, mentor students of color, and serve on diversity committees. WOC

are overburdened as token representatives for their respective racial groups (Baez, 2011; Thompson & Sekaquaptewa, 2002).

• Balancing Personal and Professional Roles: WOC faculty have to learn to negotiate family life effectively, commit to service in the community, and advance their own career goals (Mason, Goulden, & Wolfinger, 2006; Turner, 2002).

Other factors contributing to the slow ascension of women of color in academia are unfair recruiting and hiring practices (Mertz, 2011) and the glass-ceiling effect. The "pipeline" theory (White, 2005) also offers an explanation for the underrepresentation of women of color in senior leadership positions in the academy. Although the number of students of color completing undergraduate programs continues to increase, the same results are not true at the graduate and doctoral level. Subsequently, women of color are not filling the pipeline and are not available for recruitment as assistant professors earning tenured positions. Their absence makes them ineligible for senior ranks of the faculty and administrative leadership positions. Low numbers of women of color with doctoral degrees in the educational pipeline contribute to their underrepresentation in top senior positions (see Stiemke & Santamaría, this volume). In 2012, people of color earned merely 24.4% of the master's degrees awarded in the U.S.: African Americans: 9.3%, Hispanics: 5.2%, Asian Americans: 5.3%, and American Indians: 0.5%. In 2012 in the U.S., Whites, on the other hand, earned 56.8%. People of color earned only 20.5% of the doctoral degrees awarded—African Americans: 6.2%, Hispanics: 4.4%, Asian Americans: 9.4%, and American Indians: 0.6%—while Whites earned 59.9% (National Center for Education Statistics, 2014). It is imperative for people of color in general and women of color in particular to earn an advanced degree to become eligible for faculty and senior leadership positions.

Research on women of color administrators and faculty members, summarized below, offers a window into the current situation in academe. At the highest levels of higher education administration, the percentage of women in chief academic officer positions (CAOs) increased from 40% to 43% from 2008 to 2013. However, the share of African Americans in such positions fell from 3.7% to 2.3%, Asian American CAOs dropped from 3.7% to 2.4%, and Hispanic CAOs decreased from 1.5% to 0.8% (Kim & Cook, 2013). The decline in the percentage of women of color who occupy these high-ranking positions in academe merits serious investigation. These data indicate there are few women of color in senior leadership positions in academe. Further, only 23% of college and university president posts in U.S. are held by women even though they are more likely than their male counterparts to have earned a doctorate (National Center for Education Statistics, 2014). The majority of these women presidents are at two-year institutions and liberal arts and women's colleges. Nationally, fewer women than men are in upper-level administrative positions throughout higher education (i.e., presidents, provosts, vice presidents, deans, and departmental chairpersons) and particularly at four-year institutions. Although women in all racial and ethnic groups are attending college at higher rates than their male counterparts (National Center for Education Statistics, 2014) in the national landscape of institutions of higher education, men continue to dominate the senior leadership positions. Despite the dismal research findings, women of color, given their lived experiences, have cause for optimism.

Lived Experiences as Leadership Preparation

Mahatma Gandhi is credited with the quote: "You must be the change that you wish to see in the world." Valverde (2011) makes a similar charge specifically to women of color who aspire to leadership roles in academe. He argues that, in order to shape their future, they must change their practice of adapting and reacting to higher-education institutions and replace it with the critical role of change agent, augmenting it with new leadership styles. Transformational and participatory leadership styles are two approaches he advocates. By infusing their leadership style with the behavior of change agents, women of color will accomplish three major goals: eliminate societal negative forces, advance in the academy, and improve academia for the better (Valverde, p. 51). Further, the experience of social exclusion and scholarly marginalization at PWIs has the potential for situating women of color in leadership roles (Lloyd-Jones, 2014). Valverde's (2011) explanations follow:
  Women of color:

- Will be smarter because they will learn to outthink or rethink how to overcome man-made barriers placed in their path;
- Will be more experienced due to the longer time in the apprentice mode;
- Will be more adaptive because they will change themselves according to complicated situations;
- Will be stronger because of the necessity to be resilient and endure hardships and disappointments; and
- Will refashion their organizations so as to accommodate a diverse student body; they will be part of the change fabric. (p. 72)

In essence, women of color can use adverse experiences as a foundation of strength to build, develop, and perform leadership in higher education. While working on the margins in their professional careers, women of color and other historically underrepresented groups have acquired relevant cognitive and social competencies (see Stiemke & Santamaría, this volume). Shullman (2009) argues that the view from the "outside of the circle" is strikingly different to the view "from the center" and usually requires multiple sets of skills to navigate the boundaries of multiple contexts. The author concludes that this can essentially be an advantage in learning and applying leadership competencies. Unfortunately, historical leadership paradigms do not necessarily respect the power and potential of diversity (Gordon, 2009). Even so, leadership is required among visibly diverse people, who demonstrably build, and leverage, collaborative effort based on their experience of multiple angles of vision (Gordon, 2009).

Theory, Epistemology, and Methodology

In the epigraph below, Anzaldua (1990) defines the term "theory" as sources of knowledge, challenging its traditional interpretation. She implores scholars of color to transform the discourse on theorizing by contributing alternative ways of knowing and approaches to social inquiry.

> Theory, then, is a set of knowledges. Some of these knowledges have been kept from us—entry into some professions and academia denied us. Because we are not allowed to enter discourse, because we are often disqualified and excluded from it, because what passes for theory these days is forbidden territory for us, it is vital that we occupy theorizing space, that we not allow white men and women solely to occupy it. By bringing in our own approaches and methodologies, we transform that theorizing space.
>
> *(Anzaldua, 1990, p. xxv)*

Similarly to Anzaldua, and specifically referencing leadership theories, Chin (2010) argues that "theories of leadership need to be expanded to incorporate diversity if they are to be relevant for the 21st century amidst new social contexts, emerging global concerns, and changing population demographics" (p. 150). Additionally, "theories of leadership have neglected diversity issues . . . and remain silent on issues of equity, diversity, and social justice" (Chin, 2010, p. 150). Both Anzaldua and Chin affirm the standpoint that burgeoning gender, racial, and ethnic diversity merit expanded theories of leadership to include traditionally marginalized groups that have been excluded from positions of leadership.

The field of leadership is replete with multiple theories that reflect varied ideas of effective leadership. Researchers do not all agree on the meaning of what they observe, and no single theory has been able to explain all perspectives of leadership. Scholars are continually trying to support, contradict, and integrate these diverse points of views. For example, early leadership research focused on individuals in leadership positions, who were almost always White Anglo Saxon males (Rhode, 2003). Concentration on this group created the stereotype that these people were most qualified as leaders. According to Middlehurst (2008), despite the fact that some early research on leadership has been proven inaccurate, it still represents the stereotype of leadership. Fortunately, alternative approaches to theory are opening the path to change.

Applied Critical Leadership: A Practical Framework for Advancing Women of Color in Academe

The Applied Critical Leadership Difference

Critical theory questions the ways social processes in society and in academic institutions provide advantages and privileges for certain groups of people and describes how they disadvantage and marginalize other groups (Kezar, Carducci, & Contreras-McGavin, 2006). Favoring some groups' perspectives while devaluing others' points of view is done through the institutionalization of the norms and values of the dominant group as the rule or standard, (Mertz, 2011). Going beyond understanding and explaining society, critical theory is concerned with evaluating and *changing* the traditional norms of the academy that may function to disadvantage women of color in their access to and sustainability in maintaining senior leadership positions.

What is different about the ACL theoretical framework is that it intersects with transformational-leadership theory, critical pedagogy theory, and critical race theory. Although essential to the foundation of ACL, transformational leadership and critical pedagogy combined merely identify the need for change from a critical perspective (Santamaría & Santamaría, 2012). The ACL difference stems from the addition of the lens of CRT, which offers a viewpoint that gives voices to the voiceless by working toward social justice and educational equity (Santamaría & Santamaría, 2012). "One of the main functions of CRT is to feature otherwise silenced voices in empirical research" (p. 127). ACL goes beyond its individual components by empowering leaders to engage in asking questions about how specific attributes of their social identities and life experiences can support individuals in contributing to educational communities and initiatives in which they live and work.

ACL Strategies: From Personal to Professional and to Institutional

One of the primary objectives of this chapter is to present ACL strategies in an effort to support women of color who aspire to senior-level leadership roles or who currently serve in upper-level leadership positions in academe. The strategies for critical leadership practice are featured below in three broad categories: individual (which aims to develop initiatives and/or participate in activities for personal growth and understanding); professional (which aims to develop initiatives and/or participate in activities for professional development, performance, and advancement); and institutional (which aims to increase the significance, urgency, and movement of organizational change through the engagement of people, policy, and practice).

Individual Strategies for Practicing Culturally Responsive Leadership

Address Racial/Ethnic Stereotypes and Gender Biases with Counter-Storytelling

Whether one is a senior-level administrator or aspires to become one, it is important to understand that others tend to expect individuals of color to serve as representatives of their racial or ethnic groups, and when people of color occupy positions of authority the expectation is that they be exemplary role models. Hence, women of color in roles of visibility are subject to both critique and emulation and should become accustomed to close observation of their interaction with members within the academic community (e.g., faculty, students, trustees) and people external to the university (e.g., media, community leaders, legislators). Women of color who understand how their social roles have been shaped by historical and societal influences and how they as individuals are perceived in education can use CRT counter-storytelling to promote social justice by exposing and challenging deeply entrenched narratives and characterizations of racial stereotypes and gender biases (Solórzano & Yosso, 2002). The critical leadership approach promotes the process of understanding and self-identification enables women to fight for equity and opportunity in higher education while challenging the barriers that prevent or limit their participation. Committed to transforming inequitable and undemocratic social relations is characteristic of ACL.

Engage in Self-Care

Empirically documented barriers include a hostile climate in the form of distrust among peers and feelings of isolation and marginalization, which function as sources of stress for women of color in the academy. To manage stress, women academics must find an appropriate work–life balance strategy taking the necessary time for their families, employment, and themselves. Also important to high-performing faculty and administrators is their health and wellness status. In a study (Vakalahi & Starks, 2011) women of color academics completed a health and well-being questionnaire with the goal of determining the multiple factors that contribute positively and/or negatively to their health and well-being. For instance, work-related stress and anxiety, internalized unresolved experiences with racism in the workplace, isolation and withdrawal from social network due to overwhelming workload; weight problems; and financial strain were identified as negative contributors to one's health and well-being. In contrast, supportive family, friends, and mentors, spirituality, exercise and healthy diet, adequate health care, and financial security were identified as positive contributors to one's health and well-being. Using these findings, women administrators and faculty of color can design ways to reduce their own strain and increase their health and well-being status. The authors of the study concluded that research and policy practice are urgently needed to support women of color academics as they struggle to find balance between the expectations of the academy and the entities—family and friends—that contribute most to their health and well-being.

Professional Strategies for Practicing Culturally Responsive Leadership

Participate in Mentoring and Networking Programs

The practice of mentoring is commonly cited as a primary factor associated with the advancement of faculty in the academy (Stanley, 2006; Turner, 2002). Recipients of mentoring attribute career promotion, job satisfaction, and organization commitment to mentors who helped them to understand and adapt to the culture of the organization. Women faculty of color, however, often report experiences of exclusion and marginalization in academe, which challenge their retention and dissuade them from becoming productive and satisfied members of the professoriate (Lloyd-Jones, 2011).

Although mentors are critically important to helping women of color navigate the often-treacherous path to tenure, promotion, and academic survival (Lopez & Johnson, 2014), they are less likely to attain a mentor and more likely to serve as mentors in comparison to other faculty members. Few women of color are in tenure track academic positions compared to their White counterparts at PWIs and women of color tend to be the only ones of their racial or ethnic background in their respective departments in these institutions of higher education; therefore, they must be open to securing mentors who are not of their same racial group and who may not reside in their academic department or institution (Stanley, 2006).

In other words, women of color should consider securing internal and external female and male mentors. According to contemporary mentoring literature, one mentor cannot meet all the needs of a woman of color in the professoriate. Furthermore, no one person is expected to have the expertise essential for an individual to negotiate the complexities of a faculty career in higher education. Networking with individuals in upper-leadership positions in the academy with an aim to receive information on career advancement is a useful practice. Various configurations of networking and mentoring are possible in that the approach could support intergenerational, intercultural, and interdisciplinary options.

Prepare for Senior Leadership Positions

Those with an earned advanced degree have achieved the basic qualification to engage the career path for senior leadership positions in higher education

(Gasman, Abiola, & Travers, 2015). Women who aspire to senior leadership should be aware of paths that will lead to such positions, such as mid-level administration leadership positions in academic affairs. They should also take on leadership roles with incremental responsibilities including understanding effective search strategies, community relations, risk management, and financial management. In addition to securing mentors for their own career development, women of color in leadership positions will want to engage in mentoring other women of color as appropriate, thereby contributing to the education pipeline. Finally, numerous formal leadership programs are available to women who are currently in or aspiring to senior-level positions in higher education. Specific information with respect to geographic location, program contents, financial costs, and time frames of such professional development opportunities can be identified and explored on the Internet.

Institutional Strategies for Practicing Culturally Responsive Leadership

Select Battles Strategically When Addressing Organizational Change

Critical leaders are committed to transforming the academy; however, with respect to academic survival, personal stamina, and political capital, Lopez and Johnson (2014) advise individual faculty members to address challenge or change issues that are within their power. The authors suggest asking critical questions before deciding to pursue an issue: Is the issue ripe? What has happened with the issue that concerns women of color faculty and administrators and other historically underrepresented groups? Is additional information required before scheduling a meeting with the administration? Applied Critical Leadership is a promising approach for administration to use in becoming more systematic about addressing effectively social justice issues in higher education, including helping women of color overcome institutions barriers and other related challenges. Though righting the wrongs and redressing inequities are priorities for critical leaders, avoiding battle fatigue is essential for women of color. One important way to stave off possible burnout is to identify and enlist allies to take up the cause. This is a form of support that is essential for women of color in the academy.

Conclusion

Thus, I encourage all potential allies of women of color who seek culturally responsive and appropriate leadership in the academy to support an ACL approach on their campuses. And to women faculty and administrators of color, I hope the research discussed in this chapter assures you that your vision is not impaired, nor do you suffer from recurrent paranoia. Empirically speaking, your perceptions are acutely and disturbingly accurate; among senior-level leaders in the academy, women of color are few, at best. Empirical, theoretical, and anecdotal findings, explanations, and reasons for this scarcity abound, including discriminatory and biased policies and practices; hostile and unsupportive academic and social campus environments; insufficient work–family balance options; lack of leadership preparation and development opportunities; pipeline concerns related to attainment of advanced degrees, tenure, and promotion; absence of effective mentoring initiatives; and unfair recruitment, hiring, and retention practices. Critical examinations of the complexities associated with the underrepresentation of women of color in senior ranks of faculty and administrative leadership positions can be discouraging. However, ACL is a robust and optimistic option that facilitates the work of equality while simultaneously preparing for and engaging in the intricate process of transforming current professional realities.

Note

* Correspondence concerning this chapter should be addressed to Brenda Lloyd-Jones, Department of Human Relations, University of Oklahoma, Tulsa, OK 74137. Email: blloydjones@ou.edu

References

Antonio, A. L. (2002). Faculty of color reconsidered: Reassessing contributions to scholarship. *Journal of Higher Education, 73*(5), 582–602.

Anzaldua, G. (1990) *Making face, making soul: Creative and critical perspectives by women of color.* San Francisco, CA: Aunt Lute Press.

Baez, B. (2011). Mentoring and interim positions: Female faculty of color: Agency and structure in race research. In G. Jean-Marie & B. Lloyd-Jones (Eds.), *Women of color in higher education: Changing directions and new perspectives.* Diversity in Higher Education Series, vol. 10 (pp. 241–260). Bingley, UK: Emerald Group.

Bennefield, R. M. (1999). Trench warriors: On the front lines. *Black Issues in Higher Education, 16,* 69–71.

Bernal, G., Trimble, J., Burlew, A., & Leong, F. (2003). *Handbook of racial and ethnic minority psychology.* Thousand Oaks CA: Sage.

Blackwood, J., & Brown-Welty, S. (2011). Mentoring and interim positions: Pathways to leadership for women of color. In G. Jean-Marie & B. Lloyd-Jones (Eds.), *Women of color in higher education: Changing directions and new perspectives.* Diversity in Higher Education Series, vol. 10 (pp. 109–133). Bingley, UK: Emerald Group.

Chen, E.W.C., & Hune, S. (2011). Asian American Pacific Islander women from Ph.D. to campus president: Gains and leaks in the pipeline. In G. Jean-Marie & B. Lloyd-Jones (Eds.), *Women of color in higher education: Changing directions and new perspectives.* Diversity in Higher Education Series, vol. 10 (pp. 163–190). Bingley, UK: Emerald Group.

Chin, J. (2010). Introduction to the special issue on diversity and leadership. *American Psychologist, 65*(3), 150–156.

Chronicle of Higher Education. (2012). *Diversity in the academy: The 2011 issue.* Washington, DC: Author.

Ford, K. A. (2011). Race, gender, and bodily (mis) recognitions: Women of color faculty experiences with White students in the college classroom. *Journal of Higher Education, 82*(4), 444–478.

Gangone, L. (2013). *Benchmarking women's leadership in the United States, 2013.* Colorado Women's College, Denver, Colorado. Retrieved from http://www.womenscollege.du.edu/media/documents/academia.pdf

Gasman, M., Abiola, U., & Travers, C. (2015). Diversity and senior leadership at elite institutions of higher education. *Journal of Diversity in Higher Education, 8*(1), 1–14.

Gordon, T. (2009). Leadership: Values in action. *Communique: Ethnic minority leadership.* Retrieved from http://www.apa.org/pi/oema/resources/communique/2009/08/august-special.pdf

Harlow, R. (2003). "Race doesn't matter, but . . . ": The effect of race on professors' experiences and emotion management in the undergraduate college classroom. *Social Psychology Quarterly, 66*(4), 348–363.

Huang, B. L., & Yamagata-Noji, A. (2010, November). *Invisible, marginalized but strong as bamboo: Asian Pacific American president leaders of academe.* Paper presented at the Association for Studies in Higher Education Conference, Indianapolis, IN.

Hune, S. (2011). Asian American women faculty and the contested space of the classroom: Navigating student resistance and (Reclaiming authority and their rightful place). In G. Jean-Marie & B. Lloyd-Jones (Eds.), *Women of color in higher education: Turbulent past, promising future.* Diversity in Higher Education Series, vol. 10 (pp. 307–335). Bingley, UK: Emerald Group.

Jackson, J. F. L., & O'Callaghan, E. M. (2009). Ethnic and racial administrative diversity—understanding work life realities and experiences in higher education [Special issue]. *ASHE Higher Education Report, 35*(3), 1–95.

Jackson, J. F. L., & O'Callaghan, E. M. (2011). Understanding employment disparities using glass ceiling effects criteria: An examination of race/ethnicity and senior-level position attainment across the academic workforce. *Journal of the Professoriate, 5*(2), 67–99.

Jean-Marie, G. (2011). "Unfinished agendas": Trends in women of color's status in higher education. In G. Jean-Marie & B. Lloyd-Jones (Eds.), *Women of color in higher education: Turbulent past, promising future.* Diversity in Higher Education Series, vol. 9 (pp. 3–20). Bingley, UK: Emerald Group.

Kezar, A. J., Carducci, R., & Contreras-McGavin, M. (2006). Rethinking the "L" word in higher education. *ASHE Higher Education Report, 31*(6), 1–218.

Kim, Y. M., & Cook, B. J. (2013). *On the pathway to the presidency 2013: Characteristics of higher education's senior leadership.* Washington, DC: American Council on Education.

Lloyd-Jones, B. (2009). Implications of race and gender in higher education administration: An African American woman's perspective. *Advances in Developing Human Resources, 11*(5), 606–618.

Lloyd-Jones, B. (2011). Diversification in higher education administration: Leadership paradigms reconsidered. In G. Jean-Marie & B. Lloyd-Jones (Eds.), *Women of color in higher education: Changing directions and new perspectives.* Diversity in Higher Education Series, vol. 10 (pp. 3–18). Bingley, UK: Emerald Group.

Lloyd-Jones, B. (2014). Remaining connected to the sociocultural experiences of underserved populations. In G. Jean-Marie, C. M. Grant, & B. Irby (Eds.), *The duality of women scholars of color: Transforming and being transformed in the academy.* Research on Women and Education Series (pp. 137–154). Charlotte, NC: Information Age.

Lopez, M. P. & Johnson, K. R. (2014). Presumed incompetent: Important lessons for university leaders on the professional lives of women faculty of color. *Berkeley Journal of Gender, Law and Justice, 29*(2), 388–404.

Mackey, H. (2014). Navigating the academy: Exploring barriers and possibilities in scholarship through the lens of an American Indian scholar. In G. Jean-Marie, C. M. Grant, & B. Irby (Eds.), *The duality of women scholars of color: Transforming and being transformed in the academy.* Research on Women and Education Series (pp. 33–54). Charlotte, NC: Information Age.

Mason, M. A., Goulden, M., & Wolfinger, N. H. (2006). Babies matter: Pushing the gender equity revolution forward. In S. J. Bracken, J. K. Allen, & D. R. Dean (Eds.), *The balancing act: Gendered perspectives in faculty roles and work lives* (pp. 9–29). Sterling, VA: Stylus.

Mertz, N. (2011). Women of color faculty: Recruitment, hiring, and retention. In G. Jean-Marie and B. Lloyd-Jones (Eds.), *Women of color in higher education: Changing directions and new perspectives.* Diversity in Higher Education Series, vol. 10 (pp. 41–71). Bingley, UK: Emerald Group.

Middlehurst, R. (2008). Not enough science or not enough learning? Exploring the gaps between leadership theory and practice. *Higher Education Quarterly, 62*(4), 322–339.

National Center for Education Statistics (2014). *The condition of education 2014.* Retrieved from http://nces.ed.gov/pubs2014/2014083.pdf

Olsen, D., Maple, S. A., & Stage, F. K. (1995). Women and minority faculty job satisfaction: Professional role interests, professional satisfactions, and institutional fit. *Journal of Higher Education, 66*(3), 267–293.

Rhode, D. L. (2003). The difference "difference" makes: Women and leadership. In D. L. Rhode (Ed.), *The difference "difference" makes* (pp. 3–50). Stanford, CA: Stanford University Press.

Ryu, M. (2010). *Minorities in higher education 2010: Twenty-fourth status report.* Washington, DC: American Council on Education.

Santamaría, L. J. (2014). Critical change for the greater good: Multicultural dimensions of educational leadership toward social justice and educational equity. *Education Administration Quarterly (EAQ), 50*(3), 347–391.

Santamaría, L. J., & Jean-Marie, G. (2014). Cross-cultural dimensions of applied, critical, and transformational leadership: Women principals advancing social justice and educational equity. *Cambridge Journal of Education, 44*(3), 333–360.

Santamaría, L. J., & Santamaría, A. P. (2012). *Applied critical leadership in education: Choosing change.* New York, NY: Routledge.

Shullman, S. L. (2009). Diversity leadership. *Communique: Ethnic minority leadership.* Retrieved from http://www.apa.org/pi/oema/resources/communique/2009/08/august-special.pdf

Solórzano, D. G., & Yosso, T. J. (2002). Critical race methodology: Counter-storytelling as an analytical framework for education research. *Qualitative Inquiry, 8*(1), 23–44.

Stanley, C. A. (2006). Coloring the academic landscape: Faculty of color breaking the silence in predominantly White colleges and universities. *American Educational Research Journal, 43*(4), 701–736.

Stogdill, R. H. (1974). *Handbook of leadership: A survey of theory and research.* New York, NY: Free Press.

Thompson, M., & Sekaquaptewa, D. (2002). When being different is detrimental: Solo status and the performance of women and racial minorities. *Analyses of Social Issues and Public Policy, 2*(1), 183–203.

Tillman, L. C. (2011). Sometimes I've felt like a motherless child. In S. Jackson & R. Gregory Johnson III (Eds.), *The Black professoriate: Negotiating a habitable space in the academy* (pp. 91–107). New York, NY: Peter Lang.

Turner, C.S.V. (2002). Women of color in academe. *Journal of Higher Education, 73*(1), 74–93.

U.S. Census Bureau (2014). *Projections of the size and composition of the U.S. population: 2014 to 2060.* Retrieved from https://www.census.gov/content/dam/Census/library/publications/2015/demo/p25–1143.pdf

Vakalahi, H. F., & Starks, S. H. (2011). Health, well-being and women of color academics. *International Journal of Humanities and Social Sciences, 1*(2), 185–190.

Valverde, L. A. (2011). Women of color: Their path to leadership makes for a better higher education for all. In G. Jean-Marie & B. Lloyd-Jones (Eds.), *Women of color in higher education: Turbulent past, promising future.* Diversity in Higher Education Series, vol. 9 (pp. 49–75). Bingley, UK: Emerald Group.

Welch, O. M. (2011). Prologue. In G. Jean-Marie & B. Lloyd-Jones (Eds.), *Women of color in higher education: Changing directions and new perspectives.* Diversity in Higher Education Series, vol. 10 (pp. xiii–xix). Bingley, UK: Emerald Group.

White, J. S. (2005). Pipeline to pathways: New directions for improving the status of women on campus. *Advance Library Collection, 19*(1), 22–27.

Yosso, T. J. (2005). Whose culture has capital? A critical race theory discussion of community cultural wealth. *Race Ethnicity and Education, 8*(1), 69–91.

Zweigenhaft, R. L., & Domhoff, G. W. (2006). *Diversity in the power elite: How it happened, why it matters.* Lanham, MD: Rowman & Littlefield.

6

HOPE REMAINS

Transcending Barriers to Advance Women of Color in Educational Leadership

Kimberley Stiemke and Lorri J. Santamaría

IDEA IN BRIEF

This inquiry explores personal, behavioral, and environmental attributes of one African American woman's journey toward opportunity recognition and educational attainment of a doctorate in educational leadership. Strategies used to overcome barriers to doctoral degree completion are revealed. These include (1) being open to the possibility there are opportunities available; (2) actively seeking opportunities to advance and enhance current opportunities; (3) actively investigating possible opportunities to determine whether they are appropriate; (4) assessing the merits of the opportunity offered; (5) recognizing, acting on, or pursuing multiple beneficial opportunities based on input from reliable sources in the environment (e.g., peers, mentors, those who care about one's well-being); (6) engaging with individuals to follow up, participate in, or engage opportunities that might result in a positive change to current circumstances. Findings further suggest networking, negotiating, mentoring, intercession, self-determination, and self-awareness are effective behavioral mechanisms resulting in barrier transcendence.

Keywords: African American women, tertiary educational attainment, educational leadership

Compelling research and experiential counter-narratives by African American, Latina, and Indigenous descent women describe common barriers that threaten their educational attainment from primary school through to postsecondary education (Jean-Marie, Grant, & Irby, 2014; Patton, 2009; Santamaría,

Jean-Marie, & Grant, 2014). Barriers to educational attainment manifest as diminished academic achievement resulting in academic achievement gaps, high drop-out rates, and low graduation rates. Women of color in the United States (U.S.) and particularly African American women, report increased barriers as they seek to attain higher levels of educational attainment (Grant & Simmons, 2008; Santamaría, 2014a, 2014b, 2014c; Stiemke, 2012). These barriers prevent many from pursuing or attaining master's degrees and doctorates. This study begins with the premise that there are unseen barriers (e.g., psychological, economic, institutional, emotional, etc.) at play impeding African American women in the U.S. from attaining doctorates.

Adding to barriers preventing access to educational degree completion is the shortage of Black women in educational leadership positions (McGee Banks, 2007). These disproportional shortages, juxtaposed with the shortage of culturally and linguistically appropriate leaders in diverse contexts (Leithwood & Riehl, 2003), render this chapter particularly relevant.

This chapter takes a strengths-based direction, demonstrating ways in which one African American woman transcended multiple barriers to her educational attainment from intermediate school years through the attainment of her doctorate in educational leadership over 15 years. Her experience is framed by literature concerning how African American women overcome barriers in education, grounded in an emergent approach called barrier transcendence theory (BTT) (Santamaría, 2009, 2012, 2014b). BTT is a working model designed to explain the ways women are able to recognize and act upon key opportunities that assist in their ability to transcend barriers formerly preventing their academic success as measured by degree attainment. The research question guiding this work is: What are some of the strategies used by an African American woman to transcend psychological, emotional, institutional or other barriers to her terminal degree attainment in educational leadership?

Literature Considered

African American Women Overcoming Educational Barriers

Findings from the field of vocational education indicate the strong influence of perceived opportunity recognition and barriers when it comes to people of color in their pursuit of occupational and educational goals (e.g., Slaney, 1980). This and related research identifies and confirms some of the barriers impeding African American women from attaining the highest levels of educational attainment compared to White people, other women of color, and men of color; though few provide insights on ways to overcome barriers.

Recently, a significant amount of research published by women scholars of color features their own strategies and the strategies of other women of color documenting counter-stories featuring descriptions of barrier transcendence in higher education (e.g., Benham & Murakami-Ramalho, 2010; Jean-Marie &

Brooks, 2011; Lloyd-Jones, 2009; Mackey, 2011; Santamaría, 2014a, 2014b, 2014c). Although largely autoethnographic, this research is nonetheless empirical and serves to counter mainstream resiliency theories that suggest some individuals are destined to 'make-it' despite the odds and are capable of overcoming any circumstances including those represented by the proverbial 'glass ceiling' (Hughes, Pennington, & Makris, 2012; Wang, Haertel, & Walberg, 1997). According to resiliency theory, which is one assumption undergirding the current study, individuals who pass through the glass ceiling do so because of their unique genetic make-up, tenacity, and strong will to change their circumstances. However, these are but a few pieces of a complex and dynamic puzzle.

Women researchers of color in academe also suggest mentoring (Grant & Simmons, 2008; Jean-Marie & Brooks, 2011; Santamaría et al., 2014) and creating supportive networks (Jean-Marie, 2011) as key elements of barrier transcendence. According to their research findings, these scholars have each transcended multiple barriers to educational attainment by way of resistance, transformation, and activism as agency (Lloyd-Jones, 2009; Mackey, 2011). Similarly, Benham and Murakami-Ramalho (2010) and Santamaría and Santamaría (2012) have found that building cross-cultural collaborations is critical to transcending barriers associated with educational attainment for women of color in leadership roles, particularly where there are few (McGee Banks, 2007). These last scholars' research findings equally suggest barrier transcendence through the creation of alternative models for more inclusive and therefore culturally responsive leadership, resulting in a sense of belonging for all women scholars of color (Santamaría et al., 2014). Applied critical leadership research further indicates that women of color leaders have the propensity to lead for equity and social justice benefitting systemically underserved students and students well served with regard to schooling (Santamaría & Jean-Marie, 2014; Santamaría, Santamaría, Webber, & Pearson, 2014).

Opportunity Recognition and Barrier Transcendence

Opportunity recognition in this context is borrowed from the disciplines of business and psychology (Ozgen & Baron, 2007). It is best described as predictive encoding or the ability for women of color to place pending goals into their memories as associations with particular environmental features. This deliberate action lets women of color know when timing is optimal to pursue advancement (Seifert & Patalano, 2001). Environmental predictive encoding can also be thought of as a personal attribute—or self-efficacy feature—that might enable women to predict what they need to do "now" in order to do what is necessary in advance, so they will be ready, in terms of skill, when they are able to recognize a future opportunity.

Opportunity recognition has also been described as entrepreneurial alertness as associated with perceptual and information-processing skills (Gaglio & Katz, 2001). So how then does opportunity recognition render the glass ceiling penetrable? The hypothesized BTT argues that it alone does not, but that a series of complex interactions among and between self-efficacy, mindfulness, flow, and predictive encoding are each components of a complex, phenomenological, and predictable model for explaining barrier transcendence for women of color (Santamaría, 2009, 2012, 2014b).

Therefore, transcendence in this model comes by *opportunity recognition* followed by opportunity realization, when optimal conditions are met. Transcendence can be any type of advancement that transports the individual from one *plane* to the next and can manifest for example as knowledge acquisition, personal growth, social enlightenment, or professional promotion. Figure 6.1 illustrates one manner in which barriers can be transcended. The model builds on self-efficacy research, which posits a triadic reciprocal causation model in which behavior (B), personal attributes (P), and the environment (E) dynamically influence each other (see Bandura, 1977). In this chapter, transcendence is educational attainment in the form of a terminal academic degree.

As such, BTT proposes to explain some of the ways in which personal attributes (P), individual behavior (B), and environmental (E) features may interact within the educational experiences of a woman of color on what can be described as a plane of experience, and the way in which her mindfulness of these factors may increase her enjoyment and engagement in purposeful activity

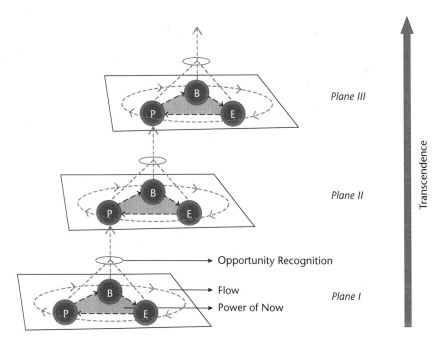

FIGURE 6.1 Barrier Transcendence Theory (BTT) Model (Santamaría, 2014b, p. 97)

and thus enhance her ability to recognize and act upon opportunities to enact change of circumstance, advancement, and movement to the next plane.

Methodological Approach

A case study was used for this study to understand the experiences of Monica (pseudonym), an African American woman working toward an Ed.D. in leadership at a research-intensive university in Southern California, as a bounded phenomenon. Monica is a first-generation college student in her late 30s. She was primarily educated in segregated urban settings in the Northeast U.S. In addition to being a wife and mother, Monica was an educational leader, teacher, and community activist. Purposeful sampling was used, as is typical in case study research, based on the researcher's positive relationship with Monica. She presented a critical convenient case based on the parameters established by Creswell (1998) and Miles and Huberman (1994). The case was critical because Monica is a self-proclaimed Black feminist who embodies intersectionality and has transcended multiple barriers toward terminal-degree attainment (Nash, 2008). Furthermore, the case was convenient because she was willing and able to engage in the inquiry process. Finally, Monica's experiences were well aligned with the literature reviewed.

Materials

Data collection included Monica's narrative account or autoethnography of educational experiences from her high school years through Ed.D. attainment; her advisor's account of the same from Monica's attainment of her teaching credential through attainment of the terminal degree and an interview using the BTT model as a scaffold for Monica to discuss opportunity recognition and barrier transcendence. Instruments offer multiple levels of critique in that they represent personal, dyadic, and institutional perspectives. Questions for the 90-minute interview were based loosely around the research questions and the BTT model in Figure 6.1.

Procedures and Analysis

Monica and her research advisor have been involved in an informal yet professional mentor/mentee arrangement for seven years. This comfortable professional relationship enabled ease of data collection, collation, and analysis. The researcher and participant discussed a research schedule from proposal through study completion and held each other accountable to the end of the project. Interview data was collected in the researcher's office or via Skype. Data analysis was completed face-to-face and online. Ethical considerations were discussed with reference to confidentiality, power relations, and intellectual property with the use of BTT.

Data was analyzed and interpreted against trends in the literature reviewed using the constant-comparative method (Bogdan & Biklen, 2007; Merriam,

1998). Analysis was iterative and cyclical, and proceeded from general to specific with parameters based on the research questions and literature reviewed combined with elements of the BTT model (Creswell, 1998; Silverman, 2000; Santamaría, 2014b). Analysis began informally with the reading and hand-coding of narrative data from the journals and continued through interviews and observations as categories emerged (Strauss & Corbin, 1998). Data was organized by placing as much as possible directly onto a conceptual map of the BTT model (Miles & Huberman, 1994). Throughout analyses, the researchers and participant functioned as a member-check in order to conduct as credible an analysis and interpretation as possible, addressing all ethical considerations, logistical issues, political realities, and related confidentiality issues (Bogdan & Biklen, 2007).

Results

This investigation produced six thematic findings in relation to Monica's journey toward gaining access and opportunity toward leadership study and position by way of barrier transcendence. First, findings indicate *networking* as a *behavior* was important in Monica's ability to recognize opportunities that resulted in her academic success. Second, the *ability to negotiate* was identified as another *behavior* crucial to Monica's acquisition of pertinent information for barrier transcendence. Third, research findings gleaned from the data validate the key role *mentor*-rich *activity as a behavior*, as well as the *presence and activity of mentors* in the *environment*, may play for Black women in the academy. The fourth finding described the role of *environmental intercession as interruption or changing course* as imperative to understand in relation to Monica's success. Fifth was the notion of *self-determination,* and finally, *self-awareness* as *personal attributes* were found to play important roles in Monica's 'way of being' that manifested throughout her journey.

The findings are presented in response to the research question by way of counter-story integrating vignettes presented in Monica's voice (Solórzano & Yosso, 2002). The counter-stories are derived from composites of data sets coded and analyzed as described in the method section: Monica's barrier-transcendence narrative, the researchers' narrative of Monica's barrier transcendence, and transcripts of a 90-minute Skype interview with Monica.

What Are Some Strategies Used by an African American Woman to Transcend Barriers to Her Terminal Degree Attainment?

Networking and Negotiation

According to the data analysis, Monica was personable. She was an effective communicator who carried herself with integrity, allowing forged relationships with people from all walks of life, particularly professionals. She considered these interfaces with people in her environment as networking activities.

Monica also employed various techniques that allowed her to think critically about situations to determine whether or not to invest her time and energy in an opportunity. Concerning this she said,

> I evaluate the environment to ascertain whether or not I will have a support system in place. I evaluate the opportunity to determine the benefits for others and myself. I look for alignment to see if the opportunity supports other areas of my life. I make a decision to see it through, and I consult with God through prayer.

She considered the processes involved in such decision making as exercising negotiation skills.

Engagement in Mentor-Rich Activity

Monica asserts that when she is connected to a group of people all working toward the same goal, she is able to learn from them and them from her in what was, at times, a peer exchange of co-learning. These relationships have been important in her ability to work through certain barriers, especially those related to academic benchmarks like high school graduation and the attainment of her college degrees. In the following passage, Monica discusses the challenges of navigating the college application process as a first-generation college student.

> My senior year was incredibly stressful. I was concentrating on building a future for my little sister and myself. I knew I had it within me to go to college, but I knew very little about the actual application process. Being the first in my family to go to college, I had to learn how to figure out the process.

At that time she had a mentor grounded in faith and community uplift, and who cared enough about her to teach Monica what she needed to know about the university application process. Monica shares that she also had a relationship with her local librarian who showed her how to research scholarships and universities that might match her interests and needs. Monica shares,

> Not only did these individuals selflessly vest themselves in my success, they challenged me to do the same for others in the future. There were others who vouched for me when my name or application turned up for a community-based scholarship . . . people who knew my family and me personally and supported me in many ways.

Monica demonstrated the need for first-generation college students to connect to people who have experienced university application procedures. She could get the assistance she needed from people who believed in reaching back and giving back to others, as someone had probably done for them. Neighbors, teachers, mentors, and community members were interceding on her behalf because she demonstrated that she was worth investing in.

Mentors

Formal mentors played a major role in Monica's life. They provided guidance and emotional support, and saw potential in her before she could see it in herself. Both Monica and her advisor reflected on Monica's decision to pursue her doctorate. Her advisor shares,

> When I became the Director of the Ed.D. program in educational leadership, Monica inquired about admission to the program and I encouraged her to apply. It was a long shot, as the program was designed for practicing educational leaders, however, I felt that she was acting as a teacher leader in so many ways and also had a history of community leadership that she could develop.

Reflecting on the same period of time Monica says,

> I had been interested in getting a doctorate for a few years before I finally applied to the program. Initially, I wasn't sure that I met the qualifications. Thankfully, I had a professor who knew better and encouraged me to apply.

Monica said she was convinced she should apply because she was encouraged and there was a mentor who would commit to her success and completion. Monica says with those conditions met, "I knew the time and place were right for me to undertake that journey."

Monica and her advisor got to know each other well enough to find value in each other's skills and abilities. Because of their student–teacher relationship, Monica's advisor felt comfortable interceding on her behalf and offering assistance and support when needed.

Environmental Intercession

When there were barriers in Monica's life that were in her geographic or physical reality (neighborhood or state of residence), removing herself from that environment allowed her to thrive. It took a physical action to interrupt her literal space and location to improve her circumstances. Monica discusses some of the challenges she faced growing up in a suppressive environment,

> My freshman year in high school was about the time that I began to process the environment around me. At home, I had an environment where

my father was an abusive alcoholic, my mother suffered from depression and other mental health issues that she did not seek treatment for, and my brother was physically abusive towards me. I sensed a lot of jealousy and resentment from my brother and sister because I was a "nerd" and was often rewarded for my scholarship.

Monica discussed negotiating barriers in her internal and external environments. She was proactive in her response to suppressive and oppressive environmental conditions. In response, she connected with community leaders and became part of a dynamic change process. She learned how to disengage from her environment and thrive in chaos.

Self-Determination

When she recognized she was growing up in a disadvantaged neighborhood, with regard to opportunity and educational success, Monica strived to turn her situation around. She was motivated to excel because she wanted more for herself and her family. Monica was goal-oriented, hard working, and stood on her principles. She shares the following,

One day I followed up with a brochure to participate in a youth leadership program. I was accepted for participation and the experience was life changing. There were a select number of students from diverse backgrounds representing eight high schools from the city and surrounding suburbs. We participated in community service, government affairs, and exchange programs with the other high schools. When I visited one of the suburban high schools, for the first time in my life I discovered I was disadvantaged. I had a front-row seat to my competition and I knew I was at a very distinct disadvantage in terms of educational opportunities. That trip to the suburbs showed me the life I wanted and motivated me to excel.

It did not take her long to realize the suburban schools offered significantly more than her segregated Black high school. Monica knew she would not have the skills to compete with her neighboring peers and that reality propelled her to excel.

Self-Awareness

Monica knew her strengths, weakness and, most of all, herself. She knew who she was and relied on her faith and her ancestors' legacies to provide her strength to push through injustices that blocked her ability to succeed in every facet of life, particularly education. She was also aware of her positionality and how it interfaced with the various environments she engaged in. Monica shared some experiences about taking advantage of learning opportunities outside her immediate environment and transcending barriers that arose. The former took place the summer of her junior year in high school. The later happened her freshman year in college. Of this, she shares,

> Over the summer, I had the opportunity to visit a boarding school in a quaint New England town. There were people from all over the world, many rich, and all very intelligent. Seven of us were African American and two of us were from my high school.

She continued to share that she initially felt slightly intimidated, until she discovered she had an advantage in some ways. She didn't have the experiences of sailing and scuba diving, but Monica knew how to take care of her basic needs like doing her own laundry, hair, shopping, and so forth. Because she felt comfortable in her own skin, she felt she could embrace and appreciate the diversity around her.

Through her educational experiences Monica could have let stigmas and scrutiny hinder her from moving forward in her life, and pursuing her goals and dreams, but she chose to press on despite what others had to say about her. She was comfortable with herself and what she had to offer.

Evidence of Barrier Transcendence

Table 6.1 reflects summative evidence for ways Monica transcended barriers toward the attainment of her doctorate.

Here evidence is organized and reflected to support personal attributes, behaviors, and environmental features that contributed to Monica's ability to transcend institutional, emotional, psychological, physical, geographic, and access to information barriers that threatened to impede the attainment of her doctorate.

Monica transcended multiple barriers throughout her educational journey that took her from depressed inner-city schools to one of the top-ranked universities globally. The counter-stories that Monica shared demonstrated that with self-determination, self-awareness, mentoring, environmental intercession, networking, and negotiating, others can push past barriers just as she has. Related research reflects Monica's experience, but her story is one of hope, promise, and alternative outcomes. Another feature in the literature, opportunity recognition, was present in Monica's quest for more information and support (Gaglio & Katz, 2001). She was almost entrepreneurial in how she advocated for herself and weighed her decisions to act or not in every aspect of her barrier transcendence.

Discussion

Women of color continue to have constraining educational experiences in the U.S. compared to their White peers (Johnson-Bailey, 2004; Stiemke, 2012); however, Monica's counter-stories demonstrate some ways barriers can be broken and

TABLE 6.1 Barrier Transcendence Strategies

Themes	Personal Attributes	Behaviors	Environment	Barriers Transcended
Networking	Personable	Connected to extended social networks / Forged trusting mentoring relationships with peers and faculty / Served as volunteer (education, community) / Surrounded self with "smart" people	Connected to extended social networks / Forged trusting mentoring relationships with peers and faculty / Served as volunteer (education, community) / Surrounded self with "smart" people	Institutional / Emotional / Psychological
Negotiating	Tenacious	Used powers of persuasion to gain access / Kept working toward goal when future looks bleak	Changed geographic location two times to change circumstance and increase opportunity	Physical / Geographic
Mentoring	Open to growing and learning from others	Connected to and extended social networks / Sought counsel when needed / Sought mentors	Talent and potential recognized by others / Supportive committee members / Culturally competent faculty / Supportive dissertation Chair	Institutional / Emotional / Psychological / Access to Information / Financial
Environmental Intercession	Strong survival skills	Followed up on opportunities to change circumstances / Sought opportunities to advance or enhance opportunity	Followed up on opportunities to change circumstances / Sought opportunities to advance or enhance opportunity	Institutional / Emotional / Psychological
Self-determination	Desire to prove self to others	Mapped out goals and educational plan / Focused on academic development / Acquired skills to navigate hurdles as necessary	When working with people who were engaged, opportunities presented themselves	Emotional / Psychological
Self-awareness	Willingness to make sacrifices to attain goals / Faith	Acquired skills to navigate hurdles as necessary. / Followed up on opportunities to change circumstances / Sought opportunities to advance or enhance situation	Followed up on opportunities to change circumstances / Sought opportunities to advance or enhance situation	Emotional / Psychological

opportunities recognized for fulfilling life-enhancing pursuits. Recognizing and taking advantage of opportunities often requires a disruption or transformation of the environment via self or others (Howard-Bostic, 2008). Findings from this study suggest women of color can transform their physical, emotional, and psychological environments through environmental interruption or intercession wherein others may intervene and disrupt an environment on their behalf. The data also indicate that women of color may find themselves in unsupportive environments where they have to negotiate racism, classism, sexism, and power-based conflict in the spaces they occupy without compromising their values and beliefs (e.g., Crenshaw, 1995).

Findings also suggest there may have been some prerequisites for Monica's documented experience with barrier transcendence. First, she demonstrated desire and self-efficacy (Wood & Bandura, 1989)—in this case, to gain access and opportunity toward attaining a doctorate. There was an element of motivation that Monica reflected from the beginning. Second, her behaviors (B) (e.g., tenacity, self-advocating, open to learn) built upon her disposition toward academic success. Third, the academic and physical environment (E) for the study was a resource-rich, research-intensive university where she had access to mentors, faculty advisors, and professional organizations. Finally, Monica demonstrated evidence of cognitions or thought processes (P) that supported her trajectory toward barrier transcendence, including questioning strategies and critical reflection. Together, complex interactions among these attributes and conditions (B, E, & P) form the triangle and the bottom of the three-dimensional model, one aspect continually feeding into the other, building momentum toward flow.

Findings from this study suggest the more Monica could disrupt old patterns of behavior and adjust her disposition (vertical axis) based on the interactions between her B, P, & E, the more able she was to transcend barriers impeding her progress (horizontal axis) (see Figure 6.2).

If Monica were to give a woman of color advice on barrier transcendence based on the counter-stories shared, there would be six steps.

1. *Remain open to the possibility there are opportunities available* for you and for your benefit.
2. *Actively seek opportunities to advance your situation* and enhance current opportunities of which you have been made aware.
3. *Actively research possible opportunities to determine whether they are right* for you.
4. *Weigh whether pursing the opportunity is a good investment of your time* and energy.
5. *Recognize, act on, or pursue multiple beneficial opportunities* based on *input from reliable sources* in your environment (e.g., peers, mentors, those who care about your well-being).
6. *Engage with whomever necessary* to follow up, participate in, or engage with opportunities that might result in a positive change to your current circumstances.

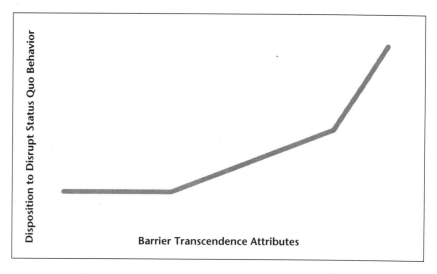

FIGURE 6.2 Disposition to Disrupt Status Quo Behaviors, Opportunity Recognition, and Barrier Transcendence

When Monica was able to operate under the conditions suggested, she enjoyed multiple educational pursuits and could transcend many barriers in the way of her educational and professional goals.

Conclusion

There are myriad barriers African American and other women of color need to overcome in order to attain terminal educational degrees and positions of influence in educational settings. In this chapter, authors considered the journey mired in hierarchical struggle, intersectionality, and multiple dimensions of identity undertaken by Black women and women of color who aspire to the highest levels of educational attainment in academe.

This chapter illuminates the ways Monica overcame barriers to educational attainment. Her narrative provides an exemplar of enduring hope for other Black women and women of color seeking doctorates or barrier transcendence toward educational and professional goals. Further, findings showcase barrier transcendence as a way of thinking about and articulating goal identification and aspirations for women of color who seek to better understand ways to overcome obstacles impeding their progress toward the study or attainment of educational leadership. Albeit dynamically diverse with regard to inter-diversity within, Monica's account reiterates that Black women are an unknown and untapped rich human resource with the potential to improve education and leadership in educational contexts at every level in the 21st century (see B. Lloyd-Jones, this volume). This contribution reveals barrier transcendence as one way of understanding viable pathways to educational leadership for these women and other systemically underserved and underrepresented groups in educational leadership in HE (see L. J. Santamaría, Jeffries, & Santamaría, this volume).

CULTURALLY RESPONSIVE LEADERSHIP IN PRACTICE

There were several applied critical leaders working on Monica's behalf in this chapter. Most of the mentoring she benefitted from came as a result of individuals inviting Monica into key positions or bringing opportunities to her attention that might benefit her in reaching educational and professional goals. Some of these leaders were formal advisors, while others she mentioned were members of her church and community. Monica shared that *they brought her in as a way of giving back to their communities*. In this way, they led by example as well as *drew on positive strengths of their identities as members of a communal organization or community*. Monica benefited from many invitations from leaders in educational settings as well as her community. They *invited her to the "table" based on her reputation* for tenacity, strong demonstrated work ethic, and commitment to social justice, as well as her demonstrated academic ability. Finally, when Monica was able to practice applied critical leadership as a developing scholar, she demonstrated the *ability to tap into personal aspects of her intersectional identity*, willingness to *initiate and engage in critical conversations with peers and instructors*, take a critical stance in her own research, and *follow up with actions that were grounded in a critical epistemological stance*. Finally, because Monica was deeply involved in her own research of women's roles in educational leadership, she was at the same time *adding to the research base and literature* on the topic. In these ways Monica has revealed a number of applied critical leadership adaptations for applied critical leaders in HE to consider and for students to apply in their contexts as well.

References

Bandura, A. (1977). Self-efficacy: Toward a unifying theory of behavioral change. *Psychological Review, 84*(2), 191–215.

Benham, M., & Murakami-Ramalho, E. (2010). Engaging in educational leadership: The generosity of spirit. *International Journal of Leadership in Education, 12*, 77–91.

Bogdan, R. C., & Biklen, S. K. (2007). *Research for education: An introduction to theories and methods* (4th ed.). Boston, MA: Allyn & Bacon.

Crenshaw, K. (1995). Mapping the margins: Intersectionality, identity, politics, and violence against women of color. In K. Crenshaw, N. Gotanda, G. Peller, & K. Thomas (Eds.), *Critical race theory: The key writings that formed the movement* (pp. 357–383). New York, NY: New Press.

Creswell, J. W. (1998). *Qualitative inquiry and research design: Choosing among five traditions.* Thousand Oaks, CA: Sage.

Gaglio, C. M., & Katz, J. (2001). The psychological basis of opportunity identification: Entrepreneurial alertness. *Journal of Small Business. Economics, 16,* 95–111.

Grant, C., & Simmons, J. (2008). Narratives on experiences of African American women in the academy: Conceptualizing effective mentoring relationships of doctoral students and faculty. *International Journal of Qualitative Studies in Education, 21,* 501–517.

Howard-Bostic, C. D. (2008, January). Stepping out of the third wave: A contemporary Black feminist paradigm. *Forum on Public Policy Online: A Journal of the Oxford Round Table,* 1–7.

Hughes, S., Pennington, J. L., & Makris, S. (2012). Translating autoethnography across the AERA standards toward understanding autoethnographic scholarship as empirical research. *Educational Researcher, 41*(6), 209–219.

Jean-Marie, G. (2011). Women of color in higher education in the 21st century. In G. Jean-Marie & B. Lloyd-Jones (Eds.), *Women of color in higher education: Changing directions and new perspectives.* Diversity in Higher Education Series, vol. 10 (pp. xxv–xxix). Bingley, UK: Emerald Group.

Jean-Marie, G., & Brooks, J. S. (2011). Mentoring and supportive networks for women of color in academe. In G. Jean-Marie & B. Lloyd-Jones (Eds.), *Women of color in higher education: Changing directions and new perspectives.* Diversity in Higher Education Series, vol. 10 (pp. 91–108). Bingley, UK: Emerald Group.

Jean-Marie, G., Grant, C., & Irby, B. (2014). *The duality of women scholars of color: Transforming and being transformed in the academy.* Research on Women and Education Series. Charlotte, NC: Information Age.

Johnson-Bailey, J. (2004). Hitting and climbing the proverbial wall: Participation and retention issues for Black graduate women. *Race Ethnicity and Education, 7*(4), 331–349.

Ladson-Billings, G. (2009). "Who you callin' nappy-headed?" A critical race theory look at the construction of Black women. *Race, Ethnicity and Education, 12,* 87–99.

Leithwood, K. A., & Riehl, C. (2003). *What we know about successful school leadership.* Philadelphia, PA: Laboratory for Student Success, Temple University. Retrieved from http://dcbsimpson.com/randd-leithwood-successful-leadership.pdf

Lloyd-Jones, B. (2009). *Implications of race and gender in higher education administration: An African American woman's perspective.* Advances in Developing Human Resources. Los Angeles, CA: Sage.

Mackey, H. (2011). Identity and research: Exploring themes of scholarship of an American Indian scholar in the academy. In G. Jean-Marie & B. Lloyd-Jones, (Eds.), *Women of color in higher education: Turbulent past, promising future.* Diversity in Higher Education Series, vol. 9 (pp. 291–305). Bingley, UK: Emerald Group.

McCall, L. (2005). The complexity of intersectionality. *Signs: Journal of Women in Culture and Society, 30*(3), 1771–1800.

McGee Banks, C. A. (2007). Gender and race as factors in educational leadership and administration. In *The Jossey-Bass reader on educational leadership* (2nd ed., pp. 299–338). San Francisco, CA: Jossey-Bass.

Merriam, S. B. (1998). *Qualitative research and case study applications in education.* San Francisco, CA: Jossey-Bass.

Miles, M. B., & Huberman, A. M. (1994). *Qualitative data analysis: A sourcebook of new methods* (2nd ed.). Thousand Oaks, CA: Sage.

Nash, J. C. (2008). Re-thinking intersectionality. *Feminist Review, 89*(1), 1–15.

Ozgen, E., & Baron, R. A. (2007). Social sources of information in opportunity recognition: Effects of mentors, industry networks and professional forums. *Journal of Business Venturing, 22*(2), 174–192.

Patton, L. D. (2009). My sister's keeper: A qualitative examination of mentoring experiences among African American women in graduate and professional schools. *Journal of Higher Education, 80*(5), 510–537.

Roth, B. (2004). *Separate roads to feminism.* New York, NY: Cambridge University Press.

Santamaría, L. J. (2009, April). *Today is tomorrow.* Keynote address. California Forum for Diversity in Graduate Education, California State University San Marcos.

Santamaría, L. J. (2012, November). *Barrier transcendence and educational leadership for women of color: Critical mentoring through sharing counter-stories.* Paper presented at the University Council on Educational Administration (UCEA) Annual Meeting, Denver, CO.

Santamaría, L. J. (2014a). Grace at the top: A Black feminist perspective on critical leadership in the academy. In G. Jean-Marie, C. Grant-Overton, & B. Irby (Eds.), *The duality of women scholars of color: Transforming and being transformed in the academy.* Research on Women and Education Series (pp. 75–95). Charlotte, NC: Information Age.

Santamaría, L. J. (2014b). Shifting, lifting and climbing: A Black feminist leadership perspective on navigating academe in Australasia. In L. J. Santamaría, G. Jean-Marie, & C. M. Grant (Eds.), *Cross cultural women scholars in academe: Intergenerational voices* (pp. 93–115). New York, NY: Routledge.

Santamaría, L. J. (2014c). Critical change for the greater good: Multicultural dimensions of educational leadership toward social justice and educational equity. *Education Administration Quarterly (EAQ), 50*(3), 347–391. doi:10.1177/0013161X13505287

Santamaría, L. J., & Jean-Marie, G. (2014). Cross-cultural dimensions of applied, critical, and transformational leadership: Women principals advancing social justice and educational equity. *Cambridge Educational Journal, 44*(3), 333–360.

Santamaría, L. J., Jean-Marie, G., & Grant, C. M. (Eds.). (2014). *Cross cultural women scholars in academe: Intergenerational voices.* New York, NY: Routledge.

Santamaría, L. J., & Santamaría, A. P. (2012). *Applied critical leadership in education: Choosing change.* New York, NY: Routledge.

Santamaría, L. J., Santamaría, A. P., Webber, M., & Pearson, H. (2014). Indigenous urban school leadership (IUSL): A critical cross-cultural comparative analysis of educational leaders in New Zealand and the United States. *Canadian and International Education (CIE), 43*(1), 1–21.

Seifert, C. M., & Patalano, A. L. (2001). Opportunism in memory: Preparing for chance encounters. *Current Directions in Psychological Science, 10,* 198–201.

Silverman, D. (2000). *Doing qualitative research: A practical handbook.* Thousand Oaks, CA: Sage.

Slaney, R. B. (1980). An investigation of racial differences on vocational variables among college women. *Journal of Vocational Behavior, 16,* 197–207.

Solórzano, D. G., & Yosso, T. J. (2002). Critical race methodology: Counter-storytelling as an analytical framework for educational research. *Qualitative Inquiry, 8*(1), 23–44.

Stiemke, K. H. (2012). *Women of color in educational leadership programs: An emic phenomenological perspective* (Doctoral dissertation). Retrieved from ProQuest Information and Learning Company. (UMI No. 3509147)

Strauss, A., & Corbin, J. (1998). *Basics of qualitative research.* Thousand Oaks, CA: Sage.

Walker, R. (1995). *To be real: Telling the truth and changing the face of feminism.* New York, NY: Anchor.

Wang, M. C., Haertel, G. D., & Walberg, H. J. (1997). Fostering educational resilience in inner-city schools. Laboratory for Student Success, the Mid-Atlantic Regional Educational Laboratory at Temple University, Center for Research in Human Development and Education.

Wood, R. E., & Bandura, A. (1989). Impact of conceptions of ability on self-regulatory mechanisms and complex decision-making. *Journal of Personality and Social Psychology, 56,* 407–415.

7

NEGOTIATING IDENTITIES, LOCATIONS, AND CREATING SPACES OF HOPE FOR ADVANCING STUDENTS OF COLOR IN UNIVERSITY SETTINGS

Miguel Zavala and Natalie A. Tran

IDEA IN BRIEF

In this chapter a conceptual expansion of the thesis that identity is central to leadership praxis, a fundamental tenet of the emerging Applied Critical Leadership (ACL) framework, is developed by analyzing the notion of "epistemic privilege" in Standpoint Theory. Emphasizing the iterative relation of cultural identity and leadership practice, the chapter builds from the voices of a Latina student leader and Latina project director as they reflect and make sense of their advocacy for students of color at a Hispanic-Serving Institution (HSI). Most important, the chapter illustrates how the marginal identities of strategically positioned women of color in leadership positions enable them to navigate and transform institutions of higher learning.

Keywords: Latina, standpoint theory, higher education, identity, marginality

In this chapter we address, albeit indirectly, the relation between the "leadership gap" in higher education and the "resource gap" that has negatively impacted historically dominated groups in the United States (Spring, 2006) in their struggle for access to higher education. Building from our own reflections as scholars of color, and through dialogues with scholars of color in leadership positions at our institution, we provide a conceptual discussion of identity and its relation to leadership that expands on the insights developed by Santamaría & Santamaría's (2012) Applied Critical Leadership (ACL) model (Santamaría, 2014; Santamaría, Santamaría, & Dam, 2014). The theoretical frameworks we bring to our praxis and our own experiences as scholars of color coalesce with a fundamental assumption in ACL, that identity is central to our praxis as leaders, and that our work as scholars advocating for increased diversity of leadership in spaces of higher learning is very much informed by our own identities. However, while identity is central to our research and advocacy work, and while we find extensive insights in the emerging body of work that uses an ACL model, with critical race theory as one of its major components, we argue that more conceptual clarity and expansion is needed in deepening our understanding of how women of color in leadership roles are positioned and how their identities serve to interpret, resist, interrupt, and transform oppressive social relations in their advocacy work. In this chapter we bring together several bodies of work, including Standpoint Theory, as a way of understanding ACL's precept that identity serves as a resource that shapes the experiences of people of color in leadership positions. Our conceptual discussion also builds into a case study of two Latina leaders, who have been advocating for increased recruitment and support of students of color at our institution. We explore the question of leadership, power, and access, and the general thesis that the marginal identity and location of women of color is a resource to facilitate institutional change.

Women of Color and Leadership in Higher Education

As strategically positioned scholars of color, one a Vietnamese American female and the other a Chicano male, working in a major Hispanic-Serving Institution (HSI) in California, we have witnessed a gradual cultural shift toward embracing the challenge of serving students of color, more generally, and Latino/a students, more specifically. While we welcome increased enrollments of students designated as "Hispanic" and the resources that an HSI designation brings with it, we are also wary of the contradictions wrought by what we, along with critical race scholars, see as the pervasiveness of racism and sexism in our society, and how these continue to shape, steer, and impact progressive policies and practices aimed at "diversifying" higher education (Santamaría, Webber, & Santamaría, 2015). Notwithstanding the fact that Latino/a students represent 33% of the student population on our campus, Latino/a faculty represent only 7%. These numbers dwindle when we consider women of color in leadership positions. Almost a decade after civil rights struggles, White men continue to maintain not just the majority, but higher positions of leadership than White women and even more so compared to women of color, who remain significantly underrepresented in these spaces.

More recently, the *Minorities in Higher Education* Report (Ryu, 2010) has documented an increase in the number of women serving in administrative positions in higher education, increasing from 45% in 1997 to 53% in 2007. Minority women accounted for 11% of full-time administrators compared to 41% accounted for by White women. The same report also indicated the growth in the number of minorities and women serving as college and university presidents in the last two decades. The data show that women represented only 10% of presidents in higher education in 1986. This number grew to 23% in 2006. The number of minority presidents showed a modest growth with an increase from 8% to 13% during this time.

Despite these relative gains by women of color, "the legislative sanctions against sex discrimination in employment and education, and the immense array of such programs, progress towards greater equality for women in management and leadership has been far slower than expected or hoped" (Ramsay, 2000, p. 5). Indeed, race and gender manifest in institutional barriers that impede the mobility of women of color into leadership positions within higher education settings and, for those who occupy leadership roles, the experience of marginalization and isolation are commonplace (Arredondo, 2011).

Centering Identity in Applied Critical Leadership (ACL)

Leadership practice in higher education has been studied for some time, yet the scholarship in this area tends to reduce identity to a cursory phenomenon, have under-theorized its role, or have, at best, studied it as a "variable" or "factor" that "impacts" leadership practice. The prevalence of rational actor models that render identity invisible has been challenged by neo-institutional perspectives that center ideology, culture, and social structure, in our understanding of leadership practices (Scott, 1998). More recently, a "distributed leadership" framework (Spillane, Halverson, & Diamond, 2004) has been offered as an alternative lens. This distributed leadership framework challenges the long-standing tradition of studying leadership as a set of traits or behaviors (Ayman & Korabik, 2010). Although a distributed leadership model re-conceptualizes leadership as a social practice that needs to be understood contextually, such that individual actors and their actions are viewed as constituted by their social environments (institutional, societal), what is missing in their discussion is an articulation of how identity mediates leadership practices and how leadership practices mediate identity.

The ACL model, on the other hand, centers identity: "Identity lies at the heart of applied critical leadership. Whether an individual chooses to look through the lens of their lived experience or through the lens of the lived experiences of others, applied critical leadership considers identity to be important," (Santamaría & Santamaría, 2012, p. 114). In the book *Applied Critical Leadership in Education: Choosing Change*, Santamaría & Santamaría (2012) highlight case studies of women-of-color leaders in higher education settings, specifically documenting how leadership practices are mediated by women's gender, sexual, and racial identities. For instance, "Kelly" foregrounds her sexual identity in her leadership practice, which leads to a fluid, adaptive leadership style (Chapter 8). "Mona," a Latina, is conscious of how she is positioned as a Latina woman, yet has developed a collaborative leadership approach informed by her political identity as a woman and Chicana (Chapter 9). And "Gina," a White woman who is conscious of her White privilege, has been strategic in using her social identity in ways that allow her to advocate for people of color (Chapter 10). For these and other women of color, their identities are inseparable from who they are and how they approach their work as women leaders (Santamaría & Santamaría, 2012, p. 148). Building on this work using Applied Critical Leadership, this chapter expands on the dialectic of identity and leadership praxis. For example, the premise that the gendered and racialized experiences of women of color are a resource in their leadership practice will be explored. Specifically, how is it that these "marginal" and contradictory locations enable women of color to navigate and contest institutions inhabited by men who often question their leadership? How do their experiences as women of color advocating for social equities generate political identities and how do their leadership practices mediate the formation of these identities? These and other questions have yet to be investigated—the ACL model opens the opportunity for the fruition of such work. In what follows, we provide a conceptual roadmap that assists critical scholars to expand on this work.

Toward a Relational View of Identity

Traditionally, identity markers such as race, gender, and social class have been conceptualized as essential qualities or properties that inhere or otherwise mark individuals. This *essentialist model* of identity has been criticized extensively by critical feminist, poststructural, and social constructionist frameworks. For instance, critical race scholars have rightly pointed to how Blackness was historically constructed and used to legitimize slavery and other systems of oppression (Crenshaw, 1988). In a parallel vein, feminists have argued against essentialist notions of gender that serve to stereotype women and their work. What critical scholars have found is that often essentialist notions of identity are used to legitimize existing relations of power and thus perpetuate the oppression against women, people of color, and others.

More recently, phenomenological approaches have re-conceptualized identity as socially, culturally, and historically mediated. This *social constructionist model* of identity has challenged essentialist models by identifying social and cultural mediations that shape our identities. In this tradition, institutions, for instance, are sites that shape who we *become* (Omi & Winant, 1993). This lens offers key insights that are subsequently developed by critical race scholars and feminists. For example, the idea that identity is "socially constructed" leads to crucial investigations as to why particular identities are constructed the way they are and to what consequence. Thus, critical race theorists have historicized "race" as a construct or invention of 18th-century European pseudo-scientists and how the basic categories used today stem in large part from the portioning of the world by Europeans into Caucasoid, Mongoloid, Negroid, and Australoid "races" (Blackburn, 2000).

A third approach to identity can be termed the *relational model* (Alcoff, 2006). This model posits that, beyond being socially, culturally, and historically mediated, identity emerges as oppositional and is constituted within a nexus of power relations. The model is *relational* because race and gender, whether self or socially ascribed, are defined in relation to their constructed opposites. Thus, from this framework, to understand gender, for instance, we not only resort to historical and social analysis of processes integral to its formation, but also must consider how, in the case of women, they are constituted vis-à-vis men; or in the case of people of color, how they are constituted vis-à-vis Whites. This framework centers social relations of power, yet it troubles essentialists due to its binary notions of gender and race. In critical race scholarship, this has been termed the *de-centering* approach to identity, which has led to the burgeoning field of Whiteness Studies (Pedersen & Samaluk, 2012; Warren, 1999). More recent developments speak of identity as social practice, performance, and enactment—yet the stage in which identity work takes shape is itself spatially, socially, and historically constructed.

We argue that intersectionality, a fundamental tenet of critical race theory (Delgado & Stefancic, 2012), represents the ways in which identities of race, gender, and class intersect. Not only are women of color racialized and thus work within/against White supremacist institutions, but they are also gendered and thus work within/against patriarchal institutions. Because systems of oppression such as patriarchy, class domination, and racism interlock, so too do our identities. For example, women of color do not experience the same oppressions of White women; they often have to endure male domination within and outside their own communities, conjoined with institutional racism at work, school, and in the broader society. One key insight we take from the work on intersectionality is that we cannot separate ourselves from our gender, race, class, sexuality: these identities are socially marked, engraved in our very bodies. However, this need not lead to a socially deterministic view of identity. In contrast, these identities are in constant flux depending on the contexts and the actors that occupy these contexts. Consequently, since our identities are represented and manifested through social, cultural, and historical interactions, our work within the institutions of unequal power relations can be turned into praxis, where identities are struggled for and become political sites for mobilization and collective action.

Standpoint Theory and Epistemic Privilege

Standpoint theorists contend that, since all knowledge is situated or embodied (i.e., it is materially produced by collective group interests), productive social justice research begins from the material conditions of the oppressed (Harding, 2004, p. 128). Jameson (2004) has argued, in his articulation of a proletarian standpoint, that standpoints are not merely perspectival but positional (p. 145). Standpoints are not simply perspectives one undertakes, but a "collective position that is achieved within concrete social movements" (Harding, personal communication, 2008). A corollary of standpoint theory is that "starting from the lives" of the oppressed provides a productive starting point for understanding oppression (Harding, 2004, p. 129). The "epistemic privilege" of the oppressed is a central thesis in standpoint theory—and one that has been greatly misunderstood. To "start from the lives of the oppressed," such as the case of women of color in the academy deploying a feminist standpoint, does not entail (a) that their own lives are the best starting point for all research projects (Harding, 2004), nor (b) that only women can study or understand gender and patriarchy (Wolf, 1996). The argument is that "starting off research from women's lives will generate less partial and distorted accounts not only of women's lives but also of men's lives and of the whole social order" (Harding, 2004, p. 128). Consequently, it follows that starting from men's lives will generate more partial and distorted accounts about women and gender relations. The phrase, "starting from" the lives of the oppressed sheds light on the dialectic between representation and location (i.e., that who we speak for is inseparable from where we speak). Moreover, in stipulating that social research begins from the lives of the oppressed because their position provides a "less partial and distorted" account of oppression in no way entails that the perspective of the oppressed, whether they are the subjects of research or researchers in the academy engaged with social justice research, is unproblematic and devoid of ideology: "To see from below is neither easily learned nor unproblematic, even if 'we' 'naturally' inhabit the great underground terrain of subjugated knowledges. The positions of the subjugated are not exempt from critical re-examination, decoding, deconstruction, and interpretation" (Haraway, 2004, p. 191).

Patricia Hill Collins (2004) explores the productive potential that Black feminist scholars bring in understanding the lives of Black women, which, within the field of sociology, have been discursively constructed through the eyes of White male academics, thus not accurately capturing the experiences of Black women, and therefore denying the ways in which Black women experience gender, race, and class oppressions. In particular, she finds the "outsider within" status of the Black intellectual as a source for enriching sociological research (p. 104). Many of these scholars, through literature and cultural criticism, have been able to challenge mainstream sociological analyses by drawing from a rich tradition of oral and written narratives produced by Black women, a tradition of work that was mostly inaccessible to the sociologist. But the limitations for non-Black women engaged in research related on social justice issues (e.g., White middle-class males) reach an insurmountable pinnacle when they encounter the edifice of theories, concepts, and sociological tools that have been taken for granted as unproblematic. Therefore, although she characterizes Black feminists' marginal position as productive and counter-hegemonic (p. 118), there are some limitations with conducting social justice research within the academy. Ultimately, Black feminists must (1) negotiate the existing patriarchal order within university life, and (2) speak a new language by appropriate (or not) ways of seeing that have been produced by White men (pp. 118–119). The "outsider within" status is used to describe the "marginal person now located at the center" (Harding, 2004, p. 134). This is the marginalized, perceived "outsider" who is now situated "within" institutions of privilege and power (e.g., see in this volume C. M. Grant; H. Mackey & G. Jean-Marie; B. Lloyd-Jones).

In this vein, the work of Méndez-Morse (2003) brings to light the question of how the institutionally marginal position of women of color, more generally, and Latinas, more specifically, is invoked as a strategic space and resource in their work as leaders. "Although the intersection of gender, class, race/ethnicity, sexual orientation, religion and language do combine to form compound means of discrimination for women of Mexican descent, within these variables there are also sources of hidden, unrecognized strengths and talents" (Méndez-Morse, 2003, p. 165).

The Voices of Latina Leaders

In the following section, we present the voices of two Latina leaders, one a student organizer and the other a project director, at a Hispanic-Serving Institution (HSI). Located in California, the institution is the largest of the 23 CSU universities, enrolling over 36,000 students. The university serves a diverse student population that is 31% White, 29% Latino/a, 21% Asian American, and 3% African American. As an HSI, it has gained national recognitions for its diversity initiatives. *Diverse Issues in Higher Education* (June, 2009) ranked the institution as a top 10 university in the nation for the number of baccalaureate degrees awarded to minority students (Borden, 2009, p. 20). *Hispanic Outlook in Higher Education* (May 2011) ranked the institution as top in the nation among top colleges and universities awarding bachelor's degrees to Hispanic students (Cooper, 2011).

As part of a broader study of women of color leaders at this institution, we use a grounded theory (Charmaz, 2006) approach that makes central the experience of women of color. We were intentional in selecting a student leader for our broader study, given her strategic position as a student leader and our interest in documenting the perspective of women of color who are often neglected in the literature, that is, student leaders who, we believe, are fundamental to social change. Following Saldaña (2013) we use interviewing, memo writing, and our own discussions of emergent themes as interpretive strategies that assist us in understanding the experiences of marginality for women of color as a resource in and through the practice of Latina leaders. Drawing primarily from semi-structured interviewing techniques, we developed a set of open-ended questions that allowed participants to critically reflect on their leadership practice. Our insights are also gleaned through structured meta-reflections via memos developed by one of the authors who has been organizing at the campus and working closely with the two Latina leaders.

Maria is a community coordinator and vice chair of the Movimiento Estudiantil Chicano de Aztlan (MEChA) chapter and president of the Educational Opportunity Program Student Association (EOPSA). She identifies herself as "Xicana," which is a political identity she has assumed. "I never check the box that says Latino or Hispanic, I always check the box that says Other and I write the word Xicana with an 'X'." She was drawn to leadership in 2007 when, as a student, she experienced limitations: "People in leadership positions at that time weren't sure how to organize people of color because most of the people in leadership positions were Anglo Saxon, White from ASI [Association Students Incorporated]." ASI is the university-sponsored student organization that coordinates student activities and events on campus. Her view of leadership is deeply informed by her leadership experience advocating for students of color on her campus. As a student organizer, she carries forward the legacy of Chicana/o activism with deep historical roots to the 1960s Chicano movement (Muñoz, 1989): "MEChA came out from this movement and the constant reminder was that movement is the reason why I'm here today. Without that movement, who knows if I would be in this institution right now."

Havana is project director of the Educational Opportunity Program (EOP), a federally funded program aimed at recruiting and retaining low-income and historically disadvantaged students. A former MEChA student organizer on campus, she has been active for the last 20 years in and outside the university, supporting student activism and creating spaces, such as a task force in support of undocumented students at the campus. In response to the identity and philosophy that guide her leadership practice, Havana iterates, "I'm a Mechista by nature, so being a Mechista, you never stop being a Mechista . . . and I think that I still continue the MEChA philosophy in all the work that I do, and that's keeping the door open to our community and fighting for injustice" (Havana, personal communication, 2012).

Identity as Integral to Leadership Practice

In our interview with Maria, when asked about the role identity plays in her leadership practice, she comments: "So my identity travels with me in the sense of where I work and with whomever I work whether it be in my own community or different community, my identity is basically like superheroes carrying their cape, it's the same, it's with me continuously." Drawing from her metaphor, identity is not only something that she "travels with" but it represents that which enables her to carry out her leadership. Congruent with ACL, Maria sees her identity as integral to her leadership practice. Havana echoes this, viewing her Chicana identity and MeChA philosophy "as a way of living" that transcends her formal role as a paid university employee. Reflecting on the spaces where identities are framed and positioned, in particular when organizing events with others who do not see themselves with a similar political–ethnic identity, Maria reminds us of the biographical trajectory of identity, as rooted in family and community: "That's why for me as a Xicana when I bring that to the table, it's a constant reminder of why I'm here, why I am working with parents like this. Because my parents were once sitting in that same boat, and knowing where my roots came from" (Maria, personal communication, 2012).

Marginality and Identity as Resources

Both Latina leaders reported experiencing marginalization as a result of being positioned as women and as members of ethnic minorities. "For us as Chicanas, we have to work twice as hard to prove our ability," Maria reminds us, in response to the question of how others view her in leadership capacities. The very marginal social location has enabled both Latinas to gain political clarity in the work they do and be able to anticipate and thus navigate spaces dominated by White males. For Maria, this experience of race, class, and gender marginalization has led to greater clarity and work toward politicizing and recruiting more Latinas into leadership positions: "That's kind of what was pushing me to be a leader, we need to give voice to *mujeres* that aren't in leadership positions and that hopefully more of them will be in leadership positions."

The question of the role identity plays in their leadership practice led to insightful comments about the intersection of identity and leadership and how it operates as a strategic space. In reflecting on her work with a community organization where Latinos/as with distinct political ideologies come together, Maria says, "working in different spaces with my identity consciously reminds me of what's going on." Being conscious of her own identity as a Chicana and marginal location given her political philosophy has allowed her to map out the different stances assumed by people with different political and ethnic identities. While her identity is marginal within this space, it allows her to see from the "margins" and anticipate with more clarity "what's going on" and the extent to which her work in the community intersects with her role in the university. We argue, and drawing from our previous discussion of the "epistemic privilege" afforded to women of color, that a particular kind of in/visibility makes this kind of seeing from the margins possible. On the one hand, Latina leaders are positioned as "outsiders," while their work is questioned due to their gender and race. Yet, this very marginality or invisibility can be an asset when they sit in the planning table with other stakeholders. While boardroom discussions are being made, they participate in the institutional roles they assume and, at the same time, strategically map out how different interests play out in particular institutional settings. This ability to navigate "inside" and "outside" of the margins places these women in the unique position where they are able to serve as a catalyst for change.

Havana also sees her marginal identity as a resource, "all the time." She acknowledges that the positions she assumes, as a Chicana and as someone very critical of the way the institution operates, are contradictory, yet this allows her to position herself strategically, depending on the situation. "Depending on who my audience is, you have to wear different roles." In staying true to her philosophy and commitment to the Latino/a community and students at her campus, she feels the need to constantly anticipate the political actions of others. In reflecting on her advocacy work she strategically asks herself, "Have you ever thought of that perspective?" Yet, at times, she finds that her own marginal perspective is acknowledged: "Say, if they're thinking of a policy, but we need to be invited in order to have that perspective, because they don't always think how we think."

Implications for Research on Leadership, Access, and Power

While race, gender, and social class identities are often thought as barriers for individuals in or aspiring to serve in leadership roles in higher education, we argue that these identities not only act as epistemic resources, but also as organizing opportunities for finding common ground in advocating for students of color and creating strategic spaces that support this goal. Rather than viewing identity as something external to leadership, the challenging work is in making our identities, as gendered and racialized groups, an explicit resource that brings people together to fight for a common struggle. The points of intersection are not predetermined, but, we argue, are achieved through the navigating and negotiating that takes place in institutional spaces and through change processes. Both Latinas in this chapter were critical of what they saw as rampant individualism that was centered on personal career advancement rather than greater social justice goals. And the greatest challenge identified by Havana has to do with ideological change: "Basically, [those in privileged positions] have to get through all their prejudice and racism views, and it's very, very hard to stop and reflect . . . You're not perfect, and here's some of the things that are maybe not so good about who you are."

With these tensions in mind, we move to a delineation of what researchers invested in not only understanding how *power* and *access* intersect with *leadership* but how leadership by and for women of color can challenge and transform institutions and spaces. We posit that relationships between power, access, and leadership are *fluid*; they rely on the context and movements within the margins in which they operate. The duality of these notions—power and powerless, access and non-access, leaders and followers—rests upon the fluidity and malleability of their opposites, thus making them vulnerable for change. More important, this duality serves as a medium in which women of color can use their identities as a vehicle to cross the "margins" while maintaining their role as an "insider" and "outsider" simultaneously. This area of research deserves further exploration.

CULTURALLY RESPONSIVE LEADERSHIP IN PRACTICE

Here the authors provide recommendations for increasing participation and engagement of women leaders of color in leadership positions in higher education with practical guidelines.

- In order to understand more intimately how power operates within the institution, we need to **prioritize the perspectives of women of color.**
- Women leaders of color recognize that **our identities and experiences allow us to serve our unique roles** in which we are both "outsiders" and "insiders" of the margins (see Lloyd-Jones, this volume).
- Institutions of higher education **embrace the unique identities of women of color** and **use their experiences as vital resources** to facilitate institutional change.
- **Preparation** for women of color in leadership roles ought to **consider integrating the role of identity** as a major component in leadership development.

Conclusion

For some, assuming one's marginal position can be quite enabling, precisely because such spaces of oppression carry with them the necessity of struggle, resistance, and the possibility of hope for a better world (hooks, 1996; Smith, 2006). Thus, some scholars have called for a re-conceptualization of leadership that makes central the perspectives of women of color (Delgado-Bernal, 1998; Méndez-Morse, 2000). In our critical re-reading of the work on standpoint theory, we do not embrace a romantic or idealistic notion that the "margins" and thus oppression are preferable, but that for women of color *choosing* the margins begins with critically embracing one's position, which grows out of a critical awareness of one's social location. So, for women of color serving in leadership positions within often hostile institutional spaces, denial and assimilation are not viable strategies for social change. Social change within these institutions begins with a critical recognition of how these institutions operate, in whose interests, and how our work, albeit limited within these spaces, is part of a broader legacy of struggle for social justice. So, the margins choose us and, in return, embracing this social location allows us to generate liberating, collective action. We further argue that it is also from those margins that the greatest movement can be achieved by women of color in leadership roles. We return therefore to the discussion of standpoint theory and the precept "epistemic privilege" in the development of social research, which we argue can be applied to the context of both the study and practice of leadership in higher education, while understanding that these practices are inseparable from access and power.

References

Alcoff, L. M. (2006). *Visible identities: Race, gender, and the self.* New York, NY: Oxford University Press.

Arredondo, P. (2011). The "borderlands" experience for women of color as higher education leaders. In J. L. Martin (Ed.), *Women as leaders in education: Succeeding despite inequity, discrimination, and other challenges* (pp. 275–298). Santa Barbara, CA: ABC-CLIO.

Ayman, R., & Korabik, K. (2010). Leadership: Why gender and culture matter. *American Psychologist, 65*(3), 157–170.

Blackburn, D. G. (2000). Why race is not a biological concept. In B. Lang (Ed.), *Race and racism in theory and practice* (pp. 3–26). Oxford, UK: Rowman & Littlefield.

Borden, V. H. (2009). Top 100 undergraduate degree producers. (Cover story). *Diverse Issues in Higher Education, 26*(10), 13–20.

Charmaz, K. (2006). *Constructing grounded theory: A practical guide through qualitative analysis.* Thousand Oaks, CA: Sage.

Collins, P. H. (2004). Learning from the outsider within: The sociological significance of Black feminist thought. In S. Harding (Ed.), *The Feminist standpoint theory reader* (pp. 103–126). New York, NY: Routledge.

Cooper, M. A. (2011, May). Top 100: Hispanic degree earners by the numbers. *The Hispanic Outlook in Higher Education Magazine.* Retrieved from http://www.hispanicoutlook.com/top-100-schools/

Crenshaw, K. W. (1988). Race, reform, and retrenchment: Transformation and legitimation in antidiscrimination law. *Harvard Law Review, 101*(7), 1331–1387.

Delgado, R., & Stefancic, J. (2012). *Critical race theory: An introduction* (2nd ed.). New York, NY: New York University Press.

Delgado-Bernal, D. (1998). Grassroots leadership reconceptualized: Chicana oral histories and the 1968 East Los Angeles blowouts. *Frontiers: A Journal of Women Studies, 19*(2), 113–142.

Haraway, D. (2004). Situated knowledges: The science question in Feminism and the privilege of partial perspective. In S. Harding (Ed.), *The Feminist standpoint theory reader* (pp. 81–102). New York, NY: Routledge.

Harding, S. (2004). *The Feminist standpoint theory reader.* New York, NY: Routledge.

hooks, b. (1996). Choosing the margins as a space of radical openness. In A. Gary & M. Pearsall (Eds.), *Women, knowledge, and reality: Explorations in feminist philosophy* (pp. 48–56). New York, NY: Routledge.

Jameson, F. (2004). History and class consciousness as an "unfinished project." In S. Harding (Ed.), *The Feminist standpoint theory reader* (pp. 143–152). New York, NY: Routledge.

Méndez-Morse, S. (2000). Claiming forgotten leadership. *Urban Education, 35*(5), 584–596.

Méndez-Morse, S. (2003). Chicana feminism and educational leadership. In M. D. Young & L. Skrla (Eds.), *Reconsidering feminist research in educational leadership* (pp. 161–178). Albany: State University of New York Press.

Muñoz, C. (1989). *Youth, identity, power: The Chicano movement.* New York, NY: Verso.

Omi, W. & Winant, H. (1993). On the theoretical concept of race. In C. McCarthy & W. Crichlow (Eds.), *Race, identity, and representation in education* (pp. 3–10). New York, NY: Routledge.

Pedersen, L. L., & Samaluk, B. (2012). Editorial: Different pathways into critical whiteness studies. *Graduate Journal of Social Science, 9*(1), 11–21.

Ramsay, E. (2000, October 30). Women and leadership in higher education: Facing international challenges and maximizing opportunities. Keynote address delivered at the international seminar Asian Women Leaders in Higher Education II: Leadership Competencies to Face the Local–Global Challenges of the Century, Universiti Kebangsaan Malaysia, Kuala Lumpur.

Ryu, M. (2010). *Minorities in higher education 2010: Twenty-fourth status report.* Washington, DC: American Council on Education.

Saldaña, J. (2013). *The coding manual for qualitative researchers.* Phoenix: Arizona State University.

Santamaría, A. P., Webber, M., & Santamaría, L. J. (2015). Māori urban school leadership (MUSL): Building capacity for indigenous and international cross-cultural collaboration. In N. D. Erbe & A. H. Normore (Eds.), *Cross-cultural collaboration and leadership in modern organizations* (pp. 99–119). Hershey, PA: IGI Global.

Santamaría, L. J. (2014). Critical change for the greater good: Multicultural dimensions of educational leadership toward social justice and educational equity. *Education Administration Quarterly (EAQ), 50*(3), 347–391. doi:10.1177/0013161X13505287

Santamaría, L. J., & Santamaría, A. P. (2012). *Applied critical leadership in education: Choosing change.* New York, NY: Routledge.

Santamaría, L. J., Santamaría, A. P., & Dam, L. I. (2014). Applied critical leadership through Latino/a lenses: An alternative approach to educational leadership. *Revista Internacional de Educación para la Justicia Social / International Journal of Education for Social Justice, 3*(2), 161–180.

Scott, W. R. (1998). *Organizations: Rational, natural, and open systems.* Upper Saddle River, NJ: Prentice Hall.

Smith, L. T. (2006). Choosing the margins: The role of research in indigenous struggles for social justice. In N. K. Denzin & M. D. Giardina (Eds.), *Qualitative inquiry: The conservative challenge* (pp. 151–174). Walnut Creek, CA: Left Coast Press.

Spillane, J. P., Halverson, R., & Diamond, J. B. (2004). Towards a theory of leadership practice: A distributed perspective. *Journal of Curriculum Studies, 36*(1), 1–34.

Spring, J. (2006). *Deculturalization and the struggle for equality: A brief history of the education of dominated cultures in the United States.* New York, NY: McGraw-Hill.

Warren, J. T. (1999). Whiteness and cultural theory: Perspectives on research and education. *Urban Review, 31*(2), 185–203.

Wolf, D. L. (1996). Situating feminist dilemmas in fieldwork. In D. L. Wolf (Ed.), *Feminist dilemmas in fieldwork* (pp. 1–56). Boulder, CO: Westview Press.

8

TOGETHER TO THE TABLE

Applying Critical Leadership in Cross-Cultural, International Research

Amani Bell, 'Ema Wolfgramm-Foliaki, Airini,
Roisin Kelly-Laubscher, Moragh Paxton,
Tepora Pukepuke, and Lorri J. Santamaría

IDEA IN BRIEF

This chapter describes the experiences of an international, inter-generational group of culturally diverse women who are higher education research leaders. We have collaborated in the planning, data collection, analysis, and dissemination of research into students who are First in the Family at University (FIFU), a project funded by the Worldwide Universities Network (WUN). We have realized that our cross-cultural collaboration and negotiation in this leadership team have been as valuable as the research itself. Our experiences are illustrative for other similar international and cross- cultural teams working for the benefit of systemically underserved learners in international contexts.

Keywords: cross-cultural leadership, Indigenous methodologies, access and equity in higher education, Applied Critical Leadership

Our First in the Family project is about pioneers, those who are first in their families to enroll and study at university (FIFU) (see Wolfgramm-Foliaki, this volume). Much has been written about university-readiness to support the retention and achievement of First in the Family students (e.g., Saenz, Hurtado, Barrera, Wolf, & Yeung, 2007). What can research tell us about how universities might better serve students who are first in their families to enter higher education and fulfil their potential for achievement and graduation? This is in large part a story of universities embracing racial/ethnic diversity and the indigenizing of higher education. It is also about expanding how we as higher education researchers within universities think about and enact research. Conventional research approaches and thinking about access and success at university have not always been up to the task of dealing with race and culture (Airini, Anae, & Mila-Schaaf, 2010).

The approach of our FIFU project is from a strengths-based and global perspective to tell multiple narratives of how this group of students experience higher education. The project looks afresh at the experience of first-generation students in higher education. Past higher education research has largely reinforced perceptions of brown people as burdened by culture, having less, and being somewhere between victim and blame—or has ignored or minimized issues of race and inequity (see, for example, Harper, 2012). Research into first-generation students tended to be about changes the learners had to make—see, for example, Devlin (2013) for further discussion of this point. Few university-based researchers asked: "What changes do we research leaders, instructors, institutions, and power holders need to make to ensure better participation and results by first-generation students?" It was timely for us as researchers to look again at Gayatri Spivak's critical theorizing on 'the gaze' (Spivak, 2009). If we did, our questions about First in the Family students would be inverted to be questions about universities themselves and we the researchers. The gaze of the researcher reveals more about the one asking the questions than those about whom we ask questions.

The FIFU project spans five nations and six universities. It began from an initial study into Pasifika student experiences at a research-intensive university in New Zealand (see Wolfgramm-Foliaki, this volume). What the initial study highlighted was the lack of research into how universities might best support the needs of First in the Family in higher education in New Zealand. While studies had been undertaken into FIFU student experiences in New Zealand, too few critically examined the role of universities themselves in attracting, retaining, and supporting successful students from underrepresented backgrounds.

Building on the findings, the lead researcher from the initial New Zealand-based research devised an international study focused on university students who are first in their families and are from underrepresented and underserved populations. In New Zealand, this was about Māori and Pasifika students; those of Indigenous ancestry from Aotearoa New Zealand and the Pacific who live in New Zealand; in South Africa: Special Admission and low socio-economic status students; in Australia: Aboriginal and Torres Strait Islander students, and low socio-economic status students; in Canada: Aboriginal students; and in the U.S.: Native American and African American students.

We quickly became aware that the research was as much about transforming our own thinking and models of higher education research as it was about transforming universities to better support first-generation students. This chapter describes the need for re-thinking and re-modeling international research team leadership, the experience of Applied Critical Leadership (ACL) in our international study, and promising practices therein (L. J. Santamaría & Santamaría, 2012; L. J. Santamaría, 2014).

Background Literature on First in the Family Students

Increasing the rates of FIFU enrollments provides a broader representation of the population within a university. While such social cohesion is important, Durie (2009) points out that Western world universities generally have an enrollment bias for students who align to Western academic conventions. The academic enrollment processes include financial barriers and are also dependent on the students' high achievement at secondary schooling. Ultimately, universities that wish to broaden FIFU representation must have both an equity perspective, as well as a university-wide culture that reflects the diverse values, customs, interests, and aspirations of groups within society (Durie, 2009).

FIFU include Indigenous students, and while there are increasing numbers of Indigenous students entering the university system as non-FIFU, they share a common need with all first-year students to develop relationships. Thomas, Ellis, Kirkham, and Parry (2014) outline a two-way exchange process to help integrate Indigenous students into university life that is aptly named 'ngapartji' (give and take). This program shows the important work of universities to better widen participation. The aim is to build a pathway from the remote rural communities and to integrate the students into university life in a way that creates real and authentic connections. This exposure to university life is considered a factor in enrollment decision-making for these students (Thomas, Ellis, Kirkham, & Parry, 2014).

There is little literature on the work done to assimilate the triangulated interests of a FIFU student—university, home, and self. Much of the literature centers on the student and progressing academic skills, addressing pastoral needs and their motivations. University-centric support may inadvertently distance students from their family by giving the message that success is dependent on assimilation to the university. An Indigenous learning advisor, Lily George, highlights that student support is only one *pillar of support* that sits alongside other complementary university services (George, 2010). George was also involved in the well-funded holistic workforce development program *Te Rau Puawai*. The name in the Māori language means "a hundred blossoms" and denotes the program's original hope to graduate 100 students. Since Te Rau Puawai's inception in 1991, the program has facilitated the students' connections to peers, staff, and university services, and has included home visits or campus events that incorporated face-to-face time with the students' families (Nikora, Levy, Henry, & Whangapirita, 2002).

FIFU students' stories show resilience and specifically rely on self-motivation, self-efficacy, and intrinsic loci of control to persist; however, more research is required on FIFU who persist to postgraduate-level studies (Gardner & Holley, 2011). Student success can be understood as widening participation, course retention and completion, pathways to employment, and a positive attitude to lifelong learning. There is also a measure of student engagement with study, and their quality of learning (Zepke, Leach, & Butler, 2011). The early departure of students is a complex mix of personal characteristics, life circumstances, and institutional factors (Harris & Barnett, 2014) and cultural commitments (Zepke, Leach, & Prebble, 2005). FIFU students are susceptible to early departure, although it is a less limiting definition of 'success' to include the FIFU student who leaves due to financial constraints, or to care for an ill family member, if they have been well informed and leave with a clear study plan to return at a later date.

Leading Research in Higher Education to Support Students Who Are FIFU

The primary investigators, representing the leading research university in New Zealand, have brought together a collaborative cross-cultural research team of women from New Zealand, Australia, South Africa, Canada, and the U.S. In keeping with tenets of Applied Critical Leadership (ACL), this cross-cultural research team of scholars, at every level, represented Indigenous and culturally diverse perspectives. The collective work aimed to impact research and leadership practices to benefit FIFU students attending the research-intensive universities where the researchers work as academics.

More specifically, the women in this initiative are of Tongan, Māori, American Indian (Oklahoma Choctaw), African American, White South African, Black South African, Samoan, White Australian, and Egyptian descent. Each has either experienced educational inequity first-hand or worked in educational environments negatively impacted by educational inequities where systemically underserved learners are affected. These direct experiences with educational inequity are what have brought the researchers together, and what have influenced the ways in which the team has engaged research that serves to support students locally and globally.

In their research on international educational leadership, Dimmock and Walker (2002) discuss cultural differences in leadership approaches in Eastern nations versus Western worldviews as being in conflict. These differences, they maintain, have to do with the cultural preferences of the local people and their ways of being. These researchers bring to light the realities of potential conflict when comparatively considering leadership practices in educational settings. Recently, L. J. Santamaría, Santamaría, Webber, and Pearson (2014) in their international comparative research work comparing leadership practices of Māori principals to culturally and linguistically diverse leaders in the U.S. found that even though those leaders have distinctly different cultural and linguistic backgrounds, their leadership approaches were quite similar. Similarities were grounded in their shared experiences with various kinds of oppression.

The FIFU leadership team has similarly come together with different experiences and thinking about the world; however, it is clear that we all want to work toward improving access and equity for the most underserved students in our communities who also happen to be first in their families to attend university. This research collaboration draws as much on our identities as women from particular cultural and linguistic traditions, as it does our professional experiences in academe (e.g., Ph.D. student, lecturer, professor), as it does our social positions (e.g., mother, grandmother, wife, sister). The strengths from these dynamic roles are interwoven into our work and practice in such a way as to yield authentic and organic research methods that are innovative and interdisciplinary (L. J. Santamaría, 2015).

The research team is made up of educational leaders pushing their professional *thinking about leadership* for social justice toward *thinking about changing leadership practice* resulting in social justice and educational equity (L. J. Santamaría, Jeffries, & Santamaría, this volume; L. J. Santamaría & Santamaría, 2012). This way of thinking, leading, and acting thus moves the leader from participating in an intellectual exercise to applying concrete and possibly measureable action. As leaders, we partner with ACL researchers and ask: In what ways does my identity enhance my ability to see alternate perspectives and practice effective leadership?

Aim of This Chapter

Our research planning and practices need to be practical, ethical, and understandable to all involved in the study, and to others. This chapter aims to highlight how our experiences of being part of a cross-cultural and intergenerational research team can be viewed as tenets of ACL. The ACL framework and approach provides a lens to illuminate practical recommendations for other higher education research teams working in culturally and linguistically diverse contexts in the U.S. and similar countries (see A. P. Santamaría, Webber, & Santamaría, 2015; L. J. Santamaría & Santamaría, 2012; L. J. Santamaría et al., 2014).

Methodology

Co-authors of this chapter wrote reflective pieces on their experiences of participating in the FIFU project. The reflective stories ranged in length from 405 to 1,577 words and were written 12 months after the project was initiated. Afterward, two of the co-authors then thematically analyzed the stories (Braun & Clarke, 2006). These themes, with representative quotes, are presented in the results section below. In the discussion we then consider which of the nine tenets of Applied Critical Leadership (L. J. Santamaría, 2014; L. J. Santamaría & Santamaría, 2012) are apparent in the reflective pieces for suitability of fit and identification of adaptations on ACL to benefit the students we serve. Authors' initials, with their permission, identify the authors of the quotes presented in the results section, as we realized that in most cases it was not possible to de-identify the source material. Further, by identifying each author we bring their voices into the narratives, hence maintaining the authenticity and validity of our work.

Results

Six themes were identified in the reflective stories: (1) Motivation, (2) Sharing food, (3) Prayer and song, (4) Teu le vā, (5) Critical conversations, and (6) Indigenous methodologies and perspectives. Elaborations for each follow below.

Motivation to Be Involved

Several team members described their motivations for being involved in the project, for example:

> The idea of critical research for greater equity in higher education in the USA, New Zealand, Australia, South Africa and Canada . . . was very appealing. . . . For me, this research about first-generation students is really about the transformation of universities. . . . It is one further contribution to the indigenisation of higher education. At this big picture level I am motivated to improve economic gains for those underserved by higher education . . . and social justice—ensuring underserved students have that opportunity from higher education. And to be honest, for me, it is also about morality and simply doing what is right.
>
> (A)

Sharing Food Together

Before the first formal meeting commenced, we shared a meal together. Here one of the project leaders explains the importance of this communal activity:

> I was extremely worried about how we would "gel" together . . . [so] . . . the most important part for me firstly was the opportunity to meet the team and to share food together. My Pacificness makes food a very significant part of any gathering. This was the opportunity to break the "ice" and I can remember thinking "God I hope this goes well." We arrived at the restaurant and immediately we looked for stories that can connect us . . . I can recall moments of slight strain but mostly there was lots of laughter. . . . Here we were engaging in building our relationship with one another.
>
> (EWF)

Prayer and Song

The first research meeting began with a prayer, and several of the participants commented on how this was unusual yet refreshing. Here prayer is seen from the perspective of one of the project leaders:

> A. and I had a brief chat about how the first part would be, and I think I asked A. to say the prayer. There was an agenda that had been circulated earlier before we arrived into Sydney but it did not drive our meeting. The power of prayer brings

a sense of calmness into a space that is occupied by Western protocol and ways of doing things. Certainly, in many research meetings I have attended, prayer is not part of the agenda. But for this meeting, it just made sense to begin with a prayer, it as an authentic way of engaging with our colleagues and thereby we were bringing ourselves to the table.

(EWF)

Singing was also part of our meetings. Of this added bonus to a research meeting, a team member shared:

I taught the group two Māori songs, and we sang them to a visitor to our meeting. An incredible shift occurred for me when we learned a South African click song. This was my first experience with song reciprocity from another culture. Singing is leading to dancing, dancing and movement brings a new type of joy to the forum. It brings us together, it lets us share in new ways, and defines the unique nature of this FIFU group.

(TP)

Teu le Vā—*To Look after the Space*

The project leaders took great care to create a supportive space in which we could work. This idea is called *Teu le vā* (Mahina, 2002; Ka'ili, 2005; Thaman, 2008). According to one of the project leaders, *va*—or *vā, va'a, vaha*—can be loosely translated as a spatial way of conceiving the secular and spiritual dimensions of relationships and relational order (Anae, 2007; Airini, Anae, & Mila-Schaaf, 2010). The word *teu* in Samoan literally means "to keep (for example, in the heart or in the mind) the space," or "to look after the space," or to "tidy up the space" (Airini et al., 2010). According to these scholars, *Teu le vā*, in educational research contexts, is involved with creating the right relational, physical, and spiritual space for educational pursuits and similarly collaborative work. Further, this way of working can be conceptualized as a tool to assist scholars in the planning and implementation of research endeavors that contribute to the development of effective policy and practice for Pasifika students in the first instance, and similarly systemically underserved students like the ones benefitting from this research project. One of the project leaders elaborates the concept:

It did not matter that we had not worked together before. What was more important was the process of establishing a relationship with one another, and then maintaining our relationship. This of course was a familiar territory to me as the concept of relational space or vā is significant to how Pacific Island peoples relate and maintain our relationship with one another.

(EWF)

Here we see the process of *Teu le vā* as experienced by one of the other participants:

> *We began [our meeting] with* whakawhanaungatanga *(Māori word), a process of sharing about our backgrounds, especially our cultural backgrounds. E., A., and L. led the way in Samoan, Tongan, Māori, and Spanish. . . . I was able to share a few words of Arabic and to talk a bit about what it was like growing up with Egyptian Muslim heritage in a very non-diverse suburb of Sydney.* Whakawhanaungatanga *was unfamiliar and unexpected but not uncomfortable. . . . It reminded me of Lucas' (2008) use of the unexpected in teaching, what she calls being "pulled up short," in order to create space for reflection and to challenge assumptions.*
>
> *(AB)*

Our first meeting concluded with a time set aside for reflection on our experiences over the two days and space for us to bid each other farewell. Each member was presented with a lei. A lei is a garland of flowers and it can be gifted upon arrival or on departure as a sign of affection and a sign that we have established a connection.

Critical Conversations within a Safe Space

Because a safe space had been created by *Teu le vā*, we were able to have critical conversations about the work we were embarking on (L. J. Santamaría & Santamaría, 2012). We listened to one another with respect. Here one of the South African team members discusses her experiences of one of our intense discussions:

> *The FIFU team is a very cross-cultural, cross-generational group and therefore it has been crucial that we understand each other and that we develop a common language that is meaningful for each and every one of us. . . . I was troubled by the emphasis on "indigenous populations" and "cultural responsiveness" in the FIFU proposal. South Africa is a country of diverse cultures and languages and the vast majority form the indigenous population. Nelson Mandela's legacy has been to encourage us to think of South Africa as a rainbow nation and move away from ethnic divisions. I was also very conscious that in this partnership, South Africa is the only representative of a Third World country, struggling to deal with desperate poverty and inequality. These differences seemed significant. However, the more we spoke, the more we found that, despite our differences, there were many commonalities among the issues that we as the FIFU team were dealing with. There was a willingness amongst the group members to engage in critical conversations around race, gender and ethnicity, and we spent an afternoon developing universal key terms i.e. "a language" for the FIFU project. By the close of the meeting I felt we had made important progress in resolving critical issues and getting to understand each other's contexts.*
>
> *(MP)*

Indigenous Methodologies and Perspectives

Some members of the group were just beginning their journeys of exploring Indigenous methodologies and perspectives, whereas others were experienced scholars. The team was encouraged to read two key texts as a starting point—Chilisa (2012) and Smith (1999). The South African team members found an appropriate methodology for their context:

> *[We have used] a methodology which has been used previously in the South African context called Participatory Learning Activity (PLA) (Bozalek & Biersteker 2010). This methodology is particularly useful for this project because it is accessible and does not disadvantage people with different levels of literacy or those who speak different languages. Furthermore it allows for different ways of thinking and knowing, and supports development of critical consciousness and reflection. Using this methodology required the students to draw their "Life River" and then present it to us. I was overwhelmed by what I saw—the different lifestyles, the creativity of the drawings, the life stories and the passion and emotion of the students as they presented. . . . By getting the students to draw their story, elements emerged that may not have if we had interviewed them.*

(RK)

Here an experienced scholar reflects on the ways in which the team is thinking about, and using Indigenous perspectives and methodologies:

> *We value indigenous research methods as expanding the research canon. But we resist "miraculating" the indigenous (Deleuze & Guattari, 2004; Spivak 2009). Criticality should be a universal tenant. In practice, that meant rethinking and negotiating research priorities and outcomes, and research team leadership models. It meant integrating diversity in language and cultural practices in the team. . . . Assumptions that all indigenous research methods are good could be fought. Similarly, we could also fight assumptions that indigenous research methods either do not exist or are bad. Either way, our own research architecture had to be forged to be indigenous specific and genuinely so. That would take effort, listening and innovation akin to Freire's (1998) idea of epistemological curiosity.*

(A)

And,

> *As an African American Spanish-born woman of Choctaw descent, I cannot take for granted the privilege of working in a cross-cultural scholarly space where indigeneity is incorporated and honored. The critical research that I have engaged has been enhanced by this work and encouraged me to write, teach, inquire and speak more boldly with regard to bringing the tenets of traditional wisdom into the academy. I am currently in a state of "unlearning" hegemonic ways associated with research*

as I integrate all elements of my self into academic work like this FIFU project and other complementary pursuits. I am convinced, as the Hopi elders affirm, that we are the ones we have been waiting for.

(LJS)

Discussion

Our international research experience highlights the importance of critical leadership that is applied in higher education settings and research. Our research design builds on previous research (rather than duplicating it in part or whole), including quantitative analysis by tapping into existing databases on participation and retention, linking to strategic plans and targets for underserved students in higher education. In this way, the research process overtly builds trust led by a "spirit" as we have described and a collaborative practice of servant leadership. On this premise, it is of no surprise that additional principles of ACL emerged from this experience. As well, there were seemingly simple, yet impactful, team-building activities that came as a result of our work together. Table 8.1 reflects ways in which core elements of ACL were adapted.

Evidence and exemplars of ACL characteristics reflect that as a team of women and inter-generational researchers we considered what these characteristics

TABLE 8.1 FIFU Adaptations and Expression of Applied Critical Leadership

ACL Characteristics	FIFU Adaptations
Initiate and engage in critical conversations as researchers	Engaging in conversations regarding race, class, gender, ethnicity, etc., because the project leaders attended to relationship building (e.g., creating a safe space).
Assume a critical race theory lens in order to consider multiple perspectives of critical issues	Consideration of multiple worldviews (e.g., utilizing Indigenous methodologies).
Use consensus building for decision-making	Key element of *Teu le va* with strong emphasis away from deficit models associated with FIFU students.
Remain consciousness of "stereotype threat" or fulfilling negative stereotypes associated with a population group, working hard to dispel negative stereotypes	Use of strengths-based approach toward underserved students and conscious work against deficit thinking, research design, and words (e.g., first in family learners as pioneers vs. needy or helpless).
Make empirical contributions and, thus, add meaningful data to academic discourse regarding underserved groups	Research contributes to improved practices regarding educational need resulting in reciprocal research giving back to marginalized communities supporting their students' success.

(Continued)

TABLE 8.1 (Continued)

ACL Characteristics	FIFU Adaptations
Honor all members of the constituencies (e.g., staff, parents, community members) and raise capability and capacity in the focus communities	Committed to legacy of research/researchers, growing pool of Indigenous and underserved researchers to undertake quality research toward improving higher education's performance for systemically underserved students.
Express leadership practices that are transformative and servant leadership for those who work ultimately to serve the greater good	Our research is a form of service wherein action and change are necessary companions to critical research leadership with practical outcomes that help transform the university environment.
Need to build trust with those who may not share critical stance or views	Rigorous scholarship findings on critical issues (e.g., race, ethnicity, gender, class) enable discussions on improvement with constituents in meaningful ways that help toward resolution.

brought to our project. At the very least, and counter to others' experiences, each voice and contribution was viewed positively; we were able to speak up (Brescoll & Uhlmann, 2008). Our work together provides affirmation that the spaces created were safe and outside the norm of other academic meetings we had each experienced. The more seasoned scholars had a wealth of experience to share with those more junior, and the junior colleagues brought fresh perspectives to the meetings. The initial leaders were willing to give the other members the opportunity to bring their ideas and perspectives to the table. In international cross-cultural research teams, each member brings a different set of values and perspectives; it is important to acknowledge this and be open to incorporating their views even if it means giving up your own.

CULTURALLY RESPONSIVE LEADERSHIP IN PRACTICE

Further to this work, the FIFU women scholars also put in place some small but meaningful activities:

- **Sharing a meal together** at the start of the research project. Sharing a meal together is common to all cultures, and being away from the academic context gives people a chance to get to know each other and share stories.
- **Having playful and fun elements within the meeting**—the researchers shared pink leis and the wearing of frangipani flowers, but it will be different for different teams depending on the cultural capital members bring. Laughter is an important part of an open and fun environment for working together.

- **Preparing in advance for the creation of an emotionally, psychologically, spiritually, and physically safe environment** for people to engage in useful discussions. Any ice-breaker should not be artificial, but rather should reflect the purpose of the meeting and the cultural space you wish to create.
- **The agenda does not drive the meeting**—give members time to speak, but not aimlessly. These scholars still ended their research meetings on time and covered the agenda items but there was not a sense of being rushed—people feel valued, heard, and respected.

Conclusion

The strength of the FIFU team lies in our different worldviews and experiences, together with our shared desire to work toward improving access and equity for underserved students in our communities. Enacting Applied Critical Leadership involves a constant process of learning and being open to learning while engaging leadership practice (L. J. Santamaría, Jeffries, & Santamaría, this volume). Here we have been open about our experiences in the hopes of helping other research teams learn from what we bring to the table.

Acknowledgments

We are grateful to the Worldwide Universities Network (WUN) for providing funding for our project, and to the partner universities for also contributing funding, including Te Whare Kura at the University of Auckland. We thank all members of the FIFU project team.

References

Airini, Anae, K., & Mila-Schaaf, K. (2010). *Teu le va—Relationships across research and policy in Pasifika education: A collective approach to knowledge generation and policy development for action towards Pasifika education success.* Wellington, New Zealand: Ministry of Education.

Anae, M. (2007). *Teu le va: Research that could make a difference to Pacific schooling in New Zealand.* Paper commissioned by Ministry of Education for "Is Your Research Making a Difference to Pasifika Education?" Retrieved from https://www.educationcounts.govt.nz/publications/pasifika/teu-le-va-relationships-across-research-and-policy-in-pasifika-education/references

Bozalek, V., & Biersteker, L. (2010). Exploring power and privilege using participatory learning and action techniques. *Social Work Education, 29*(5), 551–572.

Braun, V., & Clarke, V. (2006). Using thematic analysis in psychology. *Qualitative Research in Psychology, 3*(2), 77–101.

Brescoll, V. L., & Uhlmann, E. L. (2008). Can an angry woman get ahead? Status conferral, gender, and expression of emotion in the workplace. *Psychological Science, 19*(3), 268–275.

Chilisa, B. (2012). *Indigenous research methodologies.* Thousand Oaks, CA: Sage.

Deleuze, G., & Guattari, F. (2004). *Anti-Oedipus* (4th ed.). London, UK: Continuum.

Devlin, M. (2013). Bridging socio-cultural incongruity: Conceptualising the success of students from low socio-economic status backgrounds in Australian higher education. *Studies in Higher Education, 38*(6), 939–949.

Dimmock, C., & Walker, A. (2002). School leadership in context: Societal and organisational cultures. In T. Bush & L. Bell (Eds.), *The principles and practice of educational management* (pp. 70–85). London, UK: Paul Chapman.

Durie, M. (2009, June). *Towards social cohesion: The indigenisation of higher education in New Zealand.* Paper presented at the Vice Chancellors' Forum (VCF2009) "How Far Are Universities Changing and Shaping Our World," Kuala Lumpur, Malaysia.

Freire, P. (1998). *Pedagogy of freedom: Ethics, democracy, and civic courage.* Oxford, UK: Rowman and Littlefield.

Gardner, S. K., & Holley, K. A. (2011). "Those invisible barriers are real": The progression of First-Generation students through doctoral education. *Equity and Excellence in Education, 44*(1), 77–99.

George, L. (2010). Tradition, invention and innovation: Multiple reflections of an urban marae (Unpublished doctoral dissertation). School of Social and Cultural Studies, Massey University, Auckland, NZ.

Harper, S. R. (2012). Race without racism: How higher education researchers minimize racist institutional norms. *Review of Higher Education, 36*(1), 9–29.

Harris, M., & Barnett, T. (2014). *Thriving in transition: A model for student support in the transition to Australian higher education.* Sydney, Australia: Office for Learning and Teaching.

Ka'ili, T. (2005). Tauhi Vā: Nurturing Tongan sociospatial ties in Maui and beyond. *The Contemporary Pacific, 17*(1), 83–114.

Lucas, U. (2008). Being "pulled up short": Creating moments of surprise and possibility in accounting education. *Critical Perspectives on Accounting, 19*(3), 383–403.

Mahina, O. (2002). Tufunga Lalava: The Tongan art of lineal and spatial intersection. In S. Rees (Ed.), *Filipe Tohi: Genealogy of Lines Hohoko e Tohitohi* (pp. 5–9). New Plymouth, New Zealand: Govett Brewster Art Gallery.

Nikora, L. W., Levy, M., Henry, J., & Whangapirita, L. (2002). *An evaluation of Te Rau Puawai Workforce* 100. Technical Reports No. 1–6. Hamilton, New Zealand: Māori and Psychology Research Unit, University of Waikato.

Saenz, V., Hurtado, S., Barrera, D., Wolf, D., & Yeung, F. (2007). *First in my family: A profile of first-generation college students at four-year institutions since 1971.* Los Angeles, CA: Higher Education Research Institute, University of California Los Angeles.

Santamaría, A. P., Webber, M., & Santamaría, L. J. (2015). Māori urban school leadership (MUSL): Building capacity for indigenous and international cross-cultural collaboration. In N. D. Erbe & A. H. Normore (Eds.), *Cross-cultural collaboration and leadership in modern organizations* (pp. 99–119). Hershey, PA: IGI Global.

Santamaría, L. J. (2014). Critical change for the greater good: Multicultural dimensions of educational leadership toward social justice and educational equity. *Education Administration Quarterly (EAQ), 50*(3), 347–391.

Santamaría, L. J. (2015). Culturally responsive leadership in cross-cultural international contexts. In N. D. Erbe & A. H. Normore (Eds.), *Cross-cultural collaboration and leadership in modern organizations* (pp. 120–139). Hershey, PA: IGI Global.

Santamaría, L. J., & Santamaría, A. P. (2012). *Applied critical leadership in education: Choosing change.* New York, NY: Routledge.

Santamaría, L. J., Santamaría, A. P., Webber, M., & Pearson, H. (2014). Indigenous urban school leadership (IUSL): A critical cross-cultural comparative analysis of educational leaders in New Zealand and the United States. *Comparative and International Education/ Éducation Comparée et Internationale, 43*(1), 1–21.

Smith, L. T. (1999). *Decolonizing methodologies: Research and indigenous peoples.* London, UK: Zed Books.

Spivak, G. (2009). *Outside in the teaching machine* (2nd ed.). New York, NY: Routledge.

Thaman, K. H. (2008). Nurturing relationships and honouring responsibilities: A Pacific perspective. *International Review of Education, 54*(3/4), 459–473.

Thomas, K., Ellis, B., Kirkham, R., & Parry, L. (2014). Remote indigenous students: Raising their aspirations and awareness of tertiary pathways. *Australian and International Journal of Rural Education, 24*(2), 23–35.

Zepke, N., Leach, L., & Butler, P. (2011). Non-institutional influences and student perceptions of success. *Studies in Higher Education, 36*(2), 227–242.

Zepke, N., Leach, L., & Prebble, T. (2005). Now you've got them, can you expect to keep them? Factors that influence student departure and persistence. *New Zealand Journal of Educational Studies, 40*(2), 181–201.

PART III

Ways of Leading toward Increased Equity and Improved Student Achievement

9

"DO NOT ASSUME WE KNOW"

Perspectives of Pacific Island First in the Family Students

*'Ema Wolfgramm-Foliaki**

IDEA IN BRIEF

First in the Family (FIF) students are essentially leaders in their families and communities. They are students whose parents did not attend higher education institutions (see Bell et al., this volume). Despite what the literature says about FIF students in higher education, they are role models and pioneers within their own families and communities. This chapter reports on findings of a preliminary study that examined the experiences of Pacific Island students who are first in their families to attend a research-intensive university in New Zealand. A culturally appropriate framework is employed to gather personal narratives from the students. Insights into their experiences will give higher education leaders a better understanding of the FIF journey and ways in which to develop a culturally responsive agenda to meet their needs. This study is a strengths-based and ethical approach whereby participants are part of the research process and equal partners in the process of knowledge production.

Keywords: Pacific Island students, first in the family, culturally responsive leadership

Students who are first in their families to attend university make up a large proportion of the student population in higher education. Early literature has referred to these individuals as first-generation students (Pascarella, Wolniak, Pierson, & Terezini, 2003). Benseman, Coxon, Henderson, and Anae (2007), and local colleagues have referred to this group of students as nontraditional students, while others (Bell et al., this volume) refer to them as FIFU or first in family to attend university. It is only recently that they have been referred to as First in the Family students. This chapter adopts the recent definition as an appropriate way of describing this group of students, given that they may be first in their immediate and/or extended family to study at university. It is also a relevant way of describing this group of students who hold a significant position in their families and communities as pioneers of the educational landscape.

Context Cues

The term *Pacific Island* is used to define a very diverse group, which includes people from Samoa, Tonga, Cook Islands, Niue, Fiji, and other Pacific nations (see Fitzpatrick & Langi, this volume). According to the Ministry of Pacific Islands website, Pacific peoples as a group is a fast-growing population in New Zealand that is expected to account for 10% of the total population by 2026, in comparison to 6.5% in the 2001 Census. The majority of the Pacific population live in the greater Auckland area. For much of their limited presence in this country, the pass rates and retention of Pacific Island students has been a concern across all levels of the education sector. More specifically, the relatively low participation, achievement, and retention of Pacific Island students in higher education has been a focus of ongoing debate in this country. As a group, they have continued to achieve at a much lower rate than their counterparts. Much has been written about Pacific Island students and their demise in higher education contexts (Anae, Andersen, Benseman, & Coxon, 2002; Education Review Office, 2002). However, the literature around Pacific Island students who are first in their families to study at university is still limited. The work of Benseman et al. (2007) is one of the first to provide us with a detailed examination of issues that contribute to and hinder the participation and retention of Pacific Island students in higher education who are nontraditional or first in their families to attend university. Role models were key to the success of the students in the Benseman et al. (2007) study. Students' achievement was considered a collective effort between themselves, their families, and community, and family members looked up to these students as leaders in their own right.

Literature and Research Considered

Cultural Capital

Pike and Kuh (2005) have argued for the consequences of FIF students entering higher education with a limited understanding of what is expected and what it takes to succeed. The work of Crosnoe, Mistry, and Elder (2002) showed a strong link between parents' educational level and their children's academic achievement. This has specific implications for the future of FIF students at university, a space where their success rate is doomed, according to deficit theorizing. Evident in the literature is a long list of what FIF students lack in terms of resources and skills to succeed at university. Cultural capital, or more precisely the lack of it, has seemingly been a strong determinant to their success. Collier and Morgan (2007) pointed out that understanding and mastering the university student role is another critical ingredient for the success of First in the Family students, and is as important as knowing faculty and academic expectations.

In relation to FIF students, many have indicated that even though their families lack the cultural capital required for tertiary success, their families have been instrumental in their success (Mayeda, Keil, Dutton, & 'Ofamo'oni, 2004), which is particularly true for students who share Pacific Island backgrounds. Students who are from collective rather than individualistic cultures can see the positive contribution that their families make to their studies and lives in general, and do not attribute their low achievement to their families' lack of appropriate knowledge. Most of the work in this area, though, shows that there is a marked difference in the achievement of students who are continuing generation and those who are first in their families in higher education (Lohfink & Paulsen, 2005; Pascarella et al., 2003).

Role of Social Contexts

Our attention has also been directed to the complexity of the relationship between the institution and of students through the work of Pascarella, Edison, Nora, Hagedorn, and Terezini (1996) and Tinto (1993). Collier and Morgan (2007) applied a sociological lens of role theory to examine how First in the Family students experience university study and concluded that students who arrive at university with a good understanding of university expectations and how to respond within an academic context were likely to succeed. Given that First in the Family students were known to lack cultural capital, their future in higher education was rather dim. In order to succeed, Collier and Morgan (2007) contend that students need to understand the explicit and implicit expectations of lecturers and teachers. However, Dumais (2006) reminds us that school contexts do not often provide the opportunity for students to acquire the skills and understanding of its culture that is important for success. There has been ongoing debate about how cultural capital converts to an advantage in social contexts, especially where schooling is concerned.

In related research, Lareau and Weininger (2003) brought to light ways in which cultural capital is reproduced. Clearly, academic skills are about prior learning, whereas cultural capital is more about pre-existing knowledge and recognizing how to navigate one's way in an academic setting. This gives continuing-generation students a good basis for success in academia. First-generation students often do not have a good understanding of what is required to succeed. On the other hand, continuing-generation students, due to familial experiences, are more familiar with the demands and expectations of an academic context.

Academic Achievement for Pacific Island Students

When we examine the low achievement of Pacific Island students in New Zealand, clearly there is an imbalance of prior knowledge and also of the necessary social skills required for success within a Western academic context. Bourdieu's (1977) work has looked at how a student's cultural resources influence the student's outcome at school. He argued that schools reward students for their cultural capital. Teachers, he argued, were more likely to engage with these students and go as far as to perceive them as being more intelligent than students who lack cultural capital. Bourdieu identified cultural capital as conceptual knowledge to be passed down from one generation to the next.

As noted earlier, in the short history of Pacific Island peoples in Aotearoa New Zealand, they have remained significantly overrepresented among those that have failed to leave school with any formal achievement. As few as 10% of Pacific Island school-leavers were recorded to have qualified with university entrance accreditation, and even more worrying was the fact that over a quarter were leaving school without any qualifications whatsoever (New Zealand Ministry of Education, 2004). The students' participation rate has been slow to improve. By 2000, the statistics showed an increase in their participation from 2.5% to 4.8% of the total. However, a closer examination revealed that the majority of the increase had been from those who enrolled in certificate and diploma courses and not degree programs. Hence, in comparison to their counterparts, Pacific Island peoples are still predominantly much lower in terms of school and degree completion rates.

Sense of Belonging, Relationship, and Identity

Vincent Tinto's (1993) early work established that tertiary institutions were still not doing enough to retain nontraditional students. A main focus of his more recent work was the expectation that institutions will take responsibility for the learning environment that is offered for students (Tinto, 2004). Gee (1998) noted that institutions' failure to create engaging learning environments for nontraditional students contributed to a culture of exclusivity where the discourse and practices kept these students at the fringes of engagement. Rolleston (2004) found in his study of Māori and Pasifika students that external factors (finance, family, personal) were indicated as the main reasons why they left without completion. However, institutional reasons made up 35% of the comments from participants.

Kalavite (2010) explains the number of tensions that exist between the different relationships of Tongan university students and their wider community. She argues that their success at university is dependent on a better understanding between their social and cultural relationships and their academic relationships.

Her study demonstrated the importance of a more flexible relationship between the different contexts in order to allow students to move fluidly between them. A more fluid movement and better understanding of the different contexts would help students to better manage their studies and experience success as a consequence. Many of the students were involved in youth groups, choirs, and other groups in the wider community. Santamaría and Santamaría (2012) refer to this aspect of culturally responsive leadership as applied practice that develops as a consequence of 'lived experiences' where the participants acknowledge and uphold their cultural beliefs and community in a positive way, despite what the literature says about their lack of cultural capital and the implications this has on their studies. From FIF students' perspectives it is a strengths-based approach whereby drawing on positive attributes of one's identity will result in positive implications and eventual transformation toward educational improvement in their lives.

Culturally Responsive Research Methods

By using a culturally appropriate Pasifika research methodology, the current study gathered personal narratives from Pacific Island students who are first in their families to study at university (Halapua, 2007; Smith, 1999). Students were invited to participate in the study through networks, including student associations such as the Samoan Student Association and other university-wide support networks established to assist Māori and Pacific Island students with their studies. A comfortable space was chosen for research interactions where food was provided as well as monetary compensation ($20 grocery vouchers) to indicate a level of initial reciprocity as a normal part of the research undertaking.

Talanoa *as a Research Methodology*

Continuing this culturally responsive approach, the study employed *Talanoa* as an appropriate method of gathering personal narratives and engaging with the participants in a conversation (see Bell et al., this volume). Prior to the arrival of Western civilization in the Pacific, Talanoa was the way in which Islanders created their history, orally and through conversations where nothing was written (Halapua, 2007). Talanoa is best described as an open form of engaging in conversations similar to focus group interviews (Yin, 1994). What differentiates Talanoa from focus group interviews is the agenda and culturally embedded conversational manner of the talk. In Talanoa, there is no prescribed platform where one person's answer or position, or the research questions, drive or can sabotage the process. In Talanoa, any participant can tell his or her story according to what that person feels is important to him or her. It is not predetermined and is not about reaching a consensus. In addition, participants can be reassured of respect and trust as normal parts of the process. Halapua (2007) contended that trust and respect are the cornerstones of Talanoa.

Due to its open agenda, Talanoa gives participants the opportunity to engage in a face-to-face conversation with each other with an eventual outcome. In this way, Talanoa also helps to build a better understanding and cooperation within and across human relationships. Within the Pacific community, relationships are central to everyday life where continued maintenance of relationship is important for the well-being of everyone (Thaman, 2008). As a research methodology, Talanoa encourages peaceful and positive dialogues between individuals who may or may not be familiar with each other.

Before the Talanoa meetings (there were two sessions with seven male and female students each, from different Pacific Islands), questions were generated to guide the sessions. In aligning with the protocols of Talanoa, the questions did not restrict or prevent students from sharing their stories with each other and the two researchers. The meetings were tape recorded with the participants' permission. In terms of analysis, researchers transcribed the recordings of the narratives and then analyzed each one using a constant comparative strategy separately (Bogdan & Biklen, 2007), before the data were grouped across the researchers according to similar themes (Creswell, 1998).

Findings

Students' Voice: Family Perspectives

The majority of the students in both groups spoke positively about the institution. All saw the opportunity to study and enter higher education as a privilege and one that had long been a dream of all of their families. In addition, most of their families were also very supportive of their decision to enter university, although the students noted that most of the time their families did not have a good understanding of what university study entailed. Most of the students talked positively about being at university; one described her experiences as being enjoyable, especially being a young Pacific Island student studying at university. All agreed it was definitely something to celebrate. There was also agreement about having the opportunity to meet and connect with other Pacific Island students. This was an added bonus, particularly for those who have come out of secondary schools with a low number of Pacific students. For the mature students, their studies were more explicitly tied to their families, as the need to succeed and get employment was a priority. They were also able to articulate their strengths, which included good time-management skills and the ability to focus on their studies. Many were also connected to other mature Pacific students in different faculties, with whom they often meet for meals and for group discussion of their assignments. One student spoke of her time with fellow mature Pacific students as the most enjoyable—being together and laughing together was an important part of being a Pacific student at university. She doubted if she would still be studying if she were on her own and without her fellow Pacific peers. A number of students from both Talanoa groups were also in agreement with this. It was evident from these students that there was value in being with other Pacific students.

Most of the students agreed and acknowledged that their families viewed them as leaders and role models. While each student understood this, it often brought tensions to their relationship with their families. One student in particular spoke at length about the expectation placed upon her by her older siblings:

> *Everyone thinks that they can have a say in what I study . . . my older siblings are always suggesting other courses that I should do. They never went to university so they now think they can have a say in what I do. Being the youngest in the family also gives them the right to speak to me. And being the youngest, my family expects me to do better than my older siblings.*

The above student was not alone; another student spoke of her parents' aspirations and dreams for her to do law:

> *My parents' dream is for me to become a lawyer. That's all they talk about. When I enrolled I discovered psychology. That's what I really like. Now I am in Stage 2, I have done Law as a General Education paper, that's as far as I have gone to fulfilling my parents' dreams. I haven't told them yet . . . one day I will.*

Many also spoke of the pressure from their families and the expectations that are placed upon them. One student in particular described his feelings and belief that his parents are living their dreams through him and his studies:

> *I don't like the pressure to learn; I just want to do it for myself.*

There is an intensity regarding university study that the participants spoke about with regard to their families and their lack of understanding of the pressures they are under as students. Because of this lack of understanding, some of the students felt that this contributed to their families' unrealistic expectations of them. However, the lack of knowledge of university is not all negative. One of the students spoke of how her father supports her and her son:

> *My father comes every week with groceries for myself and my son . . . that's how he can support me. He knows that it's really important for me to study especially as a single parent.*

The findings in this study are similar to that of Benseman et al. (2007) where Pacific Island students spoke about the added pressure that their families put on them due to their lack of understanding about university study. In many cases, the demands of students' families often clashed with the requirements of academic studies. For these students, the collective nature of Pacific Island life can be in direct conflict with the demand of their studies on their time and commitment.

Family members also struggled to understand their students' course of study. For example, a student studying Early Childhood Education had to keep explaining to her elderly father what her study is about and what kind of job she was likely to have afterward. Her extended family back in Samoa often teased her about her university study. At home (Samoa), there is a local joke about university students who go to university and do not return home until very late every day. Once her father understood, he showed his support by telling her: "Do your best."

All of the students in the Talanoa groups were committed to their studies and saw it as an opportunity to get ahead in life. They understood that university was a place to learn, and an opportunity for them to obtain a qualification and then go back and work to help their families and respective communities. All spoke of their families' aspirations since leaving the Islands and migrating to New Zealand in search of a better life. A university qualification is an aspiration for all of their families. Despite the tension that exists between their studies and their way of life, each student had a deep appreciation and understanding of the leadership role they have within their families due to their being at university.

Expectations

Students talked at length about their struggles with their studies, both on a personal and pedagogical level. There was a general agreement from both groups that there was a lack of understanding on their part of the university's expectations of them as students. The implicit and unspoken expectations were most frustrating to students. For example, they felt there was an expectation that students came to university with computer skill and a specific level of competency of the English language:

> I did not know about expectations . . . technology was a huge challenge . . . didn't even know how to turn on a computer. The first tutorial task was done on a computer. I just sat there.

Learning a New Language

Knowledge and proficiency of the English language was identified by most of the students in both groups as a constant challenge. The majority of the students failed the compulsory English language diagnostic test:

> My first week as a student, I had to use the computer to take an English test. I was not very confident with using the computer let alone English is my second language. Not surprising that I failed the first time I took the assessment. I felt really bad, very disheartening. I took the semester off and just spent the time to learn how to use the computer and polish my English skills.

Most of the participants indicated that English was a second, third, and even fourth language for them. One student in particular articulated her frustration at how Pacific Island students are often misunderstood by others in Western-learning contexts:

> *They say that we never ask questions. I don't ask questions because I am trying to understand the new concepts. I am thinking and processing everything. I may have questions, but not right there and then.*

Another student agreed by stating:

> *In our culture, we are taught to respect others and not to question our elders. Here (at university) you have to ask questions, you have to find the confidence to venture out and go and get help . . .*

Learning a New Culture

Many of the participants in the study talked of their struggle to seek help. Going to seek help during the office hours of staff was a challenge for many of the participants. One student in particular spoke of her experience when she went to see her lecturer:

> *I went to see my lecturer but when I got there he wasn't available . . . they (lecturers) are really intimidating, especially for first year students . . . they don't look up . . . they are always busy. I never went back.*

A fellow student agreed:

> *Learning to function in this new culture is a real challenge. English is another big challenge.*
> *I am quiet, I am listening, I am observing. I am trying to get used to the situation. I'm quiet in class because I am trying to figure out the language, the process, the concepts. It's hard to ask a question when I'm busy trying to figure all these things in my head.*

Finding Help among Ourselves

As a consequence, students seek help from other fellow Pacific students or try to deal with it themselves. One student articulates this well:

> *We are most comfortable with other Pacific Island students . . . we have our own humor . . . we can laugh at ourselves. University as a place of study does not understand us.*

CULTURALLY RESPONSIVE LEADERSHIP IN PRACTICE

Students in the study recommended a number of ideas for how things could be improved for First in the Family students like themselves and in particular those of Pacific Island descent.

1. In general, all of the students agreed that while it is useful for the institution to employ Pacific Island staff members, **it is important to ensure Pacific staff profiles are visible** so that Pacific Island students know about them and how they can access their help.
2. Students felt strongly that **communication be used as a pathway for sharing information** and knowledge between Pacific Island and non-Pacific staff members and students so members of the community can learn from each other, share resources, inform one another of events, and discuss issues faced by Pacific Island students.
3. Students suggested **personal and cross-cultural communication as important topics for professional development** for staff.
4. Students agreed **receiving regular emails** from course instructors was a major help in terms of getting information about extra tutorials and where to go for help.
5. **"Do not assume we know"** was the message from all students.
6. Students stressed that **staff should not generalize or essentialize** Pasifika students, as they are not all the same.

Discussion

The purpose of this study was to examine the experiences of Pacific Island students who are first in their families to study at university. By employing a culturally appropriate methodology to gather narratives from students, this study demonstrated a commitment to ethical research in privileging Indigenous forms of knowledge creation. The students who participated in this study revealed in their narratives that they have a strong sense of who they are and where they come from. Many see their 'Pacificness' as a positive element in their relationship with other fellow Pacific Island students on campus. Family is also seen as an important element in each student's life and educational journey. Most expressed that their education was for themselves and for other members (immediate and extended) of their families. Each student is seen as a role model and leader in his or her own family and community. As university students, they are also seen as part of the successful migrants' dream of a better life and brighter future.

This has important implications for the expectations placed on the students and the contributions they are expected to make to the wider community.

However, even though family was considered important in students' lives, they often did not understand what university is all about and what it entails to be successful. Clearly, there was a mismatch between families' perceptions of higher education and the daily experiences of FIF students. The lack of cultural capital in FIF students' homes and wider community made FIF students feel alienated and 'out of place' at university. This contributed to FIF students' feelings of being in another culture that was very different to their own—an experience that often prompted FIF students to re-examine their identity in relation to what it takes to succeed at university. This process of negotiation of cultural obstacles in higher education can also result in a gain or loss of identity and with many FIF students feeling there is a need to take off and take on new sets of identity.

The findings have significant implications for how leaders in higher education respond to the needs of First in the Family students. Using the culturally responsive and applied critical leadership characteristics as a lens is useful in thinking about how best to support FIF students (Santamaría & Santamaría, 2012). Given that these students are systemically underserved and from sociocultural backgrounds where there is a lack of cultural capital and institutional knowledge, it is critical and only fair for appropriate support to be in place for them to ensure their success in higher education. Family and community are central to their lives and their educational journey; hence both elements need to be part of any support programs and curriculum development for FIF students. Adopting a critical lens in order to consider multiple perspectives is also key to how higher education leaders respond to the needs of FIF students including those from Pacific Island communities. Acknowledging that different viewpoints are at play will demonstrate the institution's willingness to be inclusive of all members of the academy regardless of background, color, and prior experiences. Related to this is the need to be acutely aware of the negative stereotypes that exist in our society especially in relation to the community groups where FIF students are from. Higher educational leaders will need to invest time and energy and resources to ensure that negative stereotypes are not part of institutional culture.

As with any research, there are several limitations. The cohort of participants was small and the ethnic groups were not evenly represented due mainly to the proportion of Pacific Island students at this university. While the results present a glimpse of how our Pacific Island students experience higher education, they cannot be used to generalize the experiences of First in the Family students who are at university. Although the data is dependent on personal narratives of the participants, it is the dimension of qualitative and narrative inquiry. And as a research method, it is closely aligned with the cultural practices of the participants. Vaioleti (2006) argues that through the Talanoa method, participants are able to construct their experiences by way of stories and that, in turn, gives us authentic and reliable information.

Conclusion

Education is a highly desired commodity for FIF Pacific Island students as it is seen as a pathway to social mobility via better jobs with better pay than their respective parents and other members of their families who have not been to university. As sons and daughters of migrant families to New Zealand, they are considered leaders and role models who have defied much of what has been written and presumed about them. As a cohort, FIF Pacific Island students need specific support in order to deconstruct and master the role of being a university student. The lack of cultural capital and familial experiences about university has important implications for the success of FIF students and how higher learning institutions respond to their needs. While families need a better understanding of what university study entails, there is also a need for the institutions to provide a learning environment where the implicit is made more explicit, especially for FIF students. To reiterate the words of the students in this study, "Do not assume we know."

Note

* I acknowledge the assistance and effort of Ms. Sharon Televave who helped with the data-gathering process of this project.

References

Anae, M., Andersen, H., Benseman, J., & Coxon, E. (2002). *Pacific peoples and tertiary education issues of participation.* Wellington, New Zealand: Ministry of Education.

Benseman, J., Coxon, E., Henderson, H., & Anae, M. (2007). Retaining non-traditional students: Lessons learnt from Pasifika students in New Zealand. *Higher Education Research and Development, 25*(2), 147–162.

Bogdan, R. C., & Biklen, S. K. (2007). *Research for education: An introduction to theories and methods* (4th ed.). Boston, MA: Allyn & Bacon.

Bourdieu, P. (1977). *Outline of theory of practice.* Cambridge, UK: Cambridge University Press.

Collier, P. J., & Morgan. D. L. (2007). Is that paper due today?: Differences in first generation and traditional college students' understanding of faculty expectations. *Higher Education, 55*(4), 425–446.

Creswell, J. W. (1998). *Qualitative inquiry and research design: Choosing among five traditions.* Thousand Oaks, CA: Sage.

Crosnoe, R., Mistry, R. S., & Elder, G. H. (2002). Economic disadvantages, family dynamics and adolescents enrolment in higher education. *Journal of Marriage and Family, 64*(3), 690–702.

Dumais, S. A. (2006). Early childhood, cultural capital, parental habitus and teachers' perceptions. *Poetics, 34*(2), 83–107.

Education Review Office. (2002). *Finlayson Park School.* Wellington, New Zealand: Author.

Gee, J. (1998, April). *Learning academic social languages late.* Paper presented to the writing program at Syracuse University, New York.

Halapua, S. (2007). Talanoa—Talking from the heart: Interview with Dr. Sitiveni Hapaua. *SGI Quarterly, 47,* 9–10.

Kalavite, T. (2010). *Fononga 'a Fakahalafononga: Tongan students' journey to academic achievement in New Zealand tertiary education* (Unpublished doctoral dissertation). University of Waikato, New Zealand.

Lareau, A., & Weininger, E. B. (2003). Cultural capital in educational research: A critical assessment. *Theory and Society, 32*(5/6), 567–606.

Lohfink, M. M., & Paulsen, M. B. (2005). Comparing the determinants of persistence for first generation and continuing generation students. *Journal of College Student Development, 46*(4), 409–428.

Mayeda, D., Keil, M., Dutton, H., & 'Ofamo'oni, F. (2004). You've gotta set a precedent: Māori and Pacific voices on student success in higher education. *AlterNative: An International Journal of Indigenous Peoples, 10*(2), 165–179.

New Zealand Ministry of Education. (2004). *Pasifika peoples in New Zealand education: A statistical snapshot 2004.* Wellington, New Zealand: Learning Media.

Pascarella, E., Edison, M., Nora, A., Hagedorn, L., & Terezini, P. (1996). Influences on students' openness to diversity and challenge in the first year of college. *Journal of Higher Education, 67*(2), 174–195.

Pascarella, E. T., Wolniak, G. C., Pierson, C. T., & Terezini, P. T. (2003). Experiences and outcomes of first generation students in community colleges. *Journal of College Student Development, 44*(3), 420–429.

Pike, G. R., & Kuh, G. D. (2005). First and second generation college students: A comparison of their engagement and intellectual development. *Journal of Higher Education, 76*(3), 276–300.

Rolleston, A. (2004, March). *Attrition and retention: The voices of missing students.* Paper presented to the Australian Vocational and Training Research Association Conference, Canberra, Australia.

Santamaría, L. J., & Santamaría, A. P. (2012). *Applied critical leadership in education: Choosing change.* New York, NY: Routledge.

Smith, L. T. (1999). *Decolonising methodologies: Research and indigenous peoples.* New York, NY: Palgrave.

Thaman, K. H. (2008). Nurturing relationships and honouring responsibilities: A Pacific perspective. *International Review of Education, 54*(3/4), 459–473.

Tinto, V. (1993). *Leaving college: Rethinking the causes and cures of student attrition* (2nd ed.). Chicago, IL: University of Chicago Press.

Tinto, V. (2004). *Student retention and graduation: Facing the truth, living with the consequences.* Occasional Paper 1. Pell Institute for the Study of Opportunity in Higher Education. Retrieved from http://www.pellinstitute.org

Vaioleti, T. (2006). Talanoa research methodology: A developing position on Pacific research. *Waikato Journal of Education, 12,* 21–34.

Yin, R. K. (1994). Discovering the future of the case study method in evaluation research. *Evaluation Practice, 15*(3), 283–290.

10

BEYOND CRITICAL MASS

Latina Faculty Advancing Equity in a
Hispanic-Serving Institution

Anne-Marie Núñez and Elizabeth T. Murakami

IDEA IN BRIEF

Drawing on our involvement as participant-observers in one university-based support group, we address how junior faculty can serve as agents of change to support one another to navigate the academy and to advance research to promote inclusiveness in higher education. Specifically, we employ the lens of Applied Critical Leadership (ACL) to examine how Latina faculty members in a Hispanic-Serving Institution (HSI) created a network to promote equity for Latin@s in pre-elementary through tertiary education. Our analysis of this group's collaborative activities and scholarship indicates that this group supported its members in: (1) drawing on their identities as assets to inform their faculty work, (2) managing critical steps of the tenure and promotion process, particularly during the pre-tenure phase, and (3) developing a considerable body of research to inform future scholarship and efforts to advance Latin@ educational attainment. These faculty members' experiences illustrate the potential for individual faculty to come together as agents of change to broaden educational opportunities for historically underserved groups. Because providing inclusive educational opportunities is a collective responsibility, we conclude with recommendations about how higher education leaders from all backgrounds can take active roles in advancing educational equity, particularly for faculty of color.

Keywords: Latina faculty, Hispanic-serving institution, Applied Critical Leadership, interest convergence, identity, mentoring, courageous conversations

The underrepresentation and isolation of Latina faculty in the academy is well documented (e.g., Núñez & Murakami-Ramalho, 2012). Latina faculty members who have entered the academy intending to promote societal equity can experience significant barriers in advancing this goal, as they face a myriad of responsibilities in research, teaching, and service. In fact, some Latina faculty, particularly those on the tenure track, can feel sidetracked from pursuing community-oriented goals in an effort to prove themselves in research and teaching (e.g., González & Padilla, 2008). Núñez, Murakami-Ramalho, and Cuero (2010) assert that "new faculty members, particularly those interested in promoting educational equity, often do not receive clear guidelines about socialization into the academy in a way that honors their or their students' personal and professional commitments" (p. 188). This chapter addresses how one unusually large group (a critical mass) of early-career Latina faculty members at one institution partnered with one another to challenge traditional modes of academic socialization with the aim of advancing mutual interests in advancing educational equity.

Using Applied Critical Leadership (ACL) (Santamaría & Santamaría, 2012) as a theoretical lens, we examine how Latina faculty members in a Hispanic-Serving Institution (HSI) created a network of support and research. Applied critical leadership "is the emancipatory practice of choosing to address educational issues and challenges using a critical race perspective to enact context-specific change in response to power, domination, access and achievement imbalances, resulting in improved academic achievement for learners at every academic level of institutional schooling in the U.S." (Santamaría & Santamaría, 2012, p. 7). Put differently, it is an assets-based model of culturally responsive leadership supported by critical race theory concepts (Ladson-Billings, 2009; Valenzuela, 1999).

This chapter builds on our prior recommendations in the American Association of University Professors (AAUP) magazine *Academe* (see Núñez & Murakami-Ramalho, 2012), and draws on six years of our own data as participant-observers in one university-based support group to conduct collaborative research to advance equity for Latinos in education, called the Research for the Educational Advancement of Latin@s Collaborative (REAL). It also draws on several publications by Latina faculty members in this group, including our own. Latina faculty in REAL have employed critical race theory and feminist theories (e.g., Collins, 1993; Solórzano & Yosso, 2001, 2002) to examine our experiences building a collaborative network of Latina faculty in one HSI university in San Antonio, Texas (e.g., Murakami-Ramalho, Núñez, & Cuero, 2010; Núñez et al., 2010; Quijada Cerecer, Ek, Alanís, & Murakami-Ramalho, 2010). Using several qualitative approaches, these publications have addressed:

- The importance of equity and voice in academia through collaborative networks (Alanís, Cuero, & Rodríguez, 2009);
- Pedagogical concerns for Latina/o students and faculty (Núñez et al., 2010);

- Building and nurturing a Latina academic identity (Ek, Quijada Cerecer, Alanís, & Rodríguez, 2010; Quijada Cerecer et al., 2010);
- Developing a personal and professional identity as one's class position shifts (Ek et al., 2010);
- Committing to advancing equity for Latina/o students and families (Quijada Cerecer et al., 2010); and
- Mentoring faculty of color (Ek et al., 2010; Núñez & Murakami-Ramalho, 2012; Núñez, Murakami-Ramalho, & Ruiz, 2013; Ek et al., 2010).

This research, described in more detail in Murakami and Núñez (2014), indicates how junior faculty can be agents of change and challenge the counter-narrative of isolation among women of color and other historically underrepresented groups in academia.

We begin this chapter by describing in more detail the evolution of this support group of Latina faculty. We continue by examining how the faculty participants in this group have employed ACL strategies (Santamaría & Santamaría, 2012) to advance equity for Latino faculty and students. These strategies have included: (a) finding areas of common interest with faculty and administrators both within and outside of the group to advance mutually held goals, (b) exercising collective reflexivity in research and practice, and (c) affirming positive social identities such as race, gender, and class. In this discussion, we highlight specific examples to illustrate how others can enact ACL at their own institutions to advance equity. However, the responsibility of advancing equity cannot only fall on the shoulders of faculty from underrepresented groups. Other faculty and leaders in the university must take responsibility to advance equity for underrepresented groups. We conclude with some recommendations about how higher education institutional leaders can also take an active role in advancing educational equity, particularly for faculty of color.

About the Research for the Educational Advancement of Latin@s Collaborative

In 2005, a group of junior Latina scholars, all of whom had recently begun as faculty in the University of Texas at San Antonio (UTSA) College of Education and Human Development (COEHD), formed the Research for the Educational Advancement of Latin@s Collaborative (REAL) (Alanís et al., 2009). UTSA is designated as a Hispanic-Serving Institution, an institution defined as having 25% or higher enrollment of Latino full-time students (*Excelencia* in Education, 2009), where Latino undergraduates constitute 45% of the undergraduate student body (www.utsa.edu). It is located in a city with a majority (almost two-thirds) Latino population.

REAL faculty members came from different departments in the college, including Interdisciplinary Learning and Teaching, Bilingual and Bicultural Studies, and Educational Leadership and Policy Studies. Each faculty member came to her position with a personal and professional commitment to broaden educational opportunities for Latinos. When these faculty members became acquainted with one another and their common interests, they decided to form a trans-disciplinary collaborative to pursue common research interests related to Latino educational advancement across the Pre-K–HE (pre-school to higher education) spectrum (Alanís et al., 2009).

Over the years, new faculty members have joined the group, so that the total number and composition has shifted, and the members now number about 10. Reflecting the location of our institution, the group has a similar proportion of Mexican Americans as in the Latin@ population in the U.S., about two-thirds. The remainder are of Central American and South American descent. The group includes first-, second-, and third-generation immigrants from different national origins, mixed-heritage individuals, and individuals with different religious orientations, reflecting the diversity of the Latino population in this country.

As part of this collaborative, faculty participants supported one another in understanding the institution's organizational culture and in navigating the tenure and promotion process. Activities included lunches and social events to discuss these issues and writing retreats to conduct joint research projects. It was paramount that all members met regularly in these events, even if for less than an hour during the day, to share and validate their experiences with one another. The group has also drawn on the wisdom and support of senior faculty Latinas (*madrinas*) at UTSA, who participated in some of these events. These activities have resulted in several publications and presentations about promoting educational equity for Latina/os (see Murakami & Núñez, 2014), as well as the emergence of several newly tenured Latina faculty at UTSA (Núñez & Murakami-Ramalho, 2011).

Applying Critical Leadership

According to Santamaría & Santamaría (see this volume), a focus on educational equity underlies the activities of those agents who apply critical culturally responsive leadership. REAL members articulate a commitment to intercultural traditions, educational equity, and access through the organization's mission statement (Alanís et al., 2009) as well as in written publications. For example, Maya (a pseudonym), articulated her orientation toward social justice, within the context of REAL:

> It's all about human rights and equity, . . . trying to create an equal playing field so that everyone has the opportunities, whether it's to pursue an education, or health. I think it's all about fairness and providing equal opportunities so that everyone has the same opportunities.
>
> *(Ek et al., 2010, p. 543)*

Through their scholarship and support of one another, REAL members aim to promote the equity of Latino students at all stages of the educational pipeline, as well as of Latino faculty and administrators.

What are the processes—the norms, values, and behaviors—through which REAL members enact ACL? Below, we discuss common themes that emerged from the analyses of REAL members' experiences. These themes include (a) recognizing opportunities and potential for interest convergence, (b) exercising self- and group (collective) reflexivity to serve the community in a more informed way, and (c) affirming positive identities (Santamaría & Santamaría, 2012). Accordingly, we illustrate how these faculty have purposefully chosen change as their self-described leadership practice toward educational equity for their educational contexts (Santamaría & Santamaría, 2012).

Recognizing Opportunities and Potential for Interest Convergence

As illustrated above, the formation of REAL itself involved "opportunity recognition" that there was an interest convergence among its members, and that they could choose to partner to advance their personal and professional interests regarding Latina/o educational equity (Santamaría & Santamaría, 2012, p. 117). This perspective disrupts the typical academic norm of privileging individual advancement and the competition required to achieve that. REAL members took a cooperative, rather than competitive, stance to conduct research and to navigate academia (Ek et al., 2010; Núñez et al., 2013). For example, these faculty members co-authored papers and co-presented at conferences, rotating authorship and responsibilities. Moreover, these faculty members discussed the hidden curriculum of navigating academia with one another. Similarly to a high-ranking HSI academic administrator described by Santamaría & Santamaría (2012), these faculty members at an HSI engaged in "transparency, collaboration, and consultation" with one another (Santamaría & Santamaría, 2012, p. 125).

Committing to Advance Opportunities for Diverse Students and Faculty

REAL members also practiced opportunity recognition and interest convergence as they took advantage of their positions at an HSI to strengthen their commitments to advancing Latino educational attainment. All members had earned their doctorates from research or "tier one" universities, but some turned down positions at these types of institutions to join UTSA. Here again, these faculty members chose "change" (Santamaría & Santamaría, 2012) by challenging the prevailing academic view that holding an academic position at an elite institution is the most sound career choice. In the words of Laura,

> when I left a tier one university, people were shocked that I was even applying to a teaching university and that I wanted to return to [my hometown] . . .

I think that is really part of the Americanization process—that you need to succeed as an individual and you need to be the best. Why do I want to go and be a prof at Stanford or Harvard? Why can't I be with students who I think have more my background, and maybe I can bring some background that other professors can't. So I really tried to shape my own agenda with what I wanted to teach and not follow the traditional route just taking cream from the top.

(Quijada Cerecer et al., 2010, p. 83)

Echoing Santamaría & Santamaría's (2012) high-ranking HSI academic administrator's perspective that working in an HSI was a "life-giving turn of professional events" (p. 125), one REAL member recalled seeing Chicana/Latina students speaking Spanish in graduate classes during a job interview at UTSA. She observed that "here the majority of students are Latina/Latino . . . the opportunity to teach and mentor Chicanas/Latinas is a dream come true!" (Quijada Cerecer et al., 2010, p. 89). In essence, REAL faculty were challenging traditional norms of institutional privilege by affirming a positive organizational identity for their institutions (Santamaría & Santamaría, 2012).

Another way in which REAL members practiced opportunity recognition and the pursuit of interest convergence was advocating on behalf of underrepresented faculty and students, and seeking allies in mainstream spaces. Sometimes this involved initiating "courageous conversations" (Santamaría & Santamaría, 2012, p. 117). For example, one member described how she and her Chicana/Latina colleagues advocated for linguistic minority students in their program, as a way of advancing the academic success of *all* students in the program, "because nobody else will do it" (Ek et al., 2010, p. 544). Other members supported UTSA undergraduates who led nationwide protests for immigration reform and higher education support for undocumented immigrants, engaging these students in reaching a scholarly audience by discussing their activism at the national Critical Race Studies in Education Association conference (Núñez, Sánchez, Quintanilla, Le, & Codina, 2011).

From time to time, including instances when "racial microaggressions" (Solórzano, Ceja, & Yosso, 2000) or covert forms of exclusion take place, members of the group will take the opportunity to educate other faculty using empirical research about how to improve the campus climate to be more inclusive for Latinos and other represented groups. While other faculty members do not always respond to this advocacy for courageous conversation, having other allies from similar backgrounds makes it easier for Chicana/Latina faculty here to speak up and persist on such issues over time. Like the leaders in Santamaría & Santamaría's (2012) book, REAL members take the long view and recognize that transforming the university climate to be more inclusive will take time and ongoing efforts.

Aligning REAL's Objectives with the University's

REAL members also scanned for opportunities to pursue interest convergence through initiatives to align the university's objectives with their own. Through collaborative investigations to determine funding opportunities, REAL members were able to garner financial support from the institution to advance institutional interests of (a) faculty success and (b) providing service to the community beyond the institution. To advance the first institutional interest, REAL members drew on the wisdom of senior Chicana/Latina faculty (*madrinas*) at the institution for guidance about navigating the review, tenure, and promotion process. These senior Latina faculty held a strong interest and commitment to seeing these junior Latina faculty succeed.

REAL members also applied for and received funding from both the college of education and the provost's office to conduct writing and research retreats (Núñez & Murakami-Ramalho, 2011, 2012). During these retreats, REAL members worked on joint research projects, discussed their experiences with one another (which lay groundwork for data collection on members' experiences), and shared advice with one another, making the faculty path more transparent and fostering one another's success. With respect to the objective of serving the broader community, the REAL Collaborative applied for and received funding from the provost's office to conduct a one-day professional development workshop for which local K–12 teachers, counselors, and administrators could receive continuing education credits. In this workshop, REAL members and scholars in the university conducted workshops about their research concerning effective practices for Latino students, ranging from topics like bilingual instruction to creating a college culture in schools (Núñez & Murakami-Ramalho, 2011). This event enabled REAL members to blend their research, teaching, and service work, challenging the prevailing view that faculty of color need to disengage from their communities, at least until receiving tenure, because such engagement can interfere with academic advancement (González & Padilla, 2008; Rhoades, Kiyama, McCormick, & Quiroz, 2008).

Exercising Collective Reflexivity through Research and Practice

Santamaría & Santamaría (2012) assert that those who apply critical leadership consider self-reflexive questions, including,

> In what ways does my identity (i.e., subjectivity, biases, assumptions, race, class, gender, and traditions) enhance my ability to see other perspectives and therefore provide effective leadership? Hence, what are the positive attributes that render an individual different and unique that can be explored and developed in order to improve their leadership practice?
>
> *(p. 7)*

Members of REAL have engaged in these questions as a collective, both in their formal and informal meetings and in their research.

Create a Safe Space for Dialogue and "Courageous Conversations"

REAL's formal and informal meetings and retreats have offered a "safe space for members to articulate personal experiences related to issues of oppression and privilege" (Ek et al., 2010, p. 544). These dialogues facilitated courageous conversations about transforming typical faculty struggles (e.g., Turner, González, & Wood, 2008) into personal and professional development. REAL members cultivated collegiality through sharing these experiences. Opportunities to socialize included events like birthday parties, tamaleras (making tamales), and other social gatherings, which helped us form other kinds of connections outside of work and deepened our capacity to get to know one another (Núñez et al., 2013). Fundamentally, these events allowed us to communicate with one another in a more authentic way. In one REAL member's words, these occasions afforded us chances to "let your guard down" in front of one another (Ek et al., 2010, p. 546). Sometimes, these meals together were opportunities to develop research, gather data, listen, and/or provide support to members in immediate need.

Conduct Collaborative Research Using Self-Reflexive Methods

REAL's publications have all employed qualitative methods that center group members' experiences as newcomers to academia supporting one another. Data sources have ranged from transcripts of presentations, smaller meetings, and focus groups, some of which have been conducted during retreats or meetings, to written emails and journaling. A dialogic approach (Padilla, 1993)—one involving the participants as researchers in an ongoing and regular process of distilling and clarifying themes from individual and collective narratives—characterizes all of REAL's publications.

This dialogic approach lends itself to exploring the questions such as the ones that Santamaría & Santamaría (2012) pose above, providing space to reflect individually and collectively on our experiences in academia, and push us to take action as we refine our personal and professional consciousness and awareness. It prompts us into the cycle of being self- and communally reflexive and encourages us to cultivate a habit of stepping back and reflecting on our multiple identities and how these affect our personal and professional work (Núñez et al., 2010). These habits, in turn, encourage us to (re)cast our identities in a positive light and to draw on our identities as a source of strength in our faculty lives. We will discuss this in more detail in the next section.

Affirming Positive Identities

One dimension of ACL involves "deconstructing" and "reversing stereotypes"—that is, (re)casting traditionally marginalized identities as "positive identities" (Santamaría & Santamaría, 2012, pp. 121, 123) into assets for leadership. For instance, much like the high-level Latina administrator in Santamaría &

Santamaría's (2012) study, and many other underrepresented students and faculty in higher education, some REAL members have encountered stereotypes of Latinos by being mistaken for service workers in professional settings (Quijada Cerecer et al., 2010). Those experiences of marginalization and racial microaggressions constantly remind those individuals that they do not resemble expected images of what a university faculty member or academic administrator looks like. However, REAL members who have experienced these microaggressions unpack them to relate to and address the challenges that their colleagues and students of color face and draw on these experiences to understand better the strengths of communities of color. As Ek et al. (2010) put it, "the centering of our experiences and voices as Chicanas/Latinas highlights that our individual and collective knowledge and lived experiences are resources for negotiating the academy" (p. 542).

Draw on Identities as Resources and Strengths

REAL's collective reflexivity set the stage for its members to identify and define their multiple identities in a positive light, and to draw on these identities to strengthen their research and teaching. Laura's statement below exemplifies this stance:

> I was raised as a working-class immigrant, and I still identify with this category, even if I possess some material resources (i.e., home, care, neighborhood) that are middle class. It [my working-class identity] keeps me grounded, and I think it informs my thinking much better when I choose research topics that are also related to this identity. Of course, my goal is to continue research that undoes the deficit view of Latino immigrants in this country as well as mentor those who grew up like me.
>
> *(Quijada Cerecer et al., 2010, pp. 81–82)*

Here, Laura articulates how her identity as a working-class immigrant strengthens her research, as it helps her to advance the goal of Latino educational equity by challenging deficit notions for disparities in educational attainment rates.

Explore Flexible Identities, Affiliations, and Development of Allies

Núñez et al. (2010) discuss how their multiple identities as mixed-heritage (that is, mixed ethnicity) Latinas influence their teaching in a positive way (Pao, Wang, & Teuben-Rowe, 2007). In a related piece, Murakami-Ramalho et al. (2010) address how, as mixed-heritage Latinas, who do not resemble the stereotypical images of Latinas (Quijada Cerecer et al., 2010), they have been challenged to articulate their affiliation with and advocacy for the Latino community, something they have come to call "advocacy in the hyphen" (Murakami-Ramalho et al., 2010). Their process of self- and collective interrogation involves active engagement with Santamaría & Santamaría's (2012) questions about how identity affects educational research and leadership. The authors argue that one of the benefits of having multiple and complex racial/ethnic identities has been that interrogating the role of racial/ethnic identity in educational stratification helps them to identify their "ontological blind spots" (Scheurich, 1997) regarding the sources of educational inequities.

Murakami-Ramalho et al. (2010) admit that it has neither been an easy nor a straightforward process for them to identify as Latina and to characterize how that identity affects their work, and recognize that their privilege and oppression may differ from that of other Latino scholars. But they employ social inquiry to identify how their *Latinidad*—what Beltrán (2010) and others define as the "sociohistorical process whereby various Latin American national-origin groups are understood to have a sense of collective identity and cultural consciousness" (p. 4)—affects their pedagogy. Namely, they have found that their identity as mixed-heritage Latina has positively influenced their teaching practices in the classroom and enabled them to develop what they call a "pedagogy for equity" (Núñez et al., 2010). These teaching practices include:

- Affirming flexible modes of identity;
- Critically reflecting upon their assumptions about what students know and can do;
- Encouraging students to understand their identities in relation to their communities;
- Being responsive to students' forms of expression (which could involve language or movement, for example);
- Serving as role models for Latino and other students in their HSI; and
- Challenging inequities in the U.S. educational system (Núñez et al., 2010, pp. 181–186).

In essence, the first five strategies provide a platform for empowering students to enact the final strategy.

Create Culturally Relevant Models of Mentoring

In addition to drawing on their positive identities to build equity-oriented pedagogical approaches in the classroom, REAL members have also developed a form of pedagogy with one another that they call "muxerista mentoring" (Ek et al., 2010). According to Revilla (as cited in Ek et al., 2010), "A Muxerista is a woman-identified Chicana/Latina who considers herself a feminist or womanist. The 'x' replaces a 'j' to signify a connection to the ancestry and language of Mexico and Latin America" (p. 545). The mentoring aspect of muxerista mentoring entails "not only direct support with academic activities like teaching and research but also emotional support" (p. 545). This collegial mentoring process involves both academic and social components and supportive and validating forms of interaction with one another (Núñez et al., 2013; Rendón, 1994; Rendón Linares & Muñoz, 2011). It is also grounded in a Chicana/Latina identity that is framed as a cultural resource that is useful and supportive in navigating academic life. Laura's comment at the beginning of this section of her class consciousness as an asset in her research reflects the raced and gendered character of muxerista mentoring and how REAL has provided a space for her to articulate the role of her class identity in her research.

Following ACL, REAL scholars have drawn on lenses including Latino critical race theory (Solórzano & Yosso, 2001) and intersectionality (e.g., Collins, 1993; Dill, McLaughlin, & Nieves, 2007) to advance critical consciousness and leadership in the academy. In advancing concepts such as advocacy in the hyphen (Murakami-Ramalho et al., 2010), pedagogy for equity (Núñez et al., 2010), and muxerista mentoring (Ek et al., 2010), REAL faculty members have drawn on their positive identities to become agents and creators of new knowledge (Collins, 1993). This knowledge enhances our understanding of how to promote equity for Latinos at all levels of education—from pre-kindergarten to the faculty ranks.

Conclusion

Through identifying beliefs, norms, and behaviors that exemplify "change" (Santamaría & Santamaría, 2012) as an approach to leadership, we have offered some guidelines for how other faculty committed to educational equity can leverage their identity strengths to serve the greater good. How other faculty members and administrators in other institutional contexts apply these processes and other principles of ACL will vary. We hope that this chapter sparks further conversations and initiatives about building communities in the academy to promote educational equity.

CULTURALLY RESPONSIVE LEADERSHIP IN PRACTICE

In employing ACL, individuals draw on their community identities as strengths to advance educational equity (Santamaría & Santamaría, 2012). This chapter demonstrates how faculty can come together collectively to use principles of ACL to build an "intellectual community" (Ek et al., 2010), and begin having courageous conversations around critical issues affecting the development and promotion of Latina faculty. Illustrating the potential of ACL, one REAL member says, "Maybe I can bring some background that other professors can't" (Quijada Cerecer et al., 2010, p. 83).

Indeed, REAL faculty draw on their backgrounds: (a) to recognize opportunities and potential for interest convergence to advance equity for Latino students and faculty, (b) to practice collective reflexivity that deepens the authenticity of their research, teaching, and leadership; and (c) to define their social identities in positive ways to shape their personal and professional activities as faculty members.

ACL provides tools for identifying beliefs, norms, and behaviors that REAL faculty members enacted to enhance knowledge about broadening opportunities for Latinos at all stages of education. These faculty members drew upon their marginalized positions as Latinas to become agents and creators of new knowledge (Collins, 1993) for broadening educational opportunities for Latinos in all roles (e.g., PreK–12 and college students, faculty, staff, and administrators) and at all levels (e.g., preschool through university) of education. Their experiences with building a scholarly community toward this common aim pose a counter-narrative to the historical and contemporary isolation among women of color and other underrepresented groups in academia (Ek et al., 2010). In essence, these faculty members leveraged the potential of their critical mass to build community knowledge to promote Latino educational inclusiveness and attainment.

For faculty members in ever-shifting institutional contexts with different players, ACL requires an ongoing process of advancing social justice (Núñez et al, 2010). Latino faculty cannot advance educational equity alone. They need to work with leaders who choose to be their allies and enact transformational change across different units of the university (Núñez & Murakami-Ramalho, 2012). While we have focused on faculty agency in this chapter, we recommend that higher education leaders at higher administrative levels pursue:

- Cohort hiring to cultivate a critical mass of scholars (Ek et al., 2010);
- Engaging leaders higher up and across the university to leverage faculty diversity for social justice (Núñez et al., 2010; Smith, 2009; Smith, Turner, Osei-Kofi, & Richards, 2004); and
- Rewarding scholars who conduct research that advances equity and community interests (Hurtado & Sharkness, 2008; Núñez et al., 2010; Núñez & Murakami-Ramalho, 2011, 2012).

References

Alanís, I., Cuero, K. K., & Rodríguez, M. A. (2009). Research for the educational advancement of Latinas: A research and professional development collaborative. *NASPA Journal about Women in Higher Education, 1*(2), 243–244.

Beltrán, C. (2010). *The trouble with unity: Latino politics and the creation of identity*. New York, NY: Oxford University Press.

Bogdan, R. C., & Biklen, S. K. (2007). *Qualitative research for education: An introduction to theories and traditions* (5th ed.). New York, NY: Pearson.

Collins, P. (1993). Black feminist thought in the matrix of domination. In C. Lemert (Ed.), *Social theory: The multicultural and classic readings* (pp. 615–625). Boulder, CO: Westview Press.

Dill, B. T., McLaughlin, A., & Nieves, A. D. (2007). Future directions of feminist research: Intersectionality. In S. Hesse-Biber (Ed.), *Handbook of feminist research, theory, and praxis* (pp. 629–638). Thousand Oaks, CA: Sage.

Ek, L. D., Quijada Cerecer, P. D., Alanís, I., & Rodríguez, M. (2010). "I don't belong here": Chicanas/Latinas at a Hispanic Serving Institution creating community through muxerista-mentoring. *Equity and Excellence in Education, 43*(4), 539–553.

Excelencia in Education. (2009, December). *Lists of Hispanic-serving institutions.* Retrieved from http://www.edexcelencia.org/research/hsi/hsi-lists

González, K., & Padilla, R. (2008). *Doing the public good: Latina/o scholars engage civic participation.* Sterling, VA: Stylus.

Hurtado, S., & Sharkness, J. (2008). Scholarship is changing, and so should tenure review. *Academe, 94*(5), 37–39.

Ladson-Billings, G. (2009). "Who you callin' nappy-headed?" A critical race theory look at the construction of Black women. *Race Ethnicity and Education, 12*(1), 87–99.

Murakami, E., & Núñez, A.-M. (2014). Latina faculty transcending barriers: Peer mentoring in a Hispanic-serving institution. *Mentoring and Tutoring: Partnership in Learning, 22*(4), 284–301.

Murakami-Ramalho, E., Núñez, A.-M., & Cuero, K. (2010). Latin@ advocacy in the hyphen: Faculty identity and commitment in a Hispanic-serving institution. *International Journal of Qualitative Studies in Education, 23*(6), 699–717.

Núñez, A.-M., & Murakami-Ramalho, E. (2011). Advocacy in the hyphen: Perspectives from junior faculty at a Hispanic-serving institution. In G. Jean-Marie & B. Lloyd-Jones (Eds.), *Women of color in higher education: Turbulent past, promising future.* Diversity in Higher Education Series, vol. 9 (pp. 171–194). Bingley, UK: Emerald Group.

Núñez, A.-M., & Murakami-Ramalho, E. (2012). The demographic dividend: Why the success of Latino faculty and students is critical. *Academe, 98*(1), 32–37.

Núñez, A.-M., Murakami-Ramalho, E., & Cuero, K. (2010). Pedagogy for equity: Teaching in a Hispanic-serving institution. *Innovative Higher Education, 35*(3), 177–190.

Núñez, A.-M., Murakami-Ramalho, E., & Ruiz, E. (2013, April). *Interrupting the usual in the academy: Creating a sense of belonging among Latina faculty.* Paper presented at the Annual Meeting of the American Educational Research Association, Vancouver, BC.

Núñez, A.-M., Sánchez, C., Quintanilla, M., Le, M., & Codina, Y. (2011, May). *Critical race activism: DREAMing for immigrant opportunity.* Presentation at the Annual Meeting of the Critical Race Studies in Education Association, San Antonio, TX.

Padilla, R. V. (1993). Using dialogical research methods in group interviews. In D. L. Morgan (Ed.), *Successful focus group methods: Advancing the state of an art* (pp. 152–166). Newbury Park; CA: Sage.

Pao, D. L., Wang, S. D., & Teuben-Rowe, S. (2007). Identity formation for mixed-heritage adults and implications for educators. *TESOL Quarterly, 31*(3), 622–631.

Quijada Cerecer, P., Ek, L., Alanís, I., & Murakami-Ramalho, E. (2010). Transformative resistance as agency: Chicanas/Latinas re(creating) academic spaces. *Journal of the Professoriate, 5*(1), 70–98.

Rendón, L. I. (1994). Validating culturally diverse students: Toward a new model of learning and student development. *Innovative Higher Education, 19*(1), 33–51.

Rendón Linares, L. I., & Muñoz, S. (2011). Revisiting validation theory: Theoretical foundations, applications, and extensions. *Enrollment Management Journal, 5*(2), 12–33.

Rhoades, G., Kiyama, J. M., McCormick, R., & Quiroz, M. (2008). Local cosmopolitans and cosmopolitan locals: Towards new models of professionals in the academy. *Review of Higher Education, 31*(2), 209–235.

Santamaría, L. J., & Santamaría, A. P. (2012). *Applied critical leadership in education: Choosing change.* New York, NY: Routledge.

Scheurich, J. (1997). *Research method in the postmodern.* New York, NY: Falmer Press.

Smith, D. G. (2009). *Diversity's promise for higher education.* Baltimore, MD: Johns Hopkins University Press.

Smith, D. G., Turner, C. S., Osei-Kofi, N., & Richards, S. (2004). Interrupting the usual: Successful strategies for hiring diverse faculty. *Journal of Higher Education, 75*(2), 133–160.

Solórzano, D., Ceja, M., & Yosso, T. (2000). Critical race theory, racial microaggressions, and campus racial climate: The experiences of African American college students. *Journal of Negro Education, 69*(1/2), 60–73.

Solórzano, D., & Yosso, T. (2001). Critical race and LatCrit theory and method: Counter-storytelling. *Qualitative Studies in Education, 14*(4), 471–495.

Solórzano, D., & Yosso, T. (2002). Critical race methodology: Counter-storytelling as an analytical framework for education research. *Qualitative Inquiry, 8*(1), 23–44. doi:10.1177/107780040200800103

Turner, C.S.V., González, J. C., & Wood, J. L. (2008). Faculty of color in academe: What 20 years of literature tells us. *Journal of Diversity in Higher Education, 1*(3), 139–168.

Valenzuela, A. (1999). *Subtractive schooling: U.S. Mexican youth and the politics of caring.* New York, NY: State University of New York Press.

11

TRANSITION TO LEADERSHIP

Metamorphosis of Faculty to Academic Leaders

Hollie Mackey and Gaëtane Jean-Marie

IDEA IN BRIEF

This chapter provides insight into the ways identity development creates the lens by which leaders operationalize principles and aspirations to inform practice using Santamaría & Santamaría's (2012) Applied Critical Leadership framework. The combination of principles, practices, and identity development fosters the construction of unique approaches to critical leadership based on the social context of educational communities and individual perspectives. We consider two perspectives on the transition to leadership: first from an emerging scholar with aspirations of ascending into a leadership role; and then from an established scholar who has ascended to leadership with aspirations of taking on even greater leadership responsibilities. Gaining insight from these two perspectives will provide greater understanding of applied critical leadership principles. We conclude with strategies faculty can use to advance into positions of leadership.

Keywords: higher education, administration, transformative leadership, critical multiculturism, critical pedagogy, critical race theory, applied critical leadership

Poignantly writing about the call for leadership, Gmelch and Miskin (2011) argue that in higher education, the development of academic leaders is at a critical juncture because institutions of higher learning may still be in the Dark Ages. Effective organizational leadership demands intentional recruitment, preparation, continuing education, and long-term planning for future and sustainable leadership. However, in higher education, transitioning from a faculty position to an administrative role may involve little or no specific training (Alley, 2005; Buller, 2007; McDade, 1997). Ascending to a leadership position is frequently the result of a faculty demonstrating some level of administrative acumen, having the confidence of faculty members in their departments, and having demonstrated their willingness to balance their scholarly pursuits with the challenges of administration (Buller, 2007). This is different from other educational settings where leaders receive specific training and certification, field experiences, and mentorship prior to ascending into leadership roles (Jean-Marie & Normore, 2010). This administrative induction, along with increasing demands placed on mid-level higher education administrators, prompt the necessity of examining notions of leadership principles and practices along with individual identity development to determine how to best meet the leadership needs of today's universities.

Background

Leadership is the foundation of successful organizations; however, characteristics of effective leadership in higher education have received minimal attention. Fundamentally, leadership is the structural manifestation of an organizational social contract where individuals enter into an ostensibly agreed-upon relational hierarchy (Gallos, 2002; Rich, 2006). The effectiveness of this hierarchy is largely dependent on the leader's ability to develop a vision for moving the organization forward by identifying and strategically accessing followers' strengths. To do this, leaders must understand motivational relational aspects of leadership (Alley, 2005; McDade, 1997) and followers must trust the leader's ability to do all of the above.

Universities have been in transition as scholars seek to determine more sophisticated and applicable approaches to leadership, and identify potential leaders with the disposition and skills necessary to adjust to increasing demands (Jackson & Kelley, 2002; Young, Petersen, & Short, 2002). These demands require administrators to increasingly focus on marketing and revenue generation rather than faculty and facilitating scholarly excellence (Buller, 2007; DeYoung, 2000; Gallos, 2002; Rich, 2006). Despite this administrative shift from traditional academic goals to globally competitive corporate goals, universities continue to decline in the midst of active efforts to improve (Rich, 2006). Leadership in higher education requires creativity and a willingness to engage in the complex work of restructuring faculty and traditional university structures to meet and align to 21st-century leadership needs.

Values and Identity

Leadership practices are shaped by personal and institutional values that both inform and are informed by each leader's conceptualization of her/his identity.

As Shapiro and Stefkovich (2010) explain, this creates a complex dynamic where there is often a clash of interests between a leader's personal and professional codes of conduct. In other words, leaders must reconcile personal values with the practices inherent to the expectations of the profession, which in turn, challenge identity conceptualization.

Administrative Values

Higher education functions from the central premise that the qualities needed for positions of administrative authority are inherently developed through the socialization of faculty as they progress through their career (DeYoung, 2000; Gallos, 2002). This notion of inherent leadership ability is not much different from the expectation that faculty will be inherently skilled instructors if they have acquired adequate content knowledge from their discipline. Both premises are flawed. Leadership is no more inherent than pedagogy; yet the very institutions designed for higher-level instruction, critical thinking, scholarly debate, and knowledge creation disregard the key element to organizational and institutional success: skilled leadership (Gallos, 2002). Faculty are often reluctant and unprepared for the reality of higher education administration whereby the qualities of an academic are ill suited for administration in academe (DeYoung, 2000; Gallos, 2002). For example, successful departments are not established by chance, rather, developing these departments requires strategic leadership development at all levels of the faculty ranks with both long- and short-term organizational goals in mind (Gallos, 2002; Rich, 2006).

Further, there is a dramatic shift in faculty response from lower-level administrative roles to the role of the dean. The inherent challenge in this role is the accountability to both the internal world of the academic unit and the external world of university bureaucracy, business stakeholders and donors, policymakers, students, parents, and the like (Gallos, 2002). The position holds little actual authority, yet the dean is perceived by faculty as a bureaucratic outsider despite her/his standing as a tenured faculty member within the unit. Faculty aspiring to leadership have a front-row seat in the dynamics between senior faculty and the dean, often characterized by isolation, ridicule, and complaints (Gallos, 2002). This does not provide much incentive for those seeking administrative leadership roles and exposed to a particularly toxic side of academe.

Academic Values

There are few visible incentives for junior faculty aspiring to an administrative leadership role. At the program and department levels, these roles are often portrayed as cumbersome self-sacrificing service activities that all faculty members will be burdened with at some point post-tenure. Relegating these important leadership positions to burdensome inevitability, wherein a designated senior faculty member selflessly gives for the greater good of the faculty at large, diminishes the importance of these roles. Minimal supplemental salary, course-release time, and the opportunity for greater power and prestige coupled with tales of excessive difficulty in fulfilling the disproportionate responsibility associated with the described scant incentives does not paint an appealing picture of administrative roles (Gallos, 2002). The annual game of "not it!" played by senior faculty after demanding greater voice in decision-making further dissuades faculty from envisioning an administrative role in their future (Gallos, 2002). The complexity and importance of leadership are diminished in organizations already entrenched in the mindset that possessing leadership skills is inherent to being a professor. These portrayals of administration are often founded on the notion that it is separated from academic life. As Rich (2006) explains, "The changing political economy has reinforced this natural faculty antipathy toward administrative careers by underscoring the separation of administrative and academic work" (p. 39).

Identity Development

Identity development is influenced by the internal and external factors contributing to a person's conception of how she/he "fits" into society. This development is not naturally inclusive of others' perspectives because identity development is primarily an individual and internal process. As Gallos (2002) observes, "We all construct our social reality and only see and value what our worldview allows" (p. 175).

University Struggles/Challenges

Universities are in the midst of dramatic transformation and face unique challenges where "the new environment is more turbulent, more threatening, and more competitive than was the case only a few decades ago" (Rich, 2006, p. 37). Political support has declined as policy-makers have turned their attention toward student outcomes, affordability, and access as funding determinants. Additional pressure from the public has triggered intense competition through the integration of new technologies and alternative forms of organization (Gallos, 2002; Rich, 2006). This new environment has the potential to either foster interest or turn away faculty who might seek administrative roles. Administration in higher education has taken on a distinct market-driven characteristic whereby universities operate like corporations. This is in opposition to the basic premise of academic excellence and scholarly pursuits traditionally valued by universities. Rich (2006) asserts that universities require a restructuring, not of business practices, but of "faculty appointments and organization . . . to overcome the inertia of an ossified system of academic organization" (p. 38).

Organizational Effectiveness

Why is leadership, a critical component of organizational effectiveness, minimized by some faculty with entry-level administrative responsibilities? The answer to that question is beyond the scope of this chapter, however understanding that this phenomenon exists is central to understanding how faculty might be incentivized to engage in strategic leadership development for future administrative opportunities. The faculty governance schema of higher education colleges, departments, and programs is peculiar when compared with more familiar education and business organizational charts (Gallos, 2002). This peculiarity is juxtaposed against the bureaucratic side of higher education institutions that typically use a more traditional hierarchical organizational structure. Those faculty who have elected to move into leadership positions bridge these two distinct contexts of higher education organizations; accountable to the bureaucracy of upper administration and responsible for the effective leadership of multiple independent faculty within academic units (DeYoung, 2000; Gallos, 2002). Rich (2006) states: "Universities require administrators who effectively balance, unite and integrate business and academic priorities; respond creatively to demands for increased market competitiveness in ways that support long-term academic objectives; and connect the strategies for improvement of institutional infrastructure and fiscal resources with the requirements for strengthening the ingredients of academic progress. Universities cannot import that kind of leadership; they must produce it" (pp. 40–41).

Theoretical Framework

Transformative leadership, critical multiculturalism, and 21st-century feminist theory lay the foundation for our theoretical lens—Applied Critical Leadership (Santamaría & Santamaría, 2012). In examining the leadership aspiration and practices of women scholars of color, applied critical leadership (ACL) helps to explicate how and why they enact leadership that is premised on social justice, access, and equity (Santamaría & Jean-Marie, 2014). ACL, when practiced by women of color in particular, may take on more specific characteristics as suggested in the work of McGee Banks (2007) who asserts that gender and race have significant influences on the educational practice of leaders of color who are also women. The authors of this chapter are two women of color—a tenure-track American Indian scholar who aspires to leadership, and a tenured full professor of Haitian descent who is currently a department chair.

Transformative Leadership

There have been various lines of research with regard to alternative educational leadership approaches as they relate to social justice, access, and equity. One of the most current is the consideration of transformative leadership featuring change with regard to nurturing democratic education for the greater good (Foster, 1986; Shields, 2010). Within this paradigm, researchers consider internal organizational inequities with strong considerations for the practice of social justice and equity, accompanied by a vision of reconciled injustices. In support of this, Shields (2010) asserts that transformative leadership is possible for "deep and meaningful change in the norms of schooling" (p. 583). Current iterations of transformative leadership suggest leaders work to "unlearn power and reach beyond a fear of authority" (Quantz, Rogers, & Dantley, 1991, p. 102). This chapter begs the questions with regard to power in particular; do women leaders of color have power? The notion of fear as conceptualized as professional distress, trepidation, worry, and anxiety may play out in these leaders' practices and function as assumptions undergirding this work.

Critical Multiculturalism and Critical Pedagogy

Critical multiculturalism serves as a bridge linking transformative leadership practices to a more applied leadership paradigm, incorporating a variety of critical theoretical positions including critical race theory and critical pedagogy for the purposes of "interrogating and advancing various critical theoretical threads" (May & Sleeter, 2010, p. 10). This theory embodies tenets of critical pedagogy concerned with restructuring traditional relationships in learning communities to a point where new knowledge grounded in the collective experiences of teaching and learning community members is produced through meaningful dialogue. It also involves the development of critical consciousness to the end of emancipating individuals to positively impact their contexts (Freire, 1970). Therefore, the most important issues in critical multiculturalism are those for individuals "who fall outside the white, male, middle-class spectrum" and issues involving "powerlessness, violence, and poverty" (Kincheloe & Steinberg, 1997, p. 17). Essentially, critical multiculturalism promotes building solidarity across diverse communities as well as the need to embrace struggles against oppression faced by historically marginalized 'others.' The theory challenges educators to locate 'self' and 'own' individual and collective histories, critically and reflectively, including the associated power relations (May & Sleeter, 2010). This approach is interdisciplinary wherein culture and identities are considered to be central, multilayered, fluid, and complex, encompassing multiple social categories exemplifying a dynamic conceptualization of culture (May & Sleeter, 2010).

Critical Race Theory

At this point, there is scant evidence of critical race theory being considered in higher education settings pertaining to the life experiences and perspectives of administrative leaders linking their own stories to broader systemic issues found in comprehensive educational contexts (Alemán, 2009). Critical race theory considers race first wherein "racism is normal and not aberrant in US society, storytelling is important with regard to exploring race and racism in our society, liberalism should be critiqued, and there is an emphasis on realism with regard to racism" (Ladson-Billings & Tate, 2009, p. 58). The theory "calls for the legitimization of narratives of discrimination . . . and importance of these counter-narratives on implications for leadership and policy" (Parker & Villalpando, 2007, p. 520), thus promoting social justice and transformation challenging traditional notions of ways in which to conduct, practice, or engage in the educational politics associated with leadership (Alemán, 2009). In these ways, CRT is a powerful tool that can be used to effectively challenge conventional accounts of educational institutional and social processes that occur within various perceivably oppressive educational contexts (Powers, 2007).

Applied Critical Leadership

Understanding ways in which principles of transformative leadership, critical multiculturalism and critical pedagogy, and critical race theory interface and intersect are in the nature of how a hybridization of these constructs might be reconceptualized as applied critical leadership. Applied critical leadership is the emancipatory practice of choosing to address educational issues and challenges using a critical race perspective to enact context-specific change in response to power, domination, access, and achievement imbalances, resulting in improved academic achievement for learners at every academic level of institutional schooling in the U.S. and similar contexts (Santamaría & Santamaría, 2012). We build on the work of Santamaría & Santamaría (2012) to argue that faculty who transition to leadership roles should consider the following question: in what ways does my identity (i.e., subjectivity, biases, assumptions, race, class, gender, and traditions) enhance my ability to see other perspectives and therefore provide effective leadership? Understanding leadership identity through an ACL lens provides aspiring and practicing leaders the opportunity to gain deeper understanding of their role in changing the institution in socially just ways (Santamaría, 2014). Identity development is an internal process, therefore we sought to understand our own development prior to extending this study model to others.

Vignette 1: Aspiring to Academic Leadership in Higher Education

(First author's voice). In the first month of my first year as a new faculty member, I was confronted with a statement from a senior faculty member in my department that was, and continues to be, deserving of deep reflection. The statement was, "You will be the department head at some point; it's obvious you are meant for leadership." My early thoughts focused on the flattery embedded in the statement that validated my own understanding of leadership potential as part of my identity. Upon further reflection, the flattery diminished as I wondered what 'meant for leadership' meant and questioned how a relative stranger could confidently assess and assert my leadership potential. I thought I understood my own aspiration to leadership. Now I stand on the precipice of uncertainty, knowing my tenure review is imminent and leadership opportunities will increase once I am an associate professor. Five years of carefully observing departmental, college, and university leadership at both my own and colleagues' universities makes me question if that aspiration still exists.

Until this point, I never questioned my desire to engage in activities and professional development that would assist me in advancing toward professional leadership roles. I have always gravitated toward leadership both formally and informally, beginning with coordinating a ragtag band of seven-year-olds in raiding our neighbor's apple orchard when my brother challenged me that it could not be done. Looking back, I am sure our neighbor facilitated the raids by leaving a barbed wire gate ajar, however the exhilaration I felt while inspiring my friends to join in my endeavor, organizing the logistics, and then executing the excursions tasted sweeter than all of the apples combined. I spent a good part of my youth organizing clubs, arranging social protests, and establishing charity chapters in my community. This drive for leadership now pushes my work in American Indian and Alaska Native educational leadership; however this drive often collides head-on with the normative institutional values held by higher education in America. Further, it collides with higher education's laser-like focus on a flawed definition of prestige and educational capitalism. These conflicting values have forced me to reconceptualize my notions of leadership identity (Mackey, 2014) and determine how I might best use my strengths as contribution to my profession.

Public Exemplars of Silent Barriers

Public universities should be the exemplars of academic freedom, creative endeavors, knowledge production, and service contributions in various contexts. However, discrepancies arise in unique and interesting ways that present silent barriers to junior faculty transitions to leadership, particularly the silent barriers founded on inequity. How is this still prevalent when most public universities promote a social justice agenda? Organizational culture and developing organizational cultural competence require more than crafting a mission statement claiming value in a social justice agenda. I have not yet experienced or observed much change in organizational leadership in higher education despite the number of social justice scholars and activists within these organizations.

Higher education is entrenched in rituals and myths that underpin multiple barriers to leadership for historically marginalized faculty. Many of these comprise core values and shape the identity of a university. However, the same values that function to support organizational development and growth might serve to hinder inclusive, transformative leadership. For example, 'publish or perish' can result in a faculty member's work being viewed unworthy through the narrow lens of national and international high-ranking journals. Universities value high-quality research, but 'high-quality' rarely falls outside traditionally accepted approaches. The so-called high-quality journals attempt to publish research that has broad utility, thus often excluding the voices that fall under a social justice agenda.

Leadership for Barrier Continuity

Applying the above to the human side of university leadership provides a similar result. Senior faculty comprising progressive, socially just unit organizations fall back on traditional views of research and assess junior faculty through a similarly narrow lens that, in reality, was probably wider when they were being assessed themselves. This undermines the social justice agenda these units claim to value. This sends a clear message to junior faculty that unit leadership ultimately acts contrary to the stated mission and vision. The social justice agenda suffers from the colloquial pop music critique of: "It has a great beat but you can't dance to it." Should faculty have to relinquish their commitment to social justice and organizational change once they transition to leadership? Perhaps not, yet it is readily modeled on a daily basis. Once the status quo is comfortable for a majority of faculty, it seems as if leadership is a reward for those who maintain it.

Conversely, the reluctant, dismissive leader is also modeled on a daily basis. Junior faculty, already conditioned to remain silent, witness senior faculty dismiss the importance of departmental or college-level leadership. This establishes two additional silent barriers. First, there is a silent confirmation that administrative leadership work is a disdainful task meant for those who are not committed to research. Second, it places heavy service burdens on junior faculty who are assigned or volunteer to be on committees and task forces simply because senior faculty can, and will, refuse. The time spent on additional committee work would be better spent on leadership development and mentoring activities for junior faculty aspiring to transition to leadership. In these instances, the organizational culture places little value on leadership and burns out junior faculty to the point that they too move away from leadership opportunities once they are tenured.

Looking Inward

How do senior members of organizations mark a new faculty member for leadership when the organization regularly communicates that transition to leadership requires junior faculty to reassess their identity and conform to unjust institutional systems and structures? This assumed identity must often align to a predetermined construct whereby traditional systemic barriers to success for historically marginalized people are perpetuated. Further, the binary us/them construct of faculty and administration makes mid-level leadership responsibility look less than appealing. In this construct, the 'us' are true and dedicated research faculty while the 'them' are the faculty better suited to "administrivia" intended to buffer the unit's faculty governance from bureaucratic oversight.

Applied critical leadership is intended to promote organizational change, rather than encourage individuals to change to fit the organization. With the volumes of leadership literature available, why does academe fall back on inequitable tradition and require faculty to conform to structural and systemic injustice? Moreover, why are there so few senior faculty members willing to engage in ACL to meet the demands of a social justice agenda? Without organizational critique of traditional systems that leads to intentional leadership development and mentoring, social justice leadership for socially just organizational outcomes remains nothing more than words in a mission statement (Mackey, 2014).

The tension between bureaucracy and faculty governance, shifting political coalitions, and the seemingly thankless role of an educational leader in the context of higher education makes transition to leadership seem like a pointless and distasteful endeavor. Perhaps the nature of bureaucracy itself is responsible for this. Bureaucracy is a slow-moving animal, and at some point faculty leaders resign themselves to inch along behind it rather than give it a much-needed boost. Bureaucracy can, and often does, move very quickly to affect organizational change when it is advantageous to do so. This leaves me wondering if after one month on campus, a senior faculty pegged me for an obvious departmental leader because I appeared to passively "play the game" of tenure and promotion and exhibited all the outward signs of docility and conformity. This reveals a much different interpretation of the comment I received and continue to reflect upon. It is not flattering if the above is true, however, social justice–oriented mission statements aside, contemporary faculty governance has a dark side. Junior faculty face one last silent barrier: taking great risk in voicing contrary opinions to the generally agreed-upon status quo or supporting authentic organizational change. They become a voice to silence so as to not disrupt the harmonious façade masking the complex political phenomenon of faculty governance for the benefit of those already holding positions of leadership and power. I no longer aspire to transition to leadership; rather, I aspire to transition to *critical* leadership for socially just organizational outcomes.

Vignette 2: Practicing Academic Leadership in Higher Education

Early Formation of Leadership Identity

(Second author's voice). As early as I can remember, I have always been interested in leadership and often assumed leadership roles (e.g., I was principal when playing school with my siblings). In high school, I ran and was elected class president for my junior and senior year. At the age of 19, I was the founding director and president of a 60-member youth choir at my church, which recently celebrated its 22nd anniversary. In college, I was actively involved in student groups and often appointed to serve on committees. Those opportunities crystallized a career path that would involve leadership. The formation of my leadership identity was always premised by fairness, access, and justice. My internal drive for effective leadership sought to enact practices that would improve conditions for others. As early as I can remember, the adage grounded in my spiritual faith resonates in enacting leadership: "I am my brother's/sister's keeper."

Formal Preparation of Academic Leadership

During graduate school, I took over 24 hours of higher education courses in a master's program before applying for the Ph.D. in educational leadership and cultural foundations. As a student of my craft, I thirst to understand the context, history, and normative structure of organizations of which I am part or seeking to become a member (e.g., higher education). Enrolling in a higher education program laid the foundation to gain knowledge of and insights into the institution that would become part of my career for years to come. To be transformative, one must acquire the tools (e.g., knowledge, understanding, and dispositions) that are essential for leading "deep and meaningful change" (Shields, 2010, p. 583), which would one day lead to my career trajectory of becoming a university president. While pursuing my graduate studies, I grappled with which direction to follow after earning my doctorate—administration or professoriate. I chose the latter with the goal to still become a university president. I only entrusted a few people with my aspiration to become a university president. I did not want to be discouraged or be told that was unattainable especially for an immigrant of Haitian descent.

As I pursued promotion and tenure, I also sought opportunities to lead in my program and department level. I was actively involved on numerous committees. After successfully attaining promotion and tenure, I began to be strategic with committees or leadership roles I would assume. For example, nationally, I ran and won president/chair of a SIG/AERA—Leadership for Social Justice. This is a 400-member organization that would bring national visibility to myself and my university. I continued such efforts through UCEA's Wallace Foundation Leveraging Change inclusive of deans and faculty, and a continued role with the Carnegie Project of the Education Doctorate (CPED).

As I reflected further on my preparation beyond courses in my master's degree and the leadership roles I assumed during my career, I could have benefitted more from professional development to support my transition to administration. Learning on the job is a natural part of any position, but to have some formal preparation enables one to have a foundation. This is where higher education institutions need to be more intentional about faculty transition to leadership role. Fortunately for me, I studied organizational leadership in the broader context of leadership for social justice; therefore, while I needed professional development in management, I had some experience to help prepare me for my entry into administration.

Confronting Deeply Embedded Practices and Silos

Five years after being promoted to associate professor and tenured, I wanted to move into administration but had to attain promotion to full tenure. It was time to reconnect with the journey to become president. I wanted to build an academic administrative portfolio that would bear evidence of my trajectory toward the presidency. In 2012, when I submitted my dossier for promotion to full, I simultaneously applied for administrative positions. Almost two years since I became a department chair at my current institution, I have learned a lot in this role, and this challenged me to reflect on my preparation and the challenges I confronted to enact leadership practices premised on equity, social justice, and access.

While serving as chair, I continue to be immersed in my research about issues of social justice. In this role, I was presented with the opportunity to "walk the talk" of applied critical leadership. For example, in my first semester, I began to uncover the resource disparities among programs and faculty. Of course, there is that inclination to ignore these disparities since they were long-standing issues. I tried to turn a blind eye but my values and beliefs would not let me ignore the issues. So, I studied and considered different viewpoints but, ultimately, I would have to act. Reflecting on my administrative role, there were many moments when I wanted to throw in the towel. I made the decision that if I were going to lead, I would engage in leadership practices that address the undercurrents of inequities, raise critical issues about how we are and are not meeting the needs of students, and challenge the dogma of "she's different." As inherent in ACL, I sought alternatives by considering multiple viewpoints and questioning my perceptions before making decisions. I also reflected on my identity as a leader and worked to not internalize questionable interactions that left me pondering: "Is this because I'm a Black female?"

CULTURALLY RESPONSIVE LEADERSHIP IN PRACTICE

Within this chapter, the authors provide personal accounts for navigating through the ranks as critical leaders attempting to advance social justice and equity within university settings set on maintaining status quo. These personal accounts serve as **counter-stories** to promote the voices of two women of color representing two distinct systemically underserved populations. Oppressed by common gate-keeping leadership systems of practice inherent in higher education institutions, their stories highlight the forces present that require emerging leaders to sacrifice their identity for professional gain so as not to disrupt business as usual. With pressures to adopt traditional forms of leadership practice, a lack of appropriate professional development to acquire the skills needed for leadership positions, and being subject to public scrutiny and ridicule by one's own academic peers for going to the 'dark side,' the authors' stories reflect the challenges individuals face when trying to become **transformative, servant leaders in order to work ultimately for the greater good.**

Discussion and Conclusion

As was stated earlier, effective organizational leadership demands intentional recruitment, preparation, continuing education, and long-term planning for future leadership. This is one area where K–12 educational leadership scholars can inform and help prepare universities for meeting their leadership needs in the future. How we develop leaders must be both theoretically based and evident in practice at the university and school level. However, it is only recently that the study of leadership has moved from, essentially, good management techniques to transformational, visionary, and critical leadership to meet the complex demands of contemporary society (Santamaría, 2014; Santamaría & Santamaría, 2012). Leadership frameworks that rely on traits and behaviors do not fully consider the technological advancements, cross-cultural interconnectedness, and relational necessity for leadership in a knowledge-based, heavily networked university.

Contemporary institutional complexities call for new approaches to leadership. Gallos (2002) and Rich (2006) suggest one approach is to consider restructuring academic units in ways that foster cross-disciplinary collaboration to support universities in establishing nimble reaction to financial, political, and social pressures. In essence, these collaborations strengthen research foundations, increase donor support, and allow space for creativity. The flaw in this approach is that it continues to ignore the fundamental problems with the recruitment, development, and long-term planning needed from university leadership and further perpetuates the administrator/faculty divide. As Komives, Owen, Longerbeam, Mainella, & Osteen (2005) explain, "Many of these 'new ways of leading' include components of principle-centered leadership such as collaboration, ethical action, moral purposes and leaders who transform followers into leaders themselves" (p. 594).

Recruiting aspiring leaders for higher education should be intentional and focused on those faculty who represent qualities antithetical to perpetuating institutional barriers that make it difficult, if not impossible, for marginalized people to overcome. This requires an intentional approach to leadership development inclusive of opportunities whereby faculty are introduced to increasingly more complex leadership activities coupled with formal reflection on the part of the faculty member as she/he moves toward leadership roles. Similar to K–12 leadership, higher education should focus on a type of certification process that requires aspiring leaders to demonstrate their understanding of leadership, both in theory and practice. Finally, leadership should be assessed against the complex needs of the university with performance assessment of leaders conducted on a regular basis using multiple meaningful data points.

Leadership in higher education should be afforded the same scrutiny and application of standards as K–12 institutions. Arguably, these institutions should be held to a higher standard given the role they play in shaping society. Poor leadership recruitment, preparation, continued education, and assessment undermines faculty governance by institutionalizing leadership practices within academic units that fracture the characteristics of distributed, collegial governance.

References

Alemán, E., Jr. (2009). Through the prism of critical race theory: Niceness and Latina/o leadership in the politics of education. *Journal of Latinos and Education, 8*(4), 290–311.

Alley, N. M. (2005). Choosing or becoming an interim administrator. *Journal of Professional Nursing, 21*(5), 322–326.

Buller, J. L. (2007). *The essential academic dean: A practical guide to college leadership* (vol. 118). San Francisco, CA: Jossey-Bass.

DeYoung, S. (2000). Becoming an academic administrator: Is it for you? *Journal of Professional Nursing, 16*(2), 112–115.

Foster, W. (1986). *Paradigms and promises.* Buffalo, NY: Prometheus.

Freire, P. (1970). *Pedagogy of the oppressed.* New York, NY: Continuum.

Gallos, J. V. (2002). The dean's squeeze: The myths and realities of academic leadership in the middle. *Academy of Management Learning and Education, 1*(2), 174–184.

Gmelch, W. H., & Miskin, V. D. (2011). *Department chair leadership skills.* Madison, WI: Atwood.

Jackson, B. L., & Kelley, C. (2002). Exceptional and innovative programs in educational leadership. *Educational Administration Quarterly, 38*, 192–212.

Jean-Marie, G., & Normore, A. H. (Eds.). (2010). *Educational leadership preparation: Innovation and interdisciplinary approaches to the Ed.D. and graduate education.* New York, NY: Palgrave McMillan.

Kincheloe, J. L., & Steinberg, S. R. (1997). *Changing multiculturalism.* Philadelphia, PA: Open University Press.

Komives, S. R., Owen, J. E., Longerbeam, S. D., Mainella, F. C., & Osteen, L. (2005). Developing leadership identity: A grounded theory. *Journal of College Student Development, 46*(6), 593–611.

Ladson-Billings, G., & Tate, W. F. (2009). Toward a critical race theory of education. *Teachers College Record, 97*(1), 47–68.

Mackey, H. J. (2014). Identity and conformity: Transcending barriers of race, gender, and space to promote scholar activism in educational leadership for American Indians. In L. J. Santamaría, G. Jean-Marie, & C. O. Grant (Eds.), *Cross-cultural women scholars in academe: Intergenerational voices* (pp. 116–133). New York, NY: Routledge.

May, S., & Sleeter, C. E. (Eds.). (2010). *Critical multiculturalism: Theory and praxis.* New York, NY: Routledge.

McDade, S. A. (1997). Intentions of becoming an administrator: Implications for leadership learning and practice. *Journal of Continuing Higher Education, 45*(2), 2–13.

McGee Banks, C. A. (2007). Gender and race as factors in educational leadership and administration. In *The Jossey-Bass reader on educational leadership* (2nd ed., pp. 299–338). San Francisco, CA: Jossey-Bass.

Parker, L., & Villalpando, O. (2007). A race(ialized) perspective on education leadership: Critical race theory in educational administration. *Educational Administration Quarterly, 43*(5), 519–524.

Powers, J. M. (2007). The relevance of critical race theory to educational theory and practice. *Journal of Philosophy of Education, 41*(1), 151–166.

Quantz, R. A., Rogers, J., & Dantley, M. (1991). Rethinking transformative leadership: Toward democratic reform of schools. *Journal of Education, 173*(3), 96–118.

Rich, D. (2006). Academic leadership and the restructuring of higher education. *New Directions for Higher Education, 134*, 37–48.

Santamaría, L. J. (2014). Critical change for the greater good: Multicultural dimensions of educational leadership toward social justice and educational equity. *Education Administration Quarterly (EAQ), 50*(3), 347–391.

Santamaría, L. J., & Jean-Marie, G. (2014). Cross-cultural dimensions of applied, critical, and transformational leadership: Women principals advancing social justice and educational equity. *Cambridge Educational Journal, 44*(3), 333–360.

Santamaría, L. J., & Santamaría, A. P. (2012). *Applied critical leadership in education: Choosing change.* New York, NY: Routledge.

Shapiro, J. P., & Stefkovich, J. A. (2010). *Ethical leadership and decision making in education: Applying theoretical perspectives to complex dilemmas* (3rd ed.). New York, NY: Routledge.

Shields, C. M. (2010). Transformative leadership: Working for equity in diverse contexts. *Educational Administration Quarterly, 46*(4), 558–589.

Young, M. D., Petersen, G. J., & Short, P. M. (2002). The complexity of substantive reform: A call for interdependence among key stakeholders. *Educational Administration Quarterly, 38*, 137–175.

PART IV

Institutionalized Culturally Responsive Leadership

Implementation for Social Justice and Equity

12

SMASHING THE GLASS CEILING

Accountability of Institutional Policies and Practices to Leadership Diversity in Higher Education

Cosette M. Grant

IDEA IN BRIEF

U.S. higher education institutions still have significant work to do in transforming institutional cultures to be responsive and receptive to Black women in leadership, hence diversity (Grant, 2012). Therefore, critical theories, such as Applied Critical Leadership, are used to understand complexities and issues within the context of leadership disparities for Black women in Predominantly White Institutions (PWIs) that can inform and extend traditional scholarship about educational leadership (Santamaría & Santamaría, 2012). Such perspectives can be used to advance research, policy, and practice that employs accountability for leadership diversity. The significance of this complementary chapter presents findings from a synthesis of historical and contemporary research literature that delineates the underrepresentation of Black women in leadership from an institutional perspective. Finally, recommendations are provided as a guide for university stakeholders to help advance culturally responsive and diverse leadership policies.

Keywords: Black women, critical race theory, diversity, glass ceiling, higher education

Many Predominantly White Institutions (PWIs) have failed to acknowledge the contributions of Black women in the field of education (Henry & Nixon, 1994). Notwithstanding, a genesis of the achievements of early trailblazers, few in number, who broke through historical barriers by earning doctorates and joining faculty ranks at PWIs during unpopular times (as cited in Grant, 2012). Black women have occupied marginal positions in academe for an extended period (Collins, 2003; Grant, 2012). As far back as the 19th century, education has been the familiar ground for Black women since it was always one of the respectable professions for Blacks to pursue. Black women were schoolteachers among free Blacks before and after emancipation; however, in higher education, few Black women obtained positions, but rather were consigned to Black elementary and secondary schools (Benjamin, 1997).

Researchers have documented a multitude of barriers encountered by Black women in higher education (Hughes & Howard-Hamilton, 2003). Since early on, Black women in the academy have been met with oppositional isolation from the center of authority in the hallowed halls of academia. This lack of inclusion of Black women in faculty and leadership posts has limited their access to influential academic positions (Collins, 1986). Specifically, some research findings have indicated a co-occurring discrimination related to race and gender (Zamani, 2003), lack of support systems and networks (Patton & Harper, 2003), and unwelcoming, insensitive, and isolative environments (Watt, 2003). Black women faculty in PWIs, more specifically, are less likely to gain access to networks and organizational systems in order to advance their agenda (Tillman, 2001). Very little has changed in recent years (Grant, 2012).

During the last 30 years, Black women have entered the academy in greater numbers than ever before. However, they still remain largely invisible (as cited in Grant, 2012). Even though Black women have enjoyed some gains, recent data in 2006 postulated that 88% of college presidents were White males (Association of American Colleges and Universities [AACU], 2007) and that universities have been, and continue to be, traditionally dominated and led by White men (Ross & Green, 2000). According to an Association of American Colleges and Universities (AACU) study (AACU, 2007), the "typical" college and university president was a married White male who had an earned doctorate and had served as a president for an average of nine years. The report also stated that women of color saw slight gains in comparison.

Despite substantial advancements toward gender equity, evidence of substantial disparity still exists within senior level positions in academia for Black women (Ross & Green, 2000). According to Dugger (2001) and J. C. Williams (2005), a small number of women and individuals of color progress up the academic career ladder to become institutional leaders. With the exception of certain types of institutions, such as two-year colleges and lower-tier four-year institutions (Jackson & O'Callaghan, 2009; Jackson & O'Callaghan, 2011;Trower, 2002), the number of women and people of color in senior-level positions in higher education remains low (Jackson & Daniels, 2007), and full-time faculty at highly regarded universities remain largely White and male (Trower, 2002). Researchers have underscored significant concerns that are specific to minority women administrators at PWIs (Lloyd-Jones, 2009). "Such findings reveal that Black female administrators encounter significant barriers within academia itself that discourage them from becoming productive and satisfied members" (Turner, Myers, & Creswell, 1999, p. 28).

Additionally for Black women, their dualistic roles of being women and individuals of color continue to create role incongruity (Jean-Marie, Grant, & Irby, 2014; Grant, 2012). Thus, they face perceptions of having to perform gender-stereotyped roles within academia and thereby experience greater barriers than their Black male counterparts. Nevertheless, during the 1980s, Black female administrators began increasing their share of positions in higher education (Benjamin, 1997). The American Council on Education (ACE) reported that, "in 1989 Black women made up 4.2 percent of full-time administrators, which represents 87 percent change from the previous decade" (ACE, 2012 p. 26). Between 1986 and 2006, the percentage of Black women presidents rose from 3.9 percent to 8.1 percent (AACU, 2007). And by 2011, two Black women led two prestigious PWIs, including an ivy-league institution. This reflects consistent, but nominal gains.

Following these trends, this chapter seeks to inform policy-makers, administrators, faculty, researchers, and other decision-making bodies interested in improving work environment conditions for Black women in PWIs, while also developing culturally responsive methods to increase diversity in leadership ranks. This research will be a useful tool for graduate students of color aspiring toward faculty and ultimately leadership ranks. Emphasis is on developing a clear synthesis of this research to inform effective policies and practices to increase leadership outcomes for Black women in PWIs.

However, to provide perspective on the challenges associated with Black women in leadership positions, historical data and current literature is provided to address: (1) the barriers that may prevent Black women from entering college and university administration; (2) some leadership traits of Black women leaders; (3) the glass ceiling present in academe; and (4) challenges to institutional commitments to diversity in leadership. This chapter will conclude with recommendations.

Context and Overview

With regard to U.S. colleges and universities, concern remains about institutional commitment to diversity (Jackson & Rosas, 1999; Minor, 2008). However, there is scant research that explores the leadership development of Black women in academia. It is particularly important to intensify research on Black women in higher education, given the disparities in representation, particularly the lack of senior-level positions in academia for Black women (Dugger, 2001; J. C. Williams, 2005). As it relates to the purpose of this chapter, it is important to advance policies and practices that afford Black women more leadership posts in academia. However, colleges and universities grapple with an operational framework and a productive knowledge of how to implement policies that benefit the advancement of diversity in leadership roles (Jackson & Flowers, 2003).

The Duality of Black Women

Marginal positions in educational settings have been occupied by Black women for some time (Collins, 1986). We have failed Black women when their experiences are not centered as a core consideration of what constitutes leadership. We have failed them when we resist empowering Black women as effective institutional leaders. We have also failed them when we encourage or force them to choose between their gender and their race; and when we question their duality as women when they foreground critical perspectives that transform educational settings, while being transformed (Jean-Marie et al., 2014). So what has to happen? We have to face the hard truths about racism and classism that pervades the realities of the lives of Black women.

Moreover, Black women "work to develop expertise and authority in [their] chosen field in order to balance her cultural values, beliefs, philosophies, and behaviors with those that are fundamentally different from her own" (Benjamin, 1997, p. 243). An additional burden is thereby placed on Black women, unlike their White counterparts. J. Nefta Baraka's *Collegiality in the Academy: Where Does the Black Woman Fit?* states that different cultural orientations intertwine with racism and sexism, making it difficult for Black women to fit into the White academe (as cited in Benjamin, 1997). There is a consensus that Black women in general face a myriad of challenges in the academy that impede their professional growth, which limits their ascendency to leadership participation in higher education (Battle & Doswell, 2004; Benjamin, 1997). We must work to build capacity among policy-makers and stakeholders, so that nurturing educational environments are constructed in order for Black women to ascend leadership ranks.

Literature Considered

Barriers for Black Women

Barriers to leadership opportunities are a global phenomenon where women, when compared to men, are disproportionately relegated to lower-level and lower-authoritative leadership positions (Northouse, 2010; Stiemke & Santamaría, this volume). These barriers are generally perceived to be against women and, to a larger extent, oppose Black women as leaders (Parker & Ogilvie, 1996). According to Parker and Ogilvie (1996) and Talley-Ross (1991), Black women report that racism, rather than sexism, is the greatest barrier to opportunities in dominant culture organizations (as cited in Parker & Ogilvie, 1996). Furthermore, only a few studies have examined how race impacts leadership (Santamaría &

Jean-Marie, 2014). Ransford and Miller (1983) suggested that attitudes toward and actions against Black women continue to be profoundly affected by past and current racial oppression.

Leadership Traits

Historical leadership traits have been studied in order to determine what constitutes great leaders. These theories, called the "Great Man" theories, focused on identifying the innate qualities and characteristics possessed by great social, political, and military leaders (Northouse, 2010) and mostly associated with White men (Bass, 1990; Northouse, 2010). It was believed that people were born with these traits (Northouse, 2010). Horsford (2012) stated, "Such theories have not similarly explored the natural, inborn or divine gifts and traits associated with the great woman," and certainly excludes the consideration of Black women (p. 13) (see also B. Lloyd-Jones, this volume).

Nonetheless, to capture the qualities of leaders that facilitate positive outcomes, leadership theorists are attempting to more redefine and present the qualities that constitute good leadership (Eagly, 2005). When the female gender role is inconsistent with traditionally defined leadership roles, prejudice toward women as leaders is a common outcome. People are unaccustomed in many organizational contexts to women possessing substantial authority that encompasses decision-making power (Eagly, 2005). Eagly contends that, "not only do people doubt that women possess the appropriate competencies, but also they may resent the overturning of the expected and usual hierarchical relation between the sexes" (p. 465). This is also the case for Black women. That said, research literature has been replete with studies on the differences between male and female characteristics and traits that are normally associated with leadership, such as individualism versus collaboration (Cantor & Bernay, 1992; Helgesen, 1990). Modern discussions of leadership are based upon two concepts: transactional or transformational leadership (Fisher & Koch, 2001). According to Parker (2005), transformational leadership places an emphasis on social change and emancipation. For Black women, transformational leadership has been closely aligned to their leadership style (Byrd & Stanley, 2009; Parker, 2005; Walker, 2009).

The Glass Ceiling for Black Women in Academia

Considering that 50 years have passed since the enactment of the Civil Rights Act in 1964, it is concerning that the glass ceiling still stands as a major barrier to the advancement of Black women in academia. Yet, there is little to no reference to understanding the glass ceiling phenomenon related to Black women in academia, who represent both "women" and "of color" groups (Santamaría, 2014; Stiemke & Santamaría, this volume). The understanding of its causes and its scope remains debatable; as a result, current research is needed that better measures glass-ceiling effects in order to develop effective policies and recommendations that reduce and eradicate the phenomenon (Jackson & O'Callaghan, 2009).

One of the major challenges Black women confront is that glass-ceiling effects have not generally been applied to studying leadership disparities regarding Black women in the academic workforce (Davis & Maldonado, 2015). Little is known about how to measure the presence of the glass ceiling, to determine its impact on Black women and organizations, and to generate strategies for countering a phenomenon hidden beneath layers of institutional culture (Lloyd-Jones, this volume). The lack of prior research—in particular, research that focuses on Black women—and data limitations, such as a lack of data disaggregated by race/ethnicity and gender, pose major barriers as we attempt to craft solutions to reduce or eliminate this phenomenon. Jackson and O'Callaghan (2009) contend that there is a unique intersecting relationship between gender and race with respect to glass-ceiling effects, and until there is an understanding of its relationship, important features of the glass ceiling's real negative consequences will be ignored. Among these are Black women faculty members who may face potential barriers not only as a woman but also as part of a racial group that is underrepresented in the academy.

What we do know with regard to the glass-ceiling effect on Black women is that competitive global firms are recognizing that barriers to the advancement of Black women can be detrimental to organizational effectiveness. Nohria and Khurana (2010) stated "the barriers to women's advancement undermine organizational performance and compromise fundamental principles of equal opportunity and social justice" (p. 189). Since women represent an equal share of the talent available for leadership, and with Black women making up the majority representation of any group of color in higher education, reducing the obstacles for Black women's advancement in the academy can also reduce the amount of attrition. In this case, glass-ceiling effects on Black women in higher education can be collected and analyzed to make informed decisions regarding policy and practice in colleges and universities (Jackson & O'Callaghan, 2009) to reverse this reality.

The significance of examining the glass-ceiling effect on Black women brings to light the experience of discrimination in more than one manner (Maume, 2004). Morley (2006) argued that a multitude of relationships must be considered, and as long as we continue to ignore how gender intersects with identity characteristics such as race and class, we will continue to fall short in understanding and addressing the breadth of glass-ceiling effects. And, as Jackson (2003) posits, the underrepresentation of women and people of color at the top of the organizational hierarchy may only be the tip of the iceberg. The glass ceiling will continue to subtly deter these two groups from reaching senior-level positions in higher education until we dedicate time and effort to collecting and analyzing data that provide key institutional decision-makers with valuable information to address this phenomenon.

Also, Jackson (2003) highlights how the lack of diversity in senior-level positions in institutions of higher education constitutes only the visible portion of a larger problem. When examining how the glass ceiling impacts workforce dynamics in higher education, individuals and organizations cannot ignore what underpins each institution or where unwelcoming environments are nourished by practices of discrimination and the views of a dominant majority.

Challenging Institutional Commitment to Diversity in Leadership

Research into glass-ceiling effects illustrates trends such as failures to cast broad enough nets in external searches, tendencies to hire exclusively from homogenous internal pools, salary compression, and/or pernicious cycles of negatively evaluating women and minority candidates under the aegis of not being good institutional "fits." Yet when these data are presented, what happens next? Are they translated into strategies for meaningful change that will diversify senior ranks of an institution? How does this information lead to tactics that will aggressively advance an institution's diversity agenda?

Delineated in Minor's (2014) study, too often, institutional designees will author comprehensive diversity reports that illuminate the dynamics of glass-ceiling effects—but ultimately fail to propose clear strategies of action, change management, and accountability. To take meaningful steps to overcome glass-ceiling effects, institutional research professionals and others must become strategic culturally responsive–oriented diversity leaders who are also versed in the ideas of organizational learning and change (Paul, 2003; D. A. Williams, 2013). Any philosophy of diversity leadership must learn from past mistakes, build on prior successes, ask hard questions, and move beyond flawed approaches that yield suboptimal results.

Given we are 30 years on from the inception of affirmative action programs and diversity training efforts, any success with regard to mitigating glass-ceiling effects will hinge more on understanding the processes of organizational change and less on an understanding of diversity issues. Therefore, in order to be effective, more colleges and universities must operate as learning institutions concerned with building real solutions to alter the state of these dynamics (Smith, Turner, Osei-Kofi, & Richards, 2004). But the reality is that processes of change associated with this level are generally undertaken through simple strategies and might include relocating, for example, a cultural center in the center of campus. This is often due in large part to what Schein (2004) theorizes as multiple overlapping layers in organizational cultures.

By comparison, and as pointed out in Minor's work (2014), more resilient aspects of culture exist at deeper levels, embedded in mental models and individual perceptions of diversity, excellence, and inclusion (D. A. Williams, Berger, & McClendon, 2005). For some, these deeper levels equate administrative diversification to a "lessening of quality" and "establishing quotas." Consequently, many institutional symbols, myths, traditions, processes, and behaviors do not affirm diversity but rather create a "culture of resistance" that presents a monumental challenge to diversity efforts (Alger, 2009).

Competing Institutional Priorities

Researchers have since begun to approach the idea of resistance with a focus on how positive intentions can lead to negative reactions to change (Piderit, 2000). Furthermore, these negative reactions may not be present at the outset but emerge unexpectedly as the process of change unfolds (Feldman, 2004), occurring not in the context of a single organizational culture but rather a set of diverse and sometimes competing subcultures (Jermier, Slocum, Fry, & Gaines, 1991). Minor (2014) points out that understanding this multidimensional resistance is an important first step in determining how best to implement diversity innovations.

Implications for Practice

Understanding the leadership development experiences of Black women in the academy is necessary for improving leadership development opportunities for them as emerging leaders. The facts still remain the same: Black women are not represented in leadership positions in academia. According to the American Council on Education's (2012) national data in 2012, 87% of U.S. college presidents, both male and female, were White. Out of that number, women made up 26% of all college presidents. Of the women college presidents across the nation in 2011, 81% were White and only 8% were Black (ACE, 2012). Results from the current study further substantiate the need for more women of color in academia, especially in leadership positions. It also exposes some of the barriers faced by Black women and might also provide an understanding of the experience of Black women and the contributions of these women as a collective group in executive positions. Since research on the impact of race and gender on Black women's leadership development in academia is understudied, this chapter can also serve as a reference point for those who seek to eliminate cultural barriers and obstacles that stunt the upward mobilization of Black women in academia.

Concluding Thoughts

To understand the roles cultural responsivity and diversity play in strengthening the intellectual growth and environment at colleges and universities, institutions seek to diversify all levels of participation. As such, key stakeholders see the potential benefit of including diverse approaches to leadership and policy development to build stronger institutions. The true test for a commitment to a diverse workforce at an institution is its demonstrated support of the recruitment, hiring, training, professional development, promotion, and career success of administrators and academic personnel of color.

In so doing, research in this discourse, as well as an understanding of effective policies and practices that considers the intersection of race, gender, and social class, is critical to the professional development of Black women leaders. Examining intersectionality in the leadership experiences of Black women offers opportunity for new perspectives of workplace values and beliefs to be heard (Jackson, O'Callaghan, & Adserias, 2014). Research from this paradigm seeks to explore the scientific study of domination, oppression, alienation, and struggle within institutions, organizations, and social groups for the purpose of emancipation, transformation, and social change (Creswell, 1998).

The focus on the inquiry process is on understanding ways in which individuals construct and interpret their own personal experiences and relate them to expressions of leadership in academe. Organizations, researchers, scholars, and practitioners may use the findings of the study by further exploring intersectionality as it addresses race and gender in organizations and leadership practices (Crenshaw, 1989) and to add effective policies specific to the unique situation and position of Black women in academia.

To truly overcome glass-ceiling effects in the academy, researchers and administrators must develop a clear understanding of the challenges that impede progress and develop strategies accordingly. As outlined in this chapter, several dynamics buttress the glass-ceiling effect: dynamics of the academy, including subtle bias and racism, the general lack of accountability, and powerful diversity infrastructures designed to create change at the core of institutional culture. The only way to overcome these dynamics is for leaders to implement a triple-loop organizational learning approach to change, one that is rooted in an in-depth analysis of the tactics that work, the underlying cultural dynamics that obstruct change, as well as the broader environmental dynamics that enable or constrain change in the academy (Bateson, 1973). Deeply understanding the historical and organizational nature of the problem increases the likelihood of designing policies that will result in lasting change rather than a series of incremental and ineffective stopgap measures. Additionally, establishing a shared vision and common goals is more likely to overcome those factors that contribute to a culture of resistance. Further recommendations for application follow.

CULTURALLY RESPONSIVE LEADERSHIP IN PRACTICE

With the objectives identified in the closing remarks, the following set of culturally responsive recommendations is provided and is intended to help leaders in HE to institutionalize and bring about robust, diverse applied critical leadership practices and policies:

- foster a sense of senior leadership support and engagement;
- develop an appropriate diversity infrastructure to guide change;

- implement diversity data-translation workshops;
- introduce contextually relevant diversity education programs for search committees, department chairs, faculty, and leaders;
- establish multiple diversity accountability and incentive systems at the institutional and individual levels;
- bring research home by translating scholarly research projects into campus-wide conversations that bridge theory and practice; and
- develop internal mentoring and leadership development programs designed to groom diverse faculty and staff for senior leadership roles on campus (Minor, 2014).

References

Alger, J. (2009, June). Diversity in the age of Obama: New directions or status quo? Paper presented at the Annual Meeting of the National Association of College and University Attorneys, Toronto, ON.

American Council on Education. (2012). *The American college president 2012.* Washington, DC: Center for Policy Analysis.

Association of American Colleges and Universities. (2007). *The American college president: 2007 edition.* Retrieved from http://www.aacu.org/ocww/volume36_1/data.cfm

Bass, B. M. (1990). *Bass and Stogdill's handbook of leadership: Theory, research and managerial applications* (3rd ed.). New York, NY: Free Press.

Bateson, G. (1973). *Steps to an ecology of mind.* London, UK: Palladin.

Battle, C., & Doswell, C. (2004). *Building bridges for women of color in higher education.* Lanham, MD: University Press of America.

Benjamin, L. (1997). *Black women in the academy: Promises and perils.* Gainesville, FL: University Press of Florida.

Byrd, M., & Stanley, C. (2009). Bringing the voices together. *Advances in Developing Human Resources, 11*(5), 657–666.

Cantor, D., & Bernay, T. (1992). *Women in power.* Boston, MA: Houghton-Mifflin.

Collins, P. H. (1986). Learning from the outsider within: The sociological significance of black feminist thought. *Social Problems, 33*(6), 14–32.

Collins, P. H. (2003). Intersections of race, class, gender and nation: Some implications for Black family studies. *Journal of Comparative Family Studies, 29*(1), 27–36.

Crenshaw, K. (1989). Demarginalizing the intersection of race and sex: A Black feminist critique of antidiscrimination doctrine, feminist theory and antiracist politics. *University of Chicago Legal Forum,* 139–167.

Creswell, J. W. (1998). *Qualitative inquiry and research design: The five traditions.* Thousand Oaks, CA: Sage.

Davis, D. R., & Maldonado, C. (2015). Shattering the glass ceiling: The leadership development of African American women in higher education. *Advancing Women in Leadership, 35,* 48–64.

Dugger, K. (2001). Women in higher education in the United States: Has there been progress? *International Journal of Sociology and Social Policy, 21*(1/2), 118–121.

Eagly, A. H. (2005). Achieving relational authenticity in leadership: Does gender matter? *Leadership Quarterly, 16*(2), 459–474.

Feldman, M. S. (2004). Resources in emerging structures and processes of change. *Organization Science, 15*(3), 295–309.

Fisher, J., & Koch, J. (2001). *Presidential leadership.* Phoenix, AZ: Onyx Press.

Grant, C. (2012). Advancing our legacy: A black feminist perspective on the significance of mentoring for African-American women in educational leadership [Special issue]. *International Journal of Qualitative Studies in Education, 25*(1), 101–117.

Helgesen, S. (1990). *The female advantage: Women's ways of leadership.* New York, NY: Doubleday.

Henry, W. J., & Nixon, H. L. (1994). Changing a campus climate for minorities and women. *Equity and Excellence in Education, 27*(3), 48–54.

Horsford, S. D. (2012). This bridge called my leadership: An essay on Black women as bridge leaders in education. *International Journal of Qualitative Studies in Education, 25*(1), 11–22.

Hughes, R. L., & Howard-Hamilton, M. F. (2003). Insights: Emphasizing issues that affect African American women. *New Directions for Student Services, 2003*(104), 95–104.

Jackson, J.F.L. (2003). Toward administrative diversity: An analysis of the African American male educational pipeline. *Journal of Men's Studies, 12,* 43–60.

Jackson, J.F.L., & Daniels, B. D. (2007). A national progress report of African Americans in the administrative workforce in higher education. In J.F.L. Jackson (Ed.), *Strengthening the educational pipeline for African Americans: Informing research, policy, and practice* (pp. 115–137). Albany: State University of New York Press.

Jackson, J.F.L., & Flowers, L. A. (2003). Retaining African American student affairs administrators: Voices from the field. *College Student Affairs Journal, 22*(2), 125–136.

Jackson, J.F.L., & Leon, R. A. (2010). Enlarging our understanding of glass ceiling effects with social closure theory in higher education. In J. C. Smart (Ed.), *Higher education: Handbook of theory and research* (vol. 25, pp. 351–379). London, UK/New York, NY: Springer.

Jackson, J.F.L., & O'Callaghan, E. M. (2009). What do we know about the glass ceiling effect? A taxonomy and critical review to inform higher education research. *Research in Higher Education, 50*(5), 460–482.

Jackson, J.F.L., & O'Callaghan, E. M. (2011). Understanding employment disparities using glass ceiling effects criteria: An examination of race/ethnicity and senior-level position attainment across the academic workforce. *Journal of the Professoriate, 5*(2), 67–99.

Jackson, J.F.L., O'Callaghan, E. M., & Adserias, R. P. (2014). Approximating glass ceiling effects using cross–sectional data. *New Directions for Institutional Research, 2013*(159), 37–47.

Jackson, J.F.L., & Rosas, M. (1999). Scholars of color: Are universities derailing their scholarship. In *Keeping Our Faculties Conference Proceedings* (pp. 86–107). Minneapolis, MN.

Jean-Marie, G., Grant, C., & Irby, B. (Eds.). (2014). *The duality of women scholars of color: Transforming and being transformed in the academy.* Research on Women and Education Series. Charlotte, NC: Information Age.

Jermier, J. M., Slocum Jr., J. W., Fry, L. W., & Gaines, J. (1991). Organizational subcultures in a soft bureaucracy: Resistance behind the myth and facade of an official culture. *Organization Science, 2*(2), 170–194.

Lloyd-Jones, B. (2009). Implications of race and gender in higher education administration: An African American woman's perspective. *Advances in Developing Human Resources, 11*(5), 606–618.

Maume, D. J. (2004). Is the glass ceiling a unique form of inequality? Evidence from a random-effects model of managerial attainment. *Work and Occupations, 31*(2), 250–274.

Minor, J. T. (2008). *Contemporary HBCUs: Considering institutional capacity and state priorities*. East Lansing: Michigan State University, College of Education, Department of Educational Administration.

Minor, J. T. (2014). Faculty diversity and the traditions of academic governance. *New Directions for Institutional Research, 2013*(159), 49–61.

Morley, L. (2006). Including women: Gender in commonwealth higher education. *Women's Studies International Forum, 29*(6), 539–542.

Nohria, N., & Khurana, R. (2010). *Handbook of leadership theory and practice*. Boston, MA: Harvard Business Press.

Northouse, P. G. (2010). *Leadership: Theory and practice* (5th ed.). Los Angeles, CA: Sage.

Parker, P. S. (2005). *Race, gender, and leadership: Re-envisioning organizational leadership from the perspectives of African American women executives*. Mahwah, NJ: Erlbaum.

Parker, P. S., & Ogilvie, D. T. (1996). Gender, culture, and leadership: Toward a culturally distinct model of African-American women executives' leadership strategies. *Leadership Quarterly, 7*, 189–214.

Patton, L. D., & Harper, S. R. (2003). Mentoring relationships among African American women in graduate and professional schools. *New Directions for Student Services, 2003*(104), 67–78.

Paul, M. J. (2003). Double-loop diversity: Applying adult learning theory to the cultivation of diverse learning environments in higher education. *Innovative Higher Education, 28*(1), 35–47.

Piderit, S. K. (2000). Rethinking resistance and recognizing ambivalence: A multidimensional view of attitudes toward an organizational change. *Academy of Management Review, 25*(4), 783–794.

Ransford, H. E., & Miller, J. (1983). Race, sex and feminist outlooks. *American Sociological Review, 48*(1), 46–59.

Ross, M., & Green, M. F. (2000). *The American college president* (pp. 1–114). Washington, DC: American Council on Education.

Santamaría, L. J. (2014). Critical change for the greater good: Multicultural perceptions in educational leadership toward social justice and equity. *Educational Administration Quarterly, 50*(3), 347–391.

Santamaría, L. J., & Jean-Marie, G. (2014). Cross-cultural dimensions of applied, critical, and transformational leadership: Women principals advancing social justice and educational equity. *Cambridge Journal of Education, 44*(3), 333–360.

Santamaría, L. J., & Santamaría, A. P. (2012). *Applied critical leadership in education: Choosing change*. New York, NY: Routledge.

Schein, E. H. (2004). The learning culture and the learning leader. *Organizational culture and leadership* (3rd ed., pp. 365–383). San Francisco, CA: Jossey-Bass.

Smith, D. G., Turner, C.S.V., & Osei-Kofi, N., & Richards, S. (2004). Interrupting the usual: Successful strategies for hiring diverse faculty. *Journal of Higher Education, 75*(2), 133–160.

Talley-Ross, N. (1991). *The African American woman practicing in non-traditional professions: A life history approach* (Unpublished doctoral dissertation). University of South Florida, Tampa, FL.

Tillman, L. (2001). Mentoring African American faculty in predominantly white institutions. *Research in Higher Education, 42*(3), 295–325.

Trower, C. A. (2002). Can colleges competitively recruit faculty without the prospect of tenure? In R. P. Chait (Ed.), *The questions of tenure* (pp. 182–220). Cambridge, MA: Harvard University Press.

Turner, C.S.V., Myers, S. L., Jr., & Creswell, J. W. (1999). Exploring under-representation: The case of faculty of color in the Midwest. *Journal of Higher Education, 70*(1), 27–59.

Walker, S. (2009). Reflections on leadership from the perspectives of Africa in American women of faith. *Advances in Developing Human Resources, 11*(5), 646–659.

Watt, S. K. (2003). Come to the river: Using spirituality to cope, resist, and develop identity. *New Directions for Student Services, 2003*(104), 29–40.

Williams, D. A. (2013). *Strategic diversity leadership: Activating change and transformation in higher education.* Sterling, VA: Stylus.

Williams, D. A., Berger, J. B., & McClendon, S. A. (2005). *Toward a model of inclusive excellence and change in postsecondary institutions.* Washington, DC: Association of American Colleges and Universities.

Williams, J. C. (2005). The glass ceiling and the maternal wall in academia. *New Directions for Higher Education, 20*(130), 91–105.

Zamani, E. M. (2003). African American women in higher education. *New Directions for Student Services, 2003*(104), 5–18.

13

FROM IDEAS TO ACTIONS

Institutionalizing Diversity, Social Justice, and Equity Efforts

Annette Daoud

IDEA IN BRIEF

This chapter reflects tenets of Applied Critical Leadership as practiced by a diverse group of forward-thinking scholar leaders and, as such, chronicles their efforts on a university campus to establish and maintain a center focused on promoting diversity, social justice, and equity. The chapter describes how the center's founding director applied critical race theory to practice by creating venues for faculty and staff to move from separate and often competing activities and events to college-wide collaborative and institutionalized efforts. Additionally, challenges are identified and strategies are proposed via the use of counter-storytelling to depict the center director's efforts in keeping social justice and equity at the forefront of the university's strategic plan. This chapter provides a roadmap of a journey that many leaders in higher education need to understand in order to embark on similar journeys within their own particular quests for social justice and equity in institutions where injustice has been normalized.

Keywords: critical race theory, higher education, counter-storytelling, social justice and equity, interest convergence

This chapter chronicles the efforts on a university campus to establish and maintain a center focused on promoting diversity, social justice, and equity. The center, named the Social Justice and Equity Project (SJEP), was established to bring together faculty and staff who had previously worked on diversity and social justice issues within their own contexts or silos. The chapter describes how the center's founding director created venues for faculty and staff to move from separate and often competing activities and events to college-wide collaborative and institutionalized efforts. The author, the center's director, uses the lens of critical race theory (CRT) to frame the story of the journey to create and operate the center as well as to analyze the successes and challenges along the way. Several tenets of CRT that are relevant to the story are defined: counter-storytelling, the permanence of racism, Whiteness as property, and interest convergence. Through a CRT lens, decisions made by the director are viewed as a strengths-based model of leadership "where educational leaders consider the social context of their educational communities and empower individual members of these communities based on the educational leaders' identities" (Santamaría & Santamaría, 2012, p. 5). Lessons learned from the journey are also shared to provide strategies critical leaders can use in their quest to institutionalize diversity, equity, and social justice efforts on a university campus.

As the center's director, and throughout my work as a critical leader, I use the critical pedagogy framework of problem posing where issues are not just identified, but critically examined with a lens of understanding how to address the issue and create change (Freire, 1990). When I commit to leading an effort that advances issues of diversity, equity, and social justice, I use the critical pedagogy process outlined by Wink (2011) where I name an issue, reflect critically on how to best address the issue, and then act to implement change. The effort described in this chapter is one of moving ideas of social justice and equity toward a fully operational center that encompasses the work of individuals and groups on campus through sponsored events and activities. The journey is told as a counter-story and described in phases starting with bringing together individuals and groups on campus with converging interests to form alliances where common issues are identified to create a social justice and equity center. The counter-story continues with a description of the center's approval process and strategies used to ensure support by key individuals and groups needed for successful passage and implementation. Finally, the story ends with a description of the successes and challenges of maintaining the center (the SJEP), which sponsored strategic events and activities. Counter-storytelling is one tenet of critical race theory I use in this chapter, which allows readers to fully understand the social and political context in which the development, approval, and implementation of the SJEP occurs. My intent in telling the story is to provide a roadmap for other scholars in the field so they can form alliances where they find similarities, nurture relationships for resistance, and connect tenets of CRT across stories and experiences to leverage their power (Delgado, 1989; Solórzano, Ceja, & Yasso, 2000).

Critical Race Theory Framework

This chapter uses CRT based on Derrick Bell's (1980, 1992, 1995) work that combines critical sociological theory and narrative inquiry in the field of legal scholarship as a theoretical framework. I draw from Ladson-Billings and Tate's

(1995) call for action to use CRT to expose inequities and create social justice in the field of education. Carbado (2002) identifies a first and second generation of CRT scholarship, the first is focused on overt and material manifestations of racism and inclusion of racially marginalized people, and the second generation extends the scholarship to include other markers of difference such as gender, ethnicity, language, culture, and sexuality (as cited in Lynn & Parker, 2006). This chapter represents a blending of the first and second generation of CRT as I focus on the identity markers of ethnicity, gender, and culture while recognizing race as the underlying marker of difference throughout the analysis. As a means of framing and analyzing my counter-story, I use DeCuir and Dixson's (2004) definition of CRT, which identifies the five tenets of CRT as "(a) counter-storytelling (Matsuda, 1995), (b) the permanence of racism (Bell, 1992, 1995), (c) Whiteness as property (Harris, 1995), (d) interest convergence (Bell, 1980), and (e) the critique of liberalism" (DeCuir & Dixson, 2004, p. 27). My counter-story identifies all but the last of these five tenets in this CRT framework, with the primary focus on interest convergence.

Counter-Storytelling

The first tenet of CRT from DeCuir and Dixson (2004) is counter-storytelling; to tell the stories that are unknown, unrecognized, and invalidated. Richard Delgado (1989, 1990) claims that the marginalized stories set up an alternative framework that values the marginalized voices where oppression permeates all of their experiences, and their stories are linked to liberation. Solórzano and Yosso (2009) build upon this definition by stating that "the counter story is also a tool for exposing, analyzing and challenging the majoritarian stories of racial privilege" (p. 138).

Although 'telling stories' may not appear to improve educational access, creating equity where it did not exist, or shifting the balance of an institutionalized power distribution, their value can be best understood by examining the five interrelated components of counter-storytelling: voice, alliance, navigation, survival, and change. The structure of the counter-story creates a common framework that gives power to voice by validating the sense-making of experiences individually and collectively, within and across marginalized groups (Ladson-Billings, 2009). Alliances can be formed when we find similarities (Delgado, 1989), nurture relationships for resistance (Solórzano, Ceja, & Yosso, 2000), and connect tenets of CRT across stories and experiences to leverage power. Navigation is an action taken by an individual or a group to resist oppression and survive (Chapman, 2007). Using a postmodernist approach, navigation can be viewed as a tool where the storyteller decides when, where, and who to share her multiple identities with, and how that sharing will help others avoid obstacles and make positive change (Elsbree & Daoud, 2011). Survival is the intended goal of navigation, but it is not guaranteed. Delgado (1989) claims that counter-stories are essential tools for oppressed groups' survival, but also for their liberation; namely, liberation to enact the change that individuals and marginalized groups seek. The counter-story I narrate in this chapter is important because it contests the dominant story that tells us racism is a thing of the past, issues of equity have been resolved, and thus there is no need to establish and maintain social justice and equity on campus.

The Permanence of Racism

Another central tenet of CRT is that racism is a permanent and normal part of our society (Bell, 1992). According to Vaught and Castagno (2008), the permanence of racism is the understanding that inequities between groups are expected and unavoidable. CRT "illuminates the relationship between the individual and the structure, between equality and equity" (Vaught & Castagno, 2008, p. 95). Equality and equity are unattainable constructs within a binary structure of 'us vs. them' where 'us' is permanently Whites and 'them' changes over time as the social and political context in which we live defines a new group to oppress. Given that racism is pervasive, systematic, and adaptable over time, it remains a normal part of our society (Taylor, 2009).

Whiteness as Property

Harris (1993) articulates the concept of Whiteness as property, where Whiteness is perceived as the norm giving Whites the power and privilege of domination. DeCuir and Dixson (2004) summarize how Whiteness as property functions on multiple levels through the concepts of rights: "the right of possession, the right to use, the right to disposition. Furthermore, the right to transfer, the right of use and enjoyment, and the right of exclusion are essential attributes associated with property rights" (p. 28). The privilege of Whiteness is that you have rights solely because you are White. In the field of education, Vaught and Castagno (2008) analyze how teachers sometimes substitute the concept of race with that of culture. A significant substitution that can mask racism by not acknowledging the students' race, but rather assigning their characteristics and performances to a cultural group, which in turn denies students their individuality and as a result their rights. In the context of property, passing can afford unearned privileges to those that are perceived to be part of the dominant group (Harris, 1993). The right to include/exclude plays out in the idea that the dominant group does not have to see/acknowledge race and be seen/acknowledged for race. The dominant group can then claim to be color-blind as a strategy to perpetuate racism. And, as an extension of the rights, Vaught and Castagno (2008) claim that the dominant group can modify the definition of Whiteness by clarifying who they are not and to what groups they do not belong.

Interest Convergence

Within CRT, Bell (1980) introduced the concept of interest convergence by explaining that the "interest of Blacks in achieving racial equality will be accommodated only when that interest converges with the interests of Whites in policymaking positions" (p. 69). DeCuir and Dixson (2004) extend this concept by stating, "given the vast disparities between elite Whites and most communities of color, gains that coincide with the self-interest of White elites, are not likely to make a substantive difference in the lives of people of color" (p. 28). Socially, economically, and politically, what interests of the dominant White group will ever converge to benefit marginalized groups? The answer lies in the alliances marginalized groups can form to resist, navigate, and change practices and structures that promote social justice. It is critical for marginalized groups to understand the power they possess to move issues to the forefront when alliances are formed across groups. When critical leaders of these groups understand the importance of these alliances and actively move to converge interests across groups, it can result in "sociopolitical action and decision making benefitting people of color and others who are marginalized" (Santamaría & Santamaría, 2012, p. 6).

The Journey: Moving Toward Social Justice and Equity

The Social Justice and Equity Project (SJEP) is a center located in a public university in Southern California that is over 20 years old and growing. The university serves a diverse student population, exemplified by the fact that it has been designated as a Hispanic-Serving Institution with many programs intended to support Latino and first-generation college students. At the time I was hired, the mission of the College of Education was to collaboratively transform public education. Mission statements in themselves represent a countering of the typical academic silencing on race, gender, and multiculturalism. The campus discourse in general, both official and unofficial, was inclusive and mentioned race, gender, and issues of diversity as important aspects of student learning (Elise, Daoud, & Rolinson, 2013). However, it is important to note that diversity was not clearly defined on campus and, as a result, 'diversity' programs were vulnerable to managerial change, while including diversity in the curriculum was dependent upon the faculty member assigned to teach the diversity course. Further, diversity was only one among many themes that the university faculty, staff, and administrators stated they valued, but resources allocated to technology or STEM programs and research far exceeded the value placed on diversity. Within this context, and by using a CRT lens, my narrative of establishing and institutionalizing SJEP can be understood as having an underpinning of promise and hope, even while riddled at times with perilous setbacks.

The Idea of a Social Justice and Equity Center

The story began with an idea from one of the college deans to create a multicultural center to share and house relevant research projects and teaching experiences among faculty in the college. Soon, the scope of the center had evolved into a comprehensive campus center focused on issues of diversity, social justice, and equity serving faculty, staff, students, and the local community. It was a true grassroots effort wherein faculty and staff from a broad range of colleges and units across campus worked diligently in small groups to conceptualize three overlapping sections of the center: academic programs, research, and knowledge diffusion; student life and engagement; and internal and external community connections.

For the handful of faculty members leading the effort, creating the center through collaboration and camaraderie among faculty and staff was truly inspiring. Meetings became a time when faculty and staff built alliances, sharing their work around issues of diversity, social justice, and equity, and recruiting others to participate in their group's activities and initiatives on campus. As alliances were formed and common interests discovered, faculty and staff began sharing their stories of 'diversity work' on campus, as well as their hope for the high expectations we all held for the center. After almost two years of our collaborative efforts, the group had created a proposal for a center focused on diversity, social justice, and equity, and was ready to submit it to the Academic Senate for approval. The first part of the journey was complete.

Approval Process

Moving from creating a social justice center on campus to establishing it with a budget and personnel attached was a perilous endeavor from the beginning. Opposition came from the usual suspects who did not want to invest in a center, as well as from faculty of color whose motives were self-serving—they were blocking efforts because they had no ownership in the center and thus would not receive the recognition they felt they deserved. However, along with these challenges came opportunities to create alliances across campus among individuals and groups who had previously not worked collaboratively.

The approval process began with a presentation to the Executive Committee of the Academic Senate, comprising the faculty chairs of the university's major committees and a few administrators. At the time, the spokesperson for the Social Justice Center was an African American faculty member from the Sociology Department. During the presentation, it became evident that some members of the committee had perceptions of the messenger that complicated the message. In the proposal for the center, the group had used critical pedagogy as one of the frameworks to attempt to appeal and connect with the work of the Academic Senate chair and secretary, both Latinos whom we knew also used critical pedagogy as one of the guides of their work in the field of education. However, when presented by our leader, they were offended that she used one of *their* frameworks. They expressed concern that she was trying to 'own' critical pedagogy—our intent to be inclusive had backfired. Although we believed these committee members to be allies who would support the center, our group spent the rest of our presentation time defending our proposal and the theoretical frameworks that were the underpinning of the center. At the end of our presentation, the committee asked us to re-work our proposal and present it again at a future date.

Understanding that the issue was with the messenger and not with the message, our spokesperson stepped aside for the greater good in order to receive Academic Senate approval. It was determined that since I was an Education faculty member, I should now lead the charge and steer the proposal through the approval process. Before our second presentation, there was much repair work to do and so backstage politics began. I appealed to my colleagues in Education by drawing their attention to the aspects of the center that converged with their own interests to emphasize that the center represented a reflection of their work, and was not in opposition to it. Forming an alliance with these committee members ahead of the second presentation was critical to ensuring support for the center. For the second presentation, I strategically selected the group to present the proposal with me. None of the group members had negative reputations with anyone on the Executive Committee—we were positioned to be heard. The center passed the first hurdle by receiving support from the Executive Committee and moved on to the next phase: full approval by faculty members in the Academic Senate.

The presentation to the Academic Senate proceeded as expected. There was opposition primarily from faculty members in the STEM fields and in business who couched their concerns with the center around budget issues. While the university was in a period of budget constraints, funding requested for the center was minimal. The issue was not concerning budget but rather one of value. Few, if any, STEM or business faculty members participated in any activity on campus that involved diversity. Additionally, many STEM and Business faculty members felt that their work represented valid research while that of their colleagues in the Social Sciences did not. Their opposition was rooted in their belief that a center focused on issues of diversity, equity, and social justice was not worth funding. Fortunately, there were more faculty members in the room that spoke in support of the center and voted accordingly.

The Center: Institutionalizing Diversity

After much political jockeying, the center was approved by the Academic Senate but then put on hold by the Provost who felt the scope did not "match" the definition of a center prescribed by the university's system-wide Chancellor's Office.

The group was given a small budget and a charge from the President to demonstrate what a center could do for the campus. The group decided to sponsor an all-day Social Justice and Equity Symposium and bring a national leader in the field of Multicultural Education as our guest speaker for the day. The symposium was a success and after a year of proving that the university needed the center, it was supported and funded by the President, not the Provost. While the Provost still was not convinced that the center fit into the official system-wide definition of a center, the President understood that the center had value for her and the campus for several reasons. First, the President had outlined strategic priorities for the university, one of which focused on issues of educational equity. Second, the university was undergoing an accreditation review and the center helped to "check many boxes" that ensured that the university was meeting standards involving diversity. Finally, the President would retire in the next several years and wanted to leave a legacy on campus that included a commitment to issues of diversity and equity.

The center was renamed, funded at a fraction of the proposed budget with a faculty director supported on 25% course release and a part-time staff member. The center, now called the Social Justice and Equity Project (SJEP), has never been allocated the necessary resources or status on campus to be as successful as we had envisioned in our planning phase. The center's main activities focused on signature events such as an annual Social Justice and Equity Symposium, and funding mini-grants issued to faculty and staff to sponsor their own efforts to support diversity and equity on campus. We had a difficult time attracting faculty, staff, or students who needed to learn about the injustices and inequities that they often perpetuated through their own practices. During the SJEP events, we were often "preaching to the choir" instead of contributing to real, institutionalized, and transformative change on campus.

After two years of establishing events and activities on campus, the SJEP began to lose support from some staff and administrators in the Student Affairs division. They began to realize that the SJEP's success could overshadow their ownership of how diversity is defined and enacted on campus. As a way of reclaiming diversity, several student centers within the division of Student Affairs co-opted the term *social justice* by naming the collection of their centers "social justice centers" even though it remains unclear how the mission of any of the centers relates to social justice and/or equity. When everything on campus is called "social justice," the one center approved as a social justice center becomes delegitimized. In fact, the SJEP no longer exists. It is "on hiatus" while a newly appointed Diversity Officer decides how it should continue and with what charge. A long, hard-fought faculty-driven initiative fell victim to a commonplace institutional structure—the need to have all operations on campus become the ultimate responsibility of an administrator. The SJEP has been included in the Diversity Officer's strategic plan and I have been assured that it will be re-funded and operational in the near future.

Leadership through the Lens of Critical Race Theory—An Analysis of the Journey

Tenets of critical race theory (CRT) are woven throughout this counter-story. An analysis of these tenets illustrates how the center director and other faculty leaders used CRT to analyze situations and events during planning, approval, and implementation stages of the center and made decisions to move the center forward. The first tenet of CRT that appears in this counter-story is the permanence of racism during the approval process of the center. The context of the story is a university where faculty members who teach in the sciences and in business are majority White and male. While not overtly privileged, they earn the highest salaries and have a 'legitimate' voice on campus where matters of budget are concerned. Creating this center occurs during a difficult budget crisis in the state of California, so what gets funded and what does not is in the hands of those privileged gatekeepers. While not overt, the structure of the university does not value those of us who work in fields 'on the margins.' During the approval process, the faculty leaders presenting the center to the Executive Committee and the Academic Senate were all faculty of color, faculty whose voices were not as valued as those of the keepers of the budget. Vaught and Castagno (2008) state that "racism is a pervasive, systematic condition . . . a vast system that structures our institutions and relationships" (p. 96). They also claim that racism adapts to the social and political context over time. Within the context of a budget crisis, the center represented a commitment to a social, political, and economic agenda that countered that of the university as perceived by faculty in the sciences and business allowing racism to become pervasive, systematic, and normalized (Taylor, 2009). Understanding the source of their opposition to the center and how deeply rooted it is in the operations of the institution allowed me as the lead faculty member of the group to use their reasons to frame my presentation and build consensus among faculty members in other disciplines. For some faculty members, this opposition was reason enough to support the center.

This counter-story switches from acknowledging race to culture. As an example of the CRT tenet of Whiteness as property, our dominant-culture colleagues positioned me into a culture with which they were comfortable. During the first presentation to the Executive Committee, key faculty members expressed concerns about the center because the message was being delivered by our leader at the time, an African American woman. At the second meeting, I presented virtually the same proposal for a social justice and equity center and it was accepted by the committee. Vaught and Castagno (2008) highlight how substituting culture for race is significant, because "focusing on culture provides a way to deflect power" (p. 103). Recognition of culture is superficial and "maintains the status quo and makes it look neutral, embodying the neutrality central to Whiteness as property" (p. 104). Many of my colleagues cannot identify the culture to which I belong, nor do they ever ask questions about my identity. I am an Arab American, but I have characteristics such as dark hair and olive skin that allow me to pass for multiple ethnicities. According to Cheryl I. Harris (1993), passing is a feature of subordination and she explains how racial passing is structured on White supremacy. I am able to pass because my colleagues allow it by removing the shield of interference (Harris, 1993). Color-blindness as an ideal (Dixson & Rousseau, 2005) prevents my colleagues from acknowledging my identity because it perpetuates the status quo, their dominance as members of the dominant culture and those with power. In me, they saw qualities that conformed to their own ideas—a consensus builder who appeared to value their opinions, while in reality my positions were virtually identical to those of our first leader, my African American colleague. Both of us understood how we are perceived by our colleagues and used that perception to inform our leadership decisions regarding the center, resulting in my colleague stepping down and me stepping up for the good of the cause—to get the center approved.

The final tenet of CRT represented in this counter-story during the creating, approval, and implementing phases of the center is that of interest convergence. According to Bell (1980), interest convergence occurs only when members of the dominant group deem it beneficial to themselves to support someone from a subordinate group. It is noteworthy that a consensus among faculty and staff that a center focused on social justice and equity on campus was not enough to make it a reality. It was only when the President determined that the center would be beneficial for her and the university that we were funded and began to implement activities and events. Even so, a social justice and equity center (the SJEP) never would have moved beyond an idea if faculty and staff with such vast interests were willing to find out where these interests converged. While some participants had competing interests, they were able to compromise when they envisioned the benefits to their own careers, legacies, and interests. It was only when these personal and professional benefits were no longer evident to some that the center's support diminished.

Conclusions and Implications

While the journey to institutionalize diversity, social justice, and equity efforts on my university campus is not over, I have stepped into a supporting role so that I can focus on my work in public schools in the field of multilingual education. Within each context of the university, the struggle continues to be that of elevating the status of diversity. Over the years, I have realized that accomplishments are individual and a result of the collaboration of a few rather than a collective effort of the university's faculty and staff. Additionally, the individualization of diversity efforts comes at a personal and professional cost that critical leaders must be willing to accept. In the context of my university, relationships with some of my White colleagues in Student Affairs are still strained after I asked critical questions about their competing social justice and equity efforts on campus. I was actually told that asking questions was intimidating to my White colleagues and silenced them. In order for their voices to be heard, I need to silence my own voice—an extraordinary display of White power and privilege. On the other hand, I have built alliances across campus with individuals and groups whose voices are sometimes marginalized. We strategically use our alliances to strengthen our power when we know they can move issues of diversity, equity, and social justice to the forefront of the operations of the university.

As previously stated, counter-stories are tools to expose, analyze, and challenge the majoritarian stories (Solórzano & Yosso, 2009). I share my counter-story with others to make sense of my experiences, and to use it as an entry point for conversations about contradictions and tensions I experienced when promoting diversity, social justice, and equity at the university (Rolón-Dow, 2011). I share the story to explain the process of marginalization at a university, and how it can be overcome by critically analyzing the social and political context in which diversity, social justice, and equity issues are situated. I have used critical race theory to make sense of the process and to develop the ability to recognize the marginalization, to feel validation, and to gain skills to maneuver the institution, not just for survival, but also for transforming the institution to be an environment that supports issues of diversity, equity, and social justice. Culturally responsive leadership in this context is both challenging and rewarding. Understanding the actions necessary to operationalize a center focused on diversity, equity, and social justice requires an applied critical leader to be willing to take personal and professional risks knowing that the benefits far outweigh the consequences.

CULTURALLY RESPONSIVE LEADERSHIP IN PRACTICE

Throughout the phases of the center's existence, the director used the following key leadership strategies (see Figure 13.1), as related to Wink (2011) and aligned to Applied Critical Leadership (Santamaría & Santamaría, 2012, p. 142), to keep the mission of the center alive and operational:

- Name and understand the issue from all perspectives ("Choose to assume a critical race theory lens");
- Identify your strengths and the actions you are willing to take ("Lead by example to meet an unresolved educational need or challenge");
- Identify the interests of key personnel who support the cause ("Need to honor all members of the constituency"); and
- Build consensus where you can ("Use consensus building as the preferred strategy for decision making").

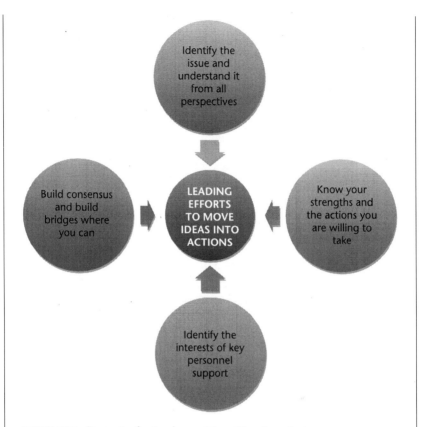

FIGURE 13.1   Strategies for Leaders to Move Ideas into Actions

While these may seem simplistic, when viewed through the lens of Applied Critical Leadership, they become culturally responsive strategies for leaders to navigate institutional practices that can serve as roadblocks when trying to make diversity efforts part of the normal and routine operations of a university. The director highlighted in this chapter used these strategies to create venues for faculty and staff to understand how their interests converged, and how moving from separate and often competing activities and events to college-wide collaborative and institutionalized efforts was beneficial to themselves, the groups whom they represented, and ultimately the culture and operations of the university.

References

Bell, D. (1980). *Brown v. Board of Education* and the interest-convergence dilemma. *Harvard Law Review, 93*(3), 518–533.

Bell, D. (1992). *And we are not saved: The elusive quest for racial justice.* New York, NY: Basic Books.

Bell, D. (1995). Who's afraid of critical race theory? *University of Illinois Law Review, 1995*(4), 893–910.

Carbado, D. (2002). Eracing education. *Equity and Excellence in Education, 35*(2), 181–194. As cited in M. Lynn & L. Parker (2006). Critical race studies in education: Examining a decade of research on U.S. schools. *Urban Review, 38*(4), 257–290.

Chapman, T. (2007). Interrogating classroom relationships and events: Using portraiture and critical race theory in education research. *Educational Researcher, 36*(3), 156–162.

DeCuir, J., & Dixson, A. (2004). "So when it comes out, they aren't that surprised that it is there": Using critical race theory as a tool of analysis of race and racism in education, *Educational Researcher, 33*(5), 26–31.

Delgado, R. (1989). Storytelling for oppositionists and others: A plea for narrative. *Michigan Law Review, 87*(8), 2411–2441.

Delgado, R. (1990). When a story is just a story: Does voice really matter? *Virginia Law Review, 76*(1), 95–111.

Dixson, A., & Rousseau, C. (2005). And we are still not saved: Critical race theory in education ten years later. *Race Ethnicity and Education, 8*(1), 7–27.

Elise, S., Daoud, A., & Rolinson, G. (2013). Perils, promise and pitfalls of diversity: One step forward, two steps back. *International Journal of Diversity in Education, 12(2),* 93–101.

Elsbree, A., & Daoud, A. (2011). "The weather is great today" and other superficial conversations to avoid acknowledging identities and inequities: A critical race theory analysis. *PRAXIS: Gender and Cultural Critiques, 23*(1), 23–30.

Freire, P. (1990). *Pedagogy of the oppressed.* New York, NY: Continuum.

Harris, C. (1993). Whiteness as property. *Harvard Law Review, 106*(8), 1707–1791.

Harris, C. I. (1995). Whiteness as property. In K. Crenshaw, N. Gotanda, G. Peller, & K. Thomas (Eds.), *Critical race theory: The key writings that formed the movement* (pp. 357–383). New York, NY: New Press.

Ladson-Billings, G. (2009). Just what is critical race theory and what's it doing in a *nice* field like education? In E. Taylor, D. Gillborn, & G. Ladson-Billings (Eds.), *Foundations of critical race theory in education* (pp. 17–36). New York, NY: Routledge.

Ladson-Billings, G., & Tate, W. (1995). Toward a theory of critical race theory in education. *Teachers College Record, 97*(1), 47–68.

Lynn, M., & Parker, L. (2006). Critical race studies in education: Examining a decade of research on U.S. schools. *Urban Review, 38*(4), 257–290.

Matsuda, M. (1995). Looking to the bottom: Critical legal studies and reparations. In K. Crenshaw, N. Gotanda, G. Peller, & K. Thomas (Eds.), *Critical race theory: The key writings that formed the movement* (pp. 63–79). New York, NY: New Press.

Rolón-Dow, R. (2011). Race(ing) stories: Digital storytelling as a tool for critical race scholarship. *Race Ethnicity and Education, 14*(2), 159–173.

Santamaría, L. J., & Santamaría, A. P. (2012). *Applied critical leadership in education: Choosing change.* New York, NY: Routledge.

Solórzano, D., Ceja, M., & Yosso, T. (2000). Critical race theory, racial microaggressions, and campus racial climate: The experiences of African American college students. *Journal of Negro Education, 69*(1–2), 60–73.

Solórzano, D., & Yosso, T. (2009). Critical race methodology: Counter-storytelling as an analytical framework for educational research. In E. Taylor, D. Gillborn, &

G. Ladson-Billings (Eds.), *Foundations of critical race theory in education* (pp. 131–147). New York, NY: Routledge.

Taylor, E. (2009). The foundations of critical race theory in education: An introduction. In E. Taylor, D. Gillborn, & G. Ladson-Billings (Eds.), *Foundations of critical race theory in education* (pp. 1–13). New York, NY: Routledge.

Vaught, S., & Castagno, A. (2008). "I don't think I'm a racist": Critical race theory, teacher attitudes, and structural racism. *Race Ethnicity and Education, 11*(2), 95–113.

Wink, J. (2011). *Critical pedagogy: Notes from the real world* (4th ed.). Boston, MA: Pearson, Allyn & Bacon.

14

SOCIAL JUSTICE LEADERSHIP

Silos to Synergies

Shaun Travers, Edwina F. Welch, and Emelyn A. dela Peña

IDEA IN BRIEF

You do not really expect them to work together, the out queer man, the established Black woman, and the fierce Pinay feminist. Certainly a university's traditional educational structure positions them against each other using identity politics, resource allocation, and historical hierarchies of underserved and disenfranchised groups. Opposing this dominant paradigm is important in reimagining new ways of leading in social justice centers, both internally and in partnership. Critical resistance to the silo structures that most colleges and universities put in place around social justice and diversity work, therefore, necessitates critical understanding of the importance of particular leadership roles and deep relationships. A combination of the lived experience and research from three social justice leaders provides numerous examples and strategies to subvert a silo paradigm. Through stories of dialogue, learning, and trust, these leaders (re)consider their own positionality from an individual, group, and systemic level in relation to each other. These collective stories create a new praxis conceptualized as *queer-brown-grrl*. Through new bosses and budget cuts, campus crises, and national diversity debates, a 10-year relationship was tested, stressed, and strengthened. The stories capture the intimate moments, the angry outbursts, and the political nuances of the synergistic, applied critical leadership practice. Utilizing this Applied Critical Leadership (ACL) lens, an understanding of the unique position occupied by social justice leaders individually and collectively within university structures is examined in more complex ways. Their stories of leadership practice and

strategies for empowering individuals to collaborate across departmental and community-specific silos inspire new ways of leading previously only imagined . . . and the silos slowly transform to synergies.
  Keywords: social justice, leadership practice, collaboration

Shaun, Emelyn, and Edwina seem to get along really well, and that surprises many people. When they first began having lunch together in the Faculty Club, other members of the University often would stop by to chat, but usually with just one of them. An awkward introduction might take place, or the other two may be totally ignored. There is a seemingly unconscious gravitational pull of individual identity-based community connections. The out gay White professor stops by to say hello to Shaun and discuss the recent marriage ruling; a member of the Black Staff Association speaks with Edwina about Black History Month; the co-chair of the Committee on the Status of Women chats with Emelyn about the students' Take Back the Night rally. Single conversations about community-specific happenings that on the surface appear to affect a specific identity-based community were common.

At the time, it was uncommon that these three campus diversity and social justice leaders be sitting together at all. Shaun, the Director of the Lesbian Gay Bisexual Transgender (LGBT) Resource Center; Emelyn, the Director of the Women's Center; and Edwina, the Director of the Cross-Cultural Center have lunch. Together? Without an agenda, a program to plan, or an outcome to be produced? From the outside it may appear to be a planning meeting over lunch. From the inside, the connection among the three of us is an act of critical resistance to the dominant narrative of social justice leadership on most college campuses.

Over the last 50 years, women's centers, ethnic-specific and/or multi-/cross-cultural centers, and LGBT resource centers have been established in higher education institutions throughout the nation (Davie, 2002; Lazarus Stewart, 2011; Patton, 2010; Sanlo, Rankin, & Schoenberg, 2002). These types of social justice centers, by virtue of their names, create physical as well as philosophical silos for members of any university community. Individual directors of campus community centers lead through their positions within these organizations, often acting as the voice and face of the community within the organization and outside to communities at large. Through the mere identification of a space, the naming geared to a particular community, a silo is built, with the inherent grain within being of one type and only one type.

So why would the directors of three different social justice centers, the de facto leaders of these community spaces for their specific communities, join together for a shared lunch? Certainly one answer might be that the three centers fall under a specific and clearly defined organizational reporting line. Within most colleges, these types of services are positioned within Student Affairs divisions (Schuh, Jones, & Harper, 2011) and more recently in newly emerging offices for Chief Diversity Officers (Williams & Wade-Golden, 2008). But structural placement within a hierarchy of the university only serves to explain meetings and co-programmatic efforts. Certainly these structures would not account for the soup and salad at the Faculty Club.

Literature Considered

A review of the literature reveals that, prior to the development of LGBT centers, little discussion of cross-issue organizing among women's centers and cross-cultural centers existed (Davie, 2002; Hord, 2005; Kasper, 2004; Stennis-Williams, Terrell, & Haynes, 1998). Thus, because of the unique role that center directors play, both as administrators and as community leaders within identity groups, they occupy unique positions to expand a campus's overall orientation toward diversity initiatives. This broader expansion of the definition of diversity challenges center staff, as well as college faculty and staff, to work together and challenge existing narrow definitions of diversity, namely—and in this order—race, gender, and sexuality (Travers, 2009).

Services for students that are historically underrepresented, marginalized, and/or experience systemic oppression vary in colleges and universities (Pascarella &Terenzini, 2005). Sadly, colleges unintentionally impose a binary and dialectic approach to identity, asking individuals to choose which piece of their identity is most salient at any given time. Leaders within these institutions are often asked to do the same in their own social justice practice. Silos abound in the ivory tower. Some leaders, however, complicate these segregated notions.

The apparent silo nature of the centers for which we as social justice leaders have responsibility does not suggest a quick answer to the lunch questions. Applied critical leadership (Santamaría, 2014; Santamaría & Santamaría, 2012), with its grounding in the work of transformational leadership, critical pedagogy, and critical race theory sheds light on the lunch in ways that illuminate the relationships beyond silos and into synergies. Through a disciplined, empirical inquiry using autoethnographic portraiture, the complexity of relationships necessary to transform silos to synergies reveals itself as a method for understanding applied critical leadership.

Research Journey

In the spring of 2008, three friends gathered on a regular basis to tell stories to one another that we recorded, transcribed, and rigorously analyzed. The three colleagues, Shaun, Emelyn, and Edwina shared a journey of research together, attempting to understand the complexities of how they enacted social justice leadership. The resulting stories began to explain the process of relationship building and navigation that characterized the evolving relationships (Travers, 2009). Trust, dialogue, and learning, when understood over a significant period of time, began to emerge as the key components to understanding silos to synergies in light of further analysis through a lens of applied critical leadership (Santamaría, 2014; Santamaría & Santamaría, 2012). In what ways do trust, dialogue, and learning occur? It is messy, and it begins with stories.

Autoethnographic portraiture blends two current methodologies in education research: autoethnography and portraiture. Portraiture (Lawrence-Lightfoot & Hoffmann Davis, 1997) builds on many qualitative data collection methods utilized in case studies (Merriam, 1998; Yin, 2003) and narrative inquiry (Clandindin, 2007; Waterhouse, 2007). Autoethnography, Chávez, Guido-DiBrito, and Mallory (2003) note, has "legitimacy as collection tools in educational environs for creating new knowledge by incorporating personal knowledge into research" (p. 453). Portraits are stories, and autoethnographic portraiture is empirical storytelling that includes the researchers.

Being Alone

We all knew the experiences of being alone. We rarely discussed it, but there we were, sitting in a room together for the first in a series of several such conversations, to deeply consider the ways in which we interacted. And through the course of the first 20 minutes of our dialogue, we learned of a common emotional feeling. Even though each of us deeply and intimately connected ourselves in an identity-based community in which we worked, we all felt isolated and alone from that community. And only through stretching away from that identity-based community, only by reaching out to others who were different from us and trusting them did we find and create community. It was a basic practice of applied critical leadership (Santamaría & Santamaría, 2012) we had in common.

Concurrently, we had stumbled into our most profound professional relationships. Shaun was hired as the first full-time Director of UC San Diego's LGBT Resource Center, and began his leadership of the center knowing he would have some level of connection to the other two established centers. Little did we know that our relationships would profoundly change each other's lives. Edwina, the Director of the Cross-Cultural Center, had come from running a women's center where notions of privilege and power made it almost impossible to lead community to an understanding of social justice practice. The collaboration with the other two centers offered a ray of hope that it was possible. For Emelyn, the Women's Center Director taking the helm after the first director parted, the relationships across the centers offered a way to combine all her passions and activism.

Having been approved for research through three intensive Human Subjects Review boards, there were many safety protocols in place. Still, the risks felt significant as the red recorder light glowed brightly, capturing our every word for later transcription, analysis, and publication. Although our personal, professional, and leadership relationships were over a half-dozen years old at the time of the research project, our conversations took on weight and importance as we imagined our stories being shared more broadly. The first step into applied critical leadership practice had started with building trust.

Emelyn's reflection on comfort sets the stage for a story related to the praxis of *queer-brown-grrl*. With typical aplomb, she said, "I've never been comfortable in all-Filipino spaces. Never; unless it was my family. But being in KP [Kaibang Pilipino—the UC San Diego Filipino student organization], even though I was the chair of KP, that just made me horribly uncomfortable."

Edwina and Shaun shared a glance, surprised by an awkward turn of conversation. Emelyn was by far one of the strongest, most powerful Pilipinas they knew; a strong voice in one of the most vocal militant feminist organizations working toward social change in the U.S. and the Philippines. Uncomfortable in the ethnic community for which she clearly had grounded her activism? It made little sense in the moment. But she started to explain more.

> I think a lot of it has to do with race, class, size issues for me. I was darker than what I perceived everybody else to be. I was fat, and I was strong, and so I think of all those coming together just kind of didn't make me a popular person, even though I was the leadership of the organization. I felt very much like an outcast most of the time.

So did Shaun. Beginning his career doing LGBT work as an openly bisexual man married to a woman, his journey through relationships and attractions had done little to inure him to many typical queer activists. His marriage often was a point of critique regarding the hetero-normative privilege that his relationship experienced. But perhaps the voices in his head were more damning than any actual words spoken to his face. Regardless, Emelyn's feelings of being outcast resonated with him. They also did with Edwina, her intense focus and eye contact markers of attention, jotted in the research notes.

Emelyn continued, saying,

> It was in SAAC [UC San Diego's Student Affirmative Action Committee— a coalition of organizations representing historically marginalized and underrepresented students], where I felt like "Oh, I love this space," and so I think that's where I found that I like to be around diverse groups of people. Working closely with two other people [referencing first Edwina, and then Shaun] kind of brings all of that together for me. It also brings this level of comfort, in that I feel very young in my profession, and to have two other people to bounce my stuff off of just makes me feel safe. Like I can't f*** up that much.

Laughter among the three of us is common, especially when we use vulgar language, a practice we refrain from in public and professional spaces, of course. But when the three of us are together, our metaphorical hair down, we often become base. We keep it real in ways that ease the difficulties of the workplace; in ways that critical race theory may even argue as necessary for applied critical leadership in higher education (Santamaría & Santamaría, 2012). Edwina echoed Emelyn's reflections with some of her own. "Being in spaces where we can be strong, but we know that it's not a space that feeds us," she begins, as she shares her own leadership experiences in identity-based organizations, "there's actually a theory out there called leadership oppression, where people like you because you're strong, but they don't like you."

As we sit together and listen to each other, there exists such a connection among the three of us, with whom, from the outside looking in, there is very little in common. We exchange nods and smiles as Edwina continues, "They really love it if you come and then lead the organization. And get the work done and crack the whip. You get everything done; that's what the organization needs. But as a way of feeding yourself, it doesn't happen." It echoes back to critical race theory and the need to ground our understanding in the voices and stories people share.

Shaun self-consciously reaches for a pastry, his outward actions belying his inward agreement—starving for community as a leader of an identity-based community that can hold complexity and critical engagement.

> We know that, and so I need different spaces to be myself, I find that even today. I can go and be in a space. And function. And like everybody. And do well. And be giving more in that space than I would necessarily be giving in this space [indicating the context of our working relationship] because I know that you all understand the days where I don't feel like giving and it won't be personal.

We are gentle with each other. Our team of three needs each other, even though we are different in so many fundamental ways. These differences and a shared passion for social justice brought us together at the very beginning, and our differences and passions continue to define us without separating us one from another. Edwina finishes, reflecting on the identity-based organizations she has led with this wry observation of human social behavior: "I can be strong for them today, but they go out after the end of the program. And nobody's asking me to go."

We commiserate, the three of us, so different from each other. We tell our own unique stories, yet they sound the same. We get angry with each other over our personal habits, our professional practices, and the privileges that one has and another will never experience. We care deeply about each other through fierce battles of space, budget, and power on the campus. There are deep truths to doing the work of social justice, applying critical leadership, especially in higher education. Those deep truths are necessary to uncover, albeit a scary process to do so, in order to truly practice the type of leadership that transforms our work in truly critical ways.

Much of what we do attempts to transform an institution mired in structurally oppressive systems that see the *queer-brown-grrl* as three distinct individuals, not as ever being embodied in one person (Crenshaw, 1989). These systems create pipelines that often, literally, have one or two Ph.D.s in certain disciplines from certain ethnic communities come through them in the nation each year. One or two people in the nation. Yet we still attempt to transform these institutions through our community building within and through different communities. Audre Lorde (1984) taught that challenging one oppression requires challenging all oppressions, even when it may feel like one group may get farther along if they go it alone. But we all know it doesn't work that way. Our stories teach us lessons of being alone in the work, especially if we do not stretch beyond our identity to form communities.

Leadership as Service

We teach lessons of community, complexity, and justice through the daily leadership practices within the communities we serve. We share critical and historical legacies and aspects of our communities directly within and across the complex web of diversity. This liberates all people from oppressive systems of knowledge that perpetuate an us-versus-them oppression Olympics many learned in early years of education—even in the most well-meaning of K–12 environments. These primary and secondary school systems are embedded in social structures that still marginalize so many, reinforcing constructions that often are critiqued only from an adult perspective, that is, when a student begins the higher education journey. As social justice leaders within a higher educational context, we train students to examine the systems of power in place, to disrupt, to challenge existing definitions of allegedly fixed categories like gender, sexuality, race, and ability (Weber, 2001).

We know our stories are powerful in the process of transforming individuals and institutions. Critical race theory (Bell, 1992; Delgado & Stefancic, 2001), queer theory, and other liberation writings (Anzaldua, 1987; Lorde, 1984) inform why we do what we do. Even as we come together to share stories, we know they exist as counter-narratives to how institutions have been historically and explicitly established. The alleged sisterhood of the women's movement has been hiding the true racial divide among White women and women of color. There is also the construction of people-of-color-in-solidarity that ignores racial tensions between and among socially defined categories of race and ethnicity. Also there are fractious divisions among LGBT communities inherent in an acronym composed of a widely divergent understanding of how sex, gender, sexual orientation, gender identity, and expression define and limit constructions of community. Our stories of leadership in higher education's social justice centers across communities and identities reveal how leaders can be truly alone if they attempt to parrot the liberal notions of feeling much, but doing little to challenge or change the status quo. We all can build our own silo, but we will be lonely within it.

Applied critical leadership intersects transformational leadership, critical pedagogy, and critical race theory (Santamaría, 2014; Santamaría & Santamaría, 2012). The interface of these three theories constructs places for conversations of the practice. These new structures can build new and more sustained communities of practice (Wenger, 2002) where the *queer-brown-grrl* can be fully herself. Returning to the director's narrative, we search for clues to navigate the experience of being alone. The stories reveal experiences that create synergies in both unexpected and typical ways.

Applied Critical Leadership Practices (or How to Begin to Honor the *Queer-Brown-Grrl*)

You can almost always count on Shaun to show up to a meeting with a type-written agenda. And you can almost always be sure that Emelyn will not. In fact, you never know from one meeting to the next whether she'll even bring her pen. But Edwina will have a pen, and will take copious hand-written notes, even if they are never, ever looked at again. But somehow we made it work, and we have all learned to utilize our particular strengths to contribute to this synergistic relationship, a hallmark of applied critical leadership (Santamaría & Santamaría, 2012).

Research on effective leadership reveals that "the most effective leaders surround themselves with the right people and then maximize their team" (Rath & Conchie, 2008, p. 2). This particular team has learned to maximize each other's strength and to trust the process in which each director exercises leadership and management. It is almost as if by design how well the directors' collective strengths came together to form our leadership synergy. Rath and Conchie (2008) describe Executing, Influencing, Relationship Building, and Strategic Thinking as the four domains of leadership strength for making a great leadership team. In their research, they found that the best teams had each of these domains represented, stating, "although individuals need not be well-rounded, teams should be" (p. 23).

In examining our own leadership strengths we found that Shaun's dominant strengths were in Executing and Influencing, Emelyn's in Relationship Building and Influencing, and Edwina's in Strategic Thinking and Relationship Building. Amazingly, our individual Strengths Finder (Buckingham & Clifton, 2001) themes collectively mapped onto all four leadership strengths domains. Shaun knew how to get things done and had a way of helping our team gain entrance into circles previously closed to us. Emelyn held the team together and provided the much-needed collective energy to the group. Edwina kept us focused on future possibilities and identified places for intellectual and professional growth (Rath & Conchie, 2008, pp. 25–26).

Our styles and approaches were so incredibly different from each other's, and yet we did not let these differences push us further into our silos, instead working through the initial discomfort and confusion to find common ground. Often the work was painful and difficult, highlighting not only differences in work style, but deeply held beliefs and assumptions about individual identities and communities and differing Diversity Paradigms (Palmer, 1989). Our willingness to engage in these critical conversations with each other was yet another example of how our leadership practice transformed us both personally and professionally.

CULTURALLY RESPONSIVE LEADERSHIP IN PRACTICE

While the above example is quite striking, however, the mundane is perhaps the most compelling illustrations of applied critical leadership. **Meet and talk** with each other. **Engage in dialogue**, not because you are supposed to, but **because the dialogue can sustain you** personally and as a leader through the loneliness of the silos in which too many of us are embedded. **Do it regularly**, without an agenda. **Tell stories to each other** of your work, your practice, your leadership. **Sustain the dialogues** for a significant period of time—an hour or two—and over a significant period of time—a semester or two. **Have the conversations with people different from you**, both in terms of identity, and of the communities they serve. Have the **conversations in public spaces**, where people see you in dialogue with each other— those public spaces where leaders come out of silos for a shared meal.

Allow the **dialogues** to happen **without an action item** on the table, but don't be afraid to take action. One idea turned up in one of our trust-building coffee hours where many ideas sparked our mutual passion. One of the stories shared among Emelyn, Edwina, and Shaun turned into work together on a significant joint project, a leadership program for undergraduates. This work was the genesis not only of the directors' collaborative relationships, but also the synergy created among all three centers and their entire staff.

Toward Institutionalizing Diversity Initiatives

The Chancellor's Undergraduate Diversity Learning Institute, or CUDLI (pronounced kud-lee) as we affectionately call it, had been an ongoing collaborative of the three directors since the fall of 2003. The three directors conceived of a year-long leadership institute, under the auspices of the Chancellor, which would train 20 first- and second-year students regarding the issues and concepts that concerned the three centers. This program concurrently moves our centers' work in new, unexpected directions.

A long summer of work began among the three directors as we examined and refined the structures, philosophies, and pedagogies that we sought to employ in a syllabus for the year. Our model built on UCLA's Social Change Model of Leadership Development (Astin & Astin, 1996), which takes students through an explicit process of self-transformation. We coupled this with a deep understanding of social justice as a theory and practice (Adams, Bell, & Griffin, 1997).

What CUDLI did for the directors was provide an intense, weekly dialogue around both the structures of the Institute itself, but also the stories, experiences, and working concepts of how we each approached our work. We were able to learn deeply about each other, both in terms of working styles and working philosophies. It was not an easy task for us to come from three distinct and individual spaces to create a joint experience that reflected the values of all three spaces and all three directors.

But the journey of CUDLI, year after year, provided space for dialogue, trust, and learning among us that served as a basis for many, many other projects. Because of the intense amount of time it took to co-create and implement the Institute, we became more intimately connected and more attuned to the similarities and differences among us. One of us needs to be at a whiteboard and front and center in his leadership, the next of us needs to take copious notes (that might never be used) to feel engaged, and one of us doodles but comes up with the most profound connecting insights.

After the third year, we gave CUDLI away. We had, at that point, spent three complete years fully invested in the concepts of CUDLI as a philosophical and leadership praxis. But concurrently, each of the centers had been growing and changing. The smallest of the three, the LGBT Resource Center, had finally added an assistant director to its full-time staff, bringing it up to three people. With that addition, the three centers had parallel structures with enough people to allow for others to do the work of CULDI beyond the directors. At the end of the third year, CUDLI was handed off to the three assistant directors, one from each center. The directors, after three years of implementing CUDLI, were done with it in many ways, and stepped completely away from the project. Here, we were able to witness the tensions around applied critical leadership when organizational structures increase the complexity for the leader.

The debt of gratitude the directors owe to the CUDLI experience is immense. Although time-consuming, intense and, at times, burdensome, the space created among the professional staff around dialogue regarding our work, working styles, and experiences with identity and community was precious. CUDLI marked the most extensive collaboration of cross-cultural, women's, and LGBT centers for many years (Travers, 2009). But even as CUDLI faded from view, new structures emerged from the synergy around student leadership.

Sharing Knowledge with Interns

At UC San Diego the Women's Center, Cross-Cultural Center, and LGBT Resource Center all have undergraduate interns. They are often student leaders in activist organizations as well as student employees of each of their respective centers. Through the experiences first developed in CUDLI, their internships are now fully academically integrated, including course work, graded papers, and academic credit earned for the internship experience. These students understand the synergy of working together, while critically examining the silos from a comprehensive curriculum that has emerged. The interns develop deep relationships with each other over the course of their academic year experience, subverting the silo that is each center, as well as the silo that is the alleged separate movements of racial justice, reproductive and gender justice, and justice for the LGBT community. Learning, trust, and dialogue over time are the bedrock of the class.

Of course, for the interns to understand this level of connection, there must be a comprehensive understanding on the part of the professional staff of social justice leaders. Each of the leaders of a community-specific center work to build the skills to train others specifically on the "other" area—for example, LGBT Center staff present trainings on racism and sexism, Women's Center staff present training on LGBT oppression and racism, and Cross-Cultural Center staff train on sexism and LGBT oppression. This level of *queer-brown-grrl* praxis does not come easily. All this happens in the constructs of the complex, intertwined system that is the modern college campus. Budget cuts are inevitable, campus crisis is common, and the national stage on which many debates occur every two to four years, depending on the political cycles, make these relationships more difficult. In fact, it may even make them seem unimportant. There are so many other things that compete for the attention of social justice leaders. What can be done?

Sometimes it has to start with trust. Do you trust enough to develop a joint philosophy or mission statement and a jointly named identity as *Campus Community Centers*? Do you trust each other enough to examine your own privilege *in front of* your colleagues? Do you trust each other enough to share *all* of your budget information—even at the risk of looking rich or feeling poor? Do you trust enough to even establish a shared financial account and decide how to spend money out of it jointly? Sometimes honoring the *queer-brown-grrl* has to start with trust.

Trust

Edwina, Shaun, and Emelyn had been discussing the barriers to their relationships, specifically regarding resources (Travers, 2009). "F*** both of you,"

Emelyn said. She didn't mean it exactly in that moment, but was tapping into past experiences that had remained unspoken among the three of us.

Emelyn: And I hear it all the time on campus. "Oh, Women's Center? What do you do over there?"

Edwina: And they don't know what the Cross does, but it's got brown people in it. So they think it's better.

Shaun: Right.

Emelyn: I think fundamentally on this campus that's what it's about. Because race is such the paradigm around diversity that that's just automatically where it's going to be the attention to "Oh, diversity that's the Cross-Cultural Center's job."

Edwina: It does suck though.

Shaun: Yeah, I mean, my question is "How do we make sense of that complexity?" . . . How then do we even sit in the room together without saying "F*** you both; I'm on my own y'all."?

Emelyn: I think that in a lot of ways . . . I try not to think about it too much. I kind of accept it for what it is. And in some ways, I think I look to you [Shaun] for support, because I feel like you understand what I'm going through. And that's been really helpful at times when I felt like "Wow, I was really just sh** upon." "That's happened to you before, Shaun, and so I find a lot of support in that, but in other ways I'm just like F***, that's just the way that it is," and if I try to think about it too hard I'm going to be like, "F*** both of you, you know?" And so I try not to think about it too much and try to understand . . . where is this coming from?

It is incredibly difficult to have a commitment to social justice, and yet at the same time attend to the communities that are the intimates to our space, and to negotiate the political realities of the three campus community centers and how we are resourced so differently. Social justice would assume that we were equally resourced. We are not. We do not necessarily share that depth of inequality with our constituents, but it is noticeable from our size of space and size of staff to any critical observer. Additionally, a social justice perspective might assume that in each of our centers we address areas of oppression (racism, sexism, etc.) equally. We do not. Our constituent communities often define the lens through which we address social justice issues, and that lens is often shaded by the identities of the people in our spaces. Directors, who have a strong commitment to social justice, navigate that reality and gently share broader understandings of social justice with our constituents.

The ease with which the laughter comes from our lips, and the same ease that we have in knowing that saying "F*** you" and going out on our own, dissolving the collaborative that is the Campus Community Centers would be a disservice to the people we have committed to this journey with through social justice work—that all comes from a trusting relationship.

The literature related to leadership in these centers won't get you there. The much-touted Council for the Advancement of Standards in Higher Education (2009) oft-used assessment will not reveal the missing *queer-brown-grrl* within your midst. The more recent guidance for cultural centers in higher education (Patton, 2010), in particular Jenkins tri-sector practitioner model from *Culture Centers in Higher Education,* will only increase your mastery of the silo, and perhaps allow you to polish the silo to a gleaming white ivory. But the tower you create may be a prison for you alone. The tower crumbles in on itself while the *queer-brown-grrl* stands alone outside of three silos, wondering which is for her, wishing for leadership from any social justice leader that affirms her existence in the world. And by affirming her existence, affirming the application of a critical leadership necessary to slowly transform the silos to synergies and help her transverse all spaces wholly and intact. And maybe even have a nice lunch.

Authors' Note

Shaun Travers, LGBT Resource Center, University of California, San Diego; Emelyn dela Peña, Office of Student Life, Harvard College; Edwina Welch, Cross-Cultural Center, University of California, San Diego.

This research and line of inquiry could not have been achieved without the personal relationships among the three authors inherent in applied critical leadership. Special thanks to Lorri J. Santamaría for her continued support of this work throughout all our educational endeavors.

Correspondence concerning this chapter should be sent to Shaun Travers, LGBT Resource Center, University of California, San Diego, La Jolla, CA 92093–0023. Email: stravers@ucsd.edu

References

Adams, M., Bell, L. A., & Griffin, P. (Eds.). (1997). *Teaching for diversity and social justice: A sourcebook.* New York, NY: Routledge.

Anzaldua, G. (1987). *Borderlands/La Frontera: The new Mestiza.* San Francisco, CA: Spinsters/Aunt Lute.

Astin, H. S., & Astin, A. W. (1996). *A social change model of leadership development guidebook, version 3.* Los Angeles, CA: Higher Education Research Institute, University of California, Los Angeles.

Bell, D. (1992). *Faces at the bottom of the well: The permanence of racism.* New York, NY: Basic Books.

Black Educator. (2007). Retrieved from http://blackeducator.blogspot.com/2007/08/blog-post.html

Buckingham, M., & Clifton, D. O. (2001). *Now, discover your strengths: How to develop your talents and those of the people you manage.* London, UK: Simon & Schuster.

Chávez, A. F., Guido-DiBrito, F., & Mallory, S. L. (2003). Learning to value the "other": A framework of individual diversity development. *Journal of College Student Development, 4*(44), 453–469.

Clandindin, D. J. (Ed.). (2007). *Handbook of narrative inquiry: Mapping a methodology.* Thousand Oaks, CA: Sage.

Council for the Advancement of Standards in Higher Education. (2009). *CAS professional standards for higher education* (7th ed.). Washington, DC: Author.

Crenshaw, K. (1989). "Demarginalizing the intersection of race and sex: A black feminist critique of antidiscrimination doctrine, feminist theory, and antiracist politics." *University of Chicago Legal Forum,* 1989, 139–167.

Davie, S. L. (2002). Drawing new maps. In S. L. Davie (Ed.), *University and college women's centers: A journey toward equity* (pp. 447–500). Westport, CT: Greenwood Press.

Delgado, R., & Stefancic, J. (2001). *Critical race theory: An introduction.* New York, NY: New York University Press.

Hord, F. L. (Ed.). (2005). *Black cultural centers: Politics of survival and identity.* Chicago, IL: Third World Press.

Kasper, B. (2004). "Campus-based women's centers: A review of problems and practices." *Affilia, 19*(2), 185–198.

Lawrence-Lightfoot, S., & Hoffmann Davis, J. (1997). *The art and science of portraiture.* San Francisco, CA: Jossey-Bass.

Lazarus Stewart, D. (2011). *Multicultural student services on campus: Building bridges, re-visioning community.* Sterling, VA: Stylus.

Lorde, A. (1984). *Sister outsider: Essays and speeches.* Berkeley, CA: Crossing Press.

Merriam, S. (1998). *Qualitative research and case study applications in education.* San Francisco, CA: Jossey-Bass.

National Association of Student Personnel Administrators and American College Personnel Association. (2004, June). *Learning reconsidered: A campus-wide focus on the student experience.* Retrieved from http://www.naspa.org

Palmer, J. (1989). Three paradigms for diversity change leaders. *OD Practitioner, 21*(1), 15–18.

Palmer, J. (1994). Diversity: Three paradigms. In E. Y. Cross, J. H. Katz, F. A. Miller, & E. W. Seashore (Eds.), *The promise of diversity* (pp. 252–258). Burr Ridge, IL: Irwin.

Pascarella, E. T., & Terenzini, P. T. (2005). *How college impacts students: A third decade of research.* Jossey-Bass Higher and Adult Education Series. San Francisco, CA: Jossey-Bass.

Patton, L. D. (2010). *Culture centers in higher education: Perspectives on identity, theory, and practice.* Sterling, VA: Stylus.

Rath, T., & Conchie, B. (2008). *Strengths based leadership: Great leaders, teams, and why people follow.* New York, NY: Gallup Press.

Rost, J. C. (1993). *Leadership for the twenty-first century.* Westport, CT: Praeger.

Sanlo, R. L., Rankin, S., & Schoenberg, R. (2002). *Our place on campus: Lesbian, gay, bisexual, transgender services and programs in higher education.* Westport, CT: Greenwood Press.

Santamaría, L. J. (2014). Critical change for the greater good: Multicultural dimensions of educational leadership toward social justice and educational equity. *Education Administration Quarterly (EAQ), 50*(3), 347–391.

Santamaría, L. J., & Santamaría, A. P. (2012). *Applied critical leadership in education: Choosing change.* New York, NY: Routledge.

Schuh, J. H., Jones, S. R., & Harper, S. R. (Eds.). (2011). *Student services: A handbook for the profession* (5th ed.). San Francisco, CA: Jossey-Bass.

Senge, P. (2006). *The fifth discipline: The art and practice of the learning organization* (2nd ed.). New York, NY: Doubleday.

Stennis-Williams, S., Terrell, M. C., & Haynes, A. W. (1998). The emergent role of multicultural education centers on predominately white campuses. In M. C. Terrell (Series Ed.) & D. J. Wright (Vol. Ed.), *From survival to success: Promoting minority student retention* [Monograph Series Vol. 9]. (ED334999) (pp. 73–98). Washington, DC: National Association of Student Personnel Administrators.

Travers, S. R. (2009). *Trust, learning and dialogue: A portrait of leadership practice in higher education's social justice centers* (Doctoral dissertation). University of California, San Diego (b6636504). Retrieved from http://escholarship.org/uc/item/2sw4r07x

Waterhouse, J. (2007). From narratives to portraits: Methodology and methods to portray leadership. *Curriculum Journal, 18*(3), 271–286.

Weber, L. (2001). *Understanding race, class, gender and sexuality: A conceptual framework.* New York, NY: McGraw-Hill.

Wenger, E. (2002). *Communities of practice: Learning, meaning, and identity.* New York, NY: Cambridge University Press.

Williams, D., & Wade-Golden, K. (2008). *The chief diversity officer: A primer for presidential leaders.* Washington, DC: American Council of Education.

Yin, R. (2003). *Case study research: Design and methods.* Thousand Oaks, CA: Sage.

15

CULTURALLY RESPONSIVE LEADERSHIP IN AOTEAROA NEW ZEALAND

Establishing Opportunities through Tertiary and Community Partnerships

Colleen Young

IDEA IN BRIEF

Access and equity for *all* students is of paramount importance if we seek to live in a world of social and economic equilibrium. This chapter combines a classic grounded theory, comparative analysis approach to the analysis of secondary data (Andrews, Higgins, Waring, & Lalor (2012). The goal of this chapter is to ascertain how, and in what ways, the key characteristics of the Applied Critical Leadership (ACL) approach (Santamaría, 2014; Santamaría & Santamaría, 2012) have been reflected through the actions of leaders and members of six Community Partnerships (CPs), as reported in a process evaluation of six Community Partnerships (CPs) (Young & Clinton, 2014). The main aim of the process evaluation was to assess how the six CPs contributed to improving opportunities for underserved students living in high-poverty regions in Auckland, New Zealand.

Keywords: New Zealand Youth Guarantee, University–Community Partnerships, Vocational Education

Auckland City has a population of just over 1.5 million people, of which the majority identify as European/Pākehā ethnicity (56%), followed by Asian (22%), Pasifika (Peoples from the Pacific Islands) (5%), Māori (New Zealand's Indigenous people) (10%), and other ethnicities (7%) (Statistics New Zealand, 2013). The establishment of CPs in New Zealand evolved from a Ministry of Education (MoE) Youth Guarantee Policy (Ministry of Education, 2015a) aimed at "bringing together education, the community and employers to deliver new vocational learning opportunities for young people." The policy specifically focuses on "priority group learners including Māori, Pasifika and learners with special needs" (Youth Guarantee, 2015). The Youth Guarantee Policy is a policy instrument to promote a mechanism to improve access and equity for all students in New Zealand. The MoE policy and related initiative to establish CPs nationwide represents a significant step toward strengthening local communities through harnessing their potential, existing resources, and building their capacity through knowledge sharing and the use of student data, in direct alignment with the ACL approach (Santamaría & Santamaría, 2012).

At this stage, it is important that I disclose my background as a researcher. First, I was the principal investigator for the MoE evaluation of the six CPs (Young & Clinton, 2014). Like many of my colleagues who were engaged participants in the initial research on CPs, I am passionate about informing and improving on secondary–tertiary interventions that re-engage priority learners and provide each one of them with improved postsecondary learning and employment opportunities.

The study findings of CPs in Auckland, New Zealand, demonstrate some of the elements of ACL well, while other elements such as critical race theory (CRT) indicate a need for a greater level of direction and attention in the context of the CPs studied. My goal for you as you read this chapter (whether you are a current leader within a secondary school, are striving to become a leader in an educational setting, are a leader in a tertiary institution, a policy-maker, an employer of youth, or a community leader) is to think about ways in which you could improve collaboration and the sharing of knowledge and resources between institutions in your community. This, in order to strengthen and build capacity to better address the needs and to improve the access of underserved students to both vocational and academic pathways within the secondary and tertiary systems.

In a practical sense, this includes considering ways you may be involved in removing barriers between institutions, and work toward a shared funding model and data system for collecting student data, developing a seamless transition process for students to move into tertiary education while continuing to study in a secondary school setting. Utilizing links between your organization, other learning institutions, or employers to intervene in the way funding is allocated to students and perhaps also partake in a conversation about how you could promote a student-centered approach, rather than an institutional approach to funding, would be a step in the right direction. In addition, I would encourage you to consider how to have the *real* conversations with your colleagues at all levels within your institution or organization. This means bringing to the surface the much-needed ACL approach and way of leading that are often thought about and discussed at some level, but not so often actioned or articulated in a way that seeps through to *evident* educational change. We need to continue to find evidence of best practice leadership, which demonstrates an increase in access and equity for underserved students to complete secondary school, and make the transition to a tertiary institution and eventually into gainful employment.

Context Matters

In New Zealand, the number of students achieving NCEA Level 2 (the New Zealand national qualification for Year 12, equivalent U.S. K–11, age 17 years) is increasing. However, evidence shows that the ethnic disparity in achievement rates for secondary school students is widening, establishing the need for culturally responsive approaches in teaching and leadership. This is highlighted in lower-than-average achievement rates for Māori and Pasifika students, indicating the average achievement rates for Māori students (55.1%), and for Pasifika students (67.6%) are still behind those of their counterparts, including European/ Pākehā (78.9%) and Asian students (87.9%) (Education Counts, 2013).

Unsurprisingly, student engagement and retention rates share similar results for students remaining in school. For example, fewer Māori (67.9%) and Pasifika students (81.3%) remain in secondary school when compared to European/ Pākehā (85.1%) and Asian (93.9%) students (Education Counts, 2013). Moreover, the Not in Education, Employment or Training (NEET) rate for all youth in 2013 was nearly 12% (Statistics New Zealand, 2014). These statistics demonstrate the significance of the ongoing challenge within New Zealand to disrupt the status quo that indicates that current overall student outcomes are acceptable by opening up the critical conversations as to *how* leaders within government and local communities can instigate *real change* for our priority students to improve access and equity outcomes for 'all.' Educational leaders need to create multiple, relevant, and meaningful pathways for all students rather than continue to rely on a one-stop shop that suits university-going students.

Similarly, from a global perspective, across the OECD countries, nearly one in every five secondary students is not equipped to compete in the job market, with an average of 20% of them not completing secondary school (OECD, 2012). These students are also recorded as being from low socioeconomic backgrounds and are "twice as likely" (OECD, 2012, p. 9) to be underachieving compared to their high socioeconomic peers. Moreover, in the United States "each year, almost one third of all public high school students—and nearly one half of all African American, Latino and American Indian descent students—fail to graduate from public high school with their class" (Bridgeland, Dilulio, & Morison, 2006, p. 3).

We know that student failure and dropout becomes both an economic and a social issue (OECD, 2012; Burrus & Roberts, 2012; Carnevale & Desrochers, 2002). For example, the International Labour Organisation indicates that up to 73 million young people are currently seeking work (International Labour Organisation, 2015) and this problem is compounded by the prediction that in 2020 there will be a worldwide shortfall of 85 million "high- and middle-skilled workers" (McKinsey Center for Government, 2013). Furthermore, it appears there is little communication between secondary, tertiary, and industry sectors. For example, a report on the transition from Education to Employment claimed that: "employers, education providers and youth live in parallel universes . . . They have fundamentally different understandings of the same situation (McKinsey Center for Government, 2013, p. 18). This means that to improve students' education and employment opportunities there is a greater need to collaborate, share knowledge, and work together, to allow underserved students to have early access to the workplace and learn the skills required for employment.

Need for Systemic Educational Change in Local Settings and the Youth Guarantee Policy

Hopkins (2007) claimed that as schools are the main vehicle for educational change, in order to rebalance power within the system, 'system leadership' within schools is required to bring about transformative changes. In other words, leaders can attempt to implement change within some schools or in some classrooms, but to progress and fight for social justice and 'whole population change' then systemic change is required over a long period of time (Hopkins, 2007, p. 3). This therefore indicates a need for educators to collaborate and share their knowledge, skills, and expertise in order to build system leadership capabilities. Establishing CPs in local communities is one way in which to build capacity and aim for continuous improvement within a local community (DuFour & Marzano, 2011; Hopkins, 2007, p. 12). Of importance is that these CPs work to gain a collective understanding of *what* work needs to be done and then create support teams to implement these changes (DuFour & Marzano, 2011, p. 61).

To meet this need, the New Zealand Youth Guarantee policy has been implemented in order to make a significant contribution toward achieving the government's Better Public Service target of 85% of 18-year-olds achieving NCEA Level 2 or an equivalent qualification by 2017 (Ministry of Education, 2015b). The achievement of this target requires a substantial lift in achievement rates across all students, but particularly for Māori and Pasifika learners (Levin, 2012) and learners with special education needs. CPs working within the parameters of the policy aim to serve the wider community including the learners, parents, *whānau* (family), and employers; improve attendance rates, retention, and engagement of learners; achieve more equitable results for priority group learners including Māori, Pasifika, and learners with special needs; deliver new vocational learning opportunities for young people; and establish equal opportunities and pathways for 70% of young people not currently attending universities (Ministry of Education, 2015a).

Literature Considered

This review begins with an overview of community partnerships. This is followed by evidence from the review, which demonstrates alignment of best practice CP elements to many ACL characteristics.

Community Partnerships

Partnerships bring people from various backgrounds and different organizations together with the goal of serving their community. Bryan and Henry (2012) aptly describe partnerships as developing:

> collaborative initiatives and relationships among school personnel, family members, and community members and representatives of community-based organizations such as universities, businesses, religious organizations, libraries, and mental health and social service agencies. Partners collaborate in planning, coordinating, and implementing programs and activities at home, at school, and in the community that build strengths and resilience in children to enhance their academic, personal, social, and college-career outcomes.
>
> *(pp. 408–409)*

Related, some of the key characteristics of Applied Critical Leadership (ACL) align with and complement best practice operations of CPs. Key characteristics of ACL include a strengths-based leadership model; honoring of all members of the community; building of trust; a consensus-driven decision-making process; a 'leading by example' approach; critical conversations; and finally, the concept of staff working to serve the greater good (Santamaría, 2014; Santamaría & Santamaría, 2012).

As a culturally responsive leadership approach, ACL encourages leaders to use "a strengths-based model of leadership practice where educational leaders consider the social context of their educational communities" (Santamaría & Santamaría, 2012, p. 5). Similarly, Bryan and Henry (2012) concur, stating that partnerships should focus on the schools, families, and wider community leaders strengths that "build resiliency in children, . . . meaningful student participation in their schools and communities, and high expectations for students' success" (p. 410). In contrast, negative attitudes from community partnerships will lead to poor family–community relationships, which are traditionally underserved backgrounds (Bryan & Henry, 2012).

Honoring All Members of the Community

When establishing CPs, leaders need to be aware of choosing members from varying and culturally and linguistically diverse groups (including parents) (Billett, Ovens, Clemans, & Seddon, 2007; Hopkins, 2007; Obeidat & Al-Hassan,

2009; Semke & Sheridan, 2012; Organization for Economic Cooperation and Development [OECD], 2012). For example, Bryan and Henry (2012) expressed the need to involve "culturally diverse and low-income parents and community members in the partnership process . . . and to regard each other as valuable resources and assets" (p. 410). Moreover, the role of business leaders and community leaders within CPs was considered to be essential (McKinsey Center for Government, 2013). Therefore, the evidence suggests that it is important for CP leaders to be inclusive when identifying prospective CP members to ensure they are honoring all members represented in their community.

Building Trust

Instilling values of trust and trustworthiness and recognition of others' differences is important for the sustainability of a CP (Billett et al., 2007). A community based on trust enables people to become genuinely engaged with a desire to serve for the greater good. Moreover, CP membership is usually mostly reliant on community volunteers. In short, a volunteer on behalf of an institution or business organization often brings about "complex relations, histories and competing interests of individuals and institutions" (Billett et al., 2007, p. 642). Therefore, building trust requires leaders to "encourage commitment and participation [to] develop processes that are inclusive and respectful" (p. 648).

Leading by Example and Having Critical Conversations

Best practice leadership and governance involves not just building trust but providing members of a CP with "transparent and workable guidelines and procedures, . . . strategic plans which are realistic . . . and communicating freely and fairly with the constituent community" (Billett et al., 2007, pp. 651–652). Furthermore, critical conversations need to be undertaken, asking questions such as: "What are the local skill shortages, youth unemployment rates, how do we build local capacity and have government assist us in the effective targeting and delivery of service provisions such as Vocational Education and Trades course provisions and what are our shared goals?" (p. 639).

In summary, the relevant ACL characteristics underlying this contribution and considered for the literature review were honoring all members within a community; building trust; 'leading by example'; and encouraging critical conversations. These will be further considered in this chapter.

Methodology

This study employed a qualitative approach using classic grounded theory and the constant comparative method to analyze secondary data reported in a process evaluation of six CPs in Auckland, New Zealand (Glaser, 1963; Glaser &

Holton, 2004). This chapter used secondary data to reanalyze how, and in what ways, the key characteristics of the ACL approach have been reflected through the actions of leaders and members of the initial process evaluation findings of the six CPs (Andrews et al., 2012). In other words, the data was originally collected for other purposes (Glaser, 1963, p. 11) but a key benefit of reanalyzing the original process evaluation data allowed the researcher to search for new insights and perspectives of leadership through an ACL lens (Andrews et al., 2012).

Findings

The data reflected perspectives of key stakeholders at the MoE, the views of CP members involved in the evaluation of the six CPs, and the analysis of documentation including CPs strategic plans and meeting minutes from the first year of CPs in operation. For this chapter the views of the CP members involved in the evaluation of the six CPs and analysis of documentation will be presented as ACL in practice.

Evidence of the ACL Approach with CP Members

There were 45 CP members who responded to the survey, with a breakdown of 15 high school participants, 11 private-training establishment participants, 5 technical institutes (U.S. equivalent: community colleges), 4 Wānanga (Māori tertiary providers), and 10 representatives from other organizations involved in either secondary, tertiary, or employment. The population of the participants was proportionate to the population served.

Honoring All Members of the Community

Representation to honor all members of the community can be a challenge, as reported by the following CP stakeholders:

> There are some great people on board in the Tertiary Education Commission and Private Training Establishment sector. However, I think the success of the Youth Guarantee network is largely dependent on the engagement and take-up from the local high schools. Sadly, whilst one or two schools are buying in, others are not and in fact have withdrawn. This is disappointing as it is not sharing the community load for our students.
>
> I do not believe that all key players are present, very few Private Training Establishments are present and the Youth Services providers have never been seen. It is very promising, however, to have one or two Independent Training Organizations involved.

Building Trust

The MoE has been instrumental in organizing workshops to enable CP members and other interested parties to share their knowledge and skills relating to the Youth Guarantee policy. This was acknowledged by CP members as they began to understand the complexity of the task at hand and the need to build long-lasting sustainable relationships with people within their community setting. This is evidenced in the remark from a CP stakeholder below:

> We are confident we will have a Health pathway operating for maybe 80–100 students in West Auckland next year—a tangible outcome which fills an identified gap in current provision. We have secured the cooperation of the Waitakere District Health Board . . . and developed four packages of standards to allow for differentiated provision for the out-of-school component of the program.

Leading by Example

Some CP participants took the time to acknowledge the difficult task faced by the MoE staff to establish CPs nationwide. This was reflected in the following remarks by a key CP member:

> I understand that establishing new initiatives comes with teething problems and in most cases MoE have supported administratively and partners have shuffled to make sure appropriate people attend the meetings.

Critical Conversations

And finally, the concept of creating CPs with the intention of involving all stakeholder groups who can make a difference to improve student outcomes from secondary to tertiary and into employment is pioneering. This is reflected in this CP stakeholder's view, which is that some members are still unclear about what the CP can actually achieve:

> I feel that many members are still unclear about what can really be accomplished within this network, but we are getting there slowly. Progress is slow and the commitment of schools is limited in terms of moving away from traditional methods and really changing the way they operate.

Also, funding remains a key challenge particularly in *how* funds are shared for each student. As one Private Training Establishment (PTE) network member appears to feel, the funds are going to stay within a school setting rather than be utilized collaboratively to provide the best outcomes for students. She remarked:

> Where I can see the direction of the Youth Guarantee networks going is that the schools will retain the learners and Youth Guarantees will no longer be available in the tertiary sector. We will be asked to help but will not have it as a main focus for business.

On the contrary, some CP stakeholders appear to understand the benefits of collaboration and sharing of resources, as this CP member commented:

> [I believe] working together as a community, sharing ideas, resources, venues, transport, and teaching—[I think] collaboration has to be a positive thing.

There are several perceived challenges that are articulated by CP members, such as whether the vocational pathways are surface measures rather than a coherent and cohesive program for the student.

> A significant issue is whether the solutions are at band-aid level or a deeper level; in which case intermediate schools should *definitely* be involved.

A CP member commented on the time commitment required:

> Over-commitment will mean that individuals withdraw from a demanding "extra" that is not key to their work role, and turnover of representatives will mean that commitment to the network will fluctuate based on personal values and beliefs.

In addition to the difficulty of conversation on the use of *time*, there are other solutions such as hiring a facilitator in the district, which some CP members have highlighted as a need for the creation of a sustainable CP:

> This is being done on goodwill with no extra support. Even with just one pathway we will need to put a considerable amount of staff time into working with these students, coordinating their programs and ensuring their pastoral care when they are outside the school. This will inevitably be a drain on staffing and time.

Simple conversations on agreements, such as transportation and payment terms between providers, are critical to a seamless educational pathway for students. This point is further addressed by this CP member's comment:

> Forging really clear agreements across multiple partners where there is no resourcing for a coordination role to manage the relationships and

coordinate all the administrative requirements of the networks [is a challenge]. This includes capacity to collect and collate progress and ensure that students' stories are captured across transition stages and into the future.

Table 15.1 illustrates the connections, validations, and examples of ACL in the implementation and institutionalized culturally responsive leadership practices (or lack thereof) for the CPs considered in this chapter. However, this is not to assert that ACL was overwhelmingly present.

Data also revealed evidence of some challenges to the implementation of some ACL characteristics and a culturally responsive leadership approach as indicated in Table 15.2.

TABLE 15.1 Community Partnerships Are Enhanced When They Use an Applied Critical Leadership Approach: Community Partnership Members Can Choose Change

Community Partnership Members: Consensus Decision-making Process	• The Ministry of Education staff encouraged Community Partnership members to lead and make decisions at a local community level and to take ownership of the challenges to improve NCEA Level 2+ achievement and student outcomes from secondary to tertiary and into employment. The Ministry staff view themselves as *facilitators of change.*
Community Partnership Members: Willingness to Engage in the Critical Conversations	• Who is represented on the Community Partnership? What is their position in terms of *Power?*
	• *Silo* versus *together*—common goals and *vision.*
	• Raising to the surface (not hiding behind the walls of the institution) conversations for individual student achievement specifically for priority learners.
	• Tracking students over time—sharing data and taking an evidence-based approach for student individual education planning.
	• Stigma behind *Vocational* versus *Academic* pathways.
	• *Funding Model*—Student-centered approach to sharing resources.
	• Commitment and goodwill; responsive to educational change.
	• What does effective transition look like for students from secondary to tertiary and into employment? Linking with employers, creating student work opportunities.
	• Agreed Memorandum of Understanding between partners.
	• Sharing knowledge and expertise on leadership, teaching, and learning practice.

(Continued)

TABLE 15.1 (Continued)

Honor All Members of the Community	• Priority population groups—invitations extended to all (e.g., Pasifika educational leaders and community leaders and Māori authorities included employers, Industry Training Organisations (ITOs), all high schools in the area, tertiary providers, Careers New Zealand, and other support groups for youth).
Community Partnership Members: Building Trust	• The need to build trusting relationships with each other, to be collaborative, honest with each other, and to focus on the core business, which is the student. • The Community Partnership members learn to understand the importance of building trust between each other within the various educational institutions but also between the employers and the educators.
Working to Serve the Greater Good	• New Zealand Government "Better Public Service Goal": that 85% of 18-year-olds gain a National Certificate of Educational Achievement Level 2 (NCEA, Level 2) or an equivalent qualification by 2017. • Youth Guarantee Networks/Community Partnerships Key Goals: improve attendance rates, retention, and engagement of our learners. • Priority group learners: Māori, Pasifika, and learners with special needs. • To serve the wider community—learners, parents, whānau (family), and employers.
Critical Race Theory	• The Ministry of Education Youth Guarantee representatives and Community Partnership members share an understanding of the need to improve opportunities and future life chances for Māori and Pasifika students by providing them with increased access to greater economic success through Vocational Pathways created through Community Partnership efforts.
Leading by Example to Solve an Unresolved Educational Need	• Understanding from a policy perspective that this is an equity issue, clear focus on priority groups—Ministry of Education running *workshops,* initially being *present at Community Partnership meetings, coaching, facilitating,* and mentoring Community Partnership members—for example: teaching them the importance of identifying each student and putting *names* to students so it is not just *those kids.* • Showing *empathy,* understanding implementation of Vocational Pathways through Community Partnerships is a *complex* process. • Leading by example, showing that an improved understanding between sectors will result in re-engaging learners, less pastoral care required, student retention, and improved family relationships.

TABLE 15.2 Evidence of Challenges Associated with an ACL Approach in CP Practice

ACL Indicator	CP Stakeholder Practice	Evidence of Challenge
Consensus in Decision-making	Difficult if leadership changes within an organization as decision-making continuity can be disrupted	"We have had several changes of leadership at school, and are just really back on track with ordinary school business so I can see that this is quite challenging to put into place right now even though it will benefit our school."
		"We need [to have] consensus on measures for success factors."
Building Trust and Working to Serve the Greater Good	Lack of clarity with a transparent funding model made it difficult to trust other providers	"Resources seem to be the biggie right now and this has caused schools (and Youth Guarantees–funded tertiary providers) to be extremely cautious about committing to anything."

Consensus Decision-Making Process and Building Trust

While there was little documentation to illustrate that CPs were ensuring consensus decision-making processes were in place, there was some evidence in the documentation that the CP members needed to be "inclusive [with their] decision making process." Thus, it is implied that they work also toward building trust.

CULTURALLY RESPONSIVE LEADERSHIP IN PRACTICE

The documentation data collected during the process evaluation provided further evidence and triangulation from the six CPs minutes of meetings, agendas, and strategic plans. These documents illustrated several areas of the ACL approach in action.

Honor Members of the Community

There were several examples where CPs discussed the honoring of all members within the community. These include:

- *Collaboration between all schools* and education providers in the area.
- *Quality, relevant curriculum* offering that corresponds with the needs of the community and industry/employers.

- *Training aligned to work* opportunities.
- *Engaging construction personnel* and professionals to find out what is needed.
- *Working with Māori/Pacific networks* creating a collaborative environment.
- *Having appropriate and relevant people present* as part of decisions being made in CP *meetings*.

Lead by Example

Documentation illustrates very clearly the ability for leaders within the CPs to lead by example. The following statements within the documentation indicate the leaders' thoughts on what they know they *should* be doing:

- We will *share learner achievement data, information*, and teaching and assessment practices within the network/partnership so that we can learn from each other and each other's organizations.
- [We need to have a] *unity of effort* rather than a division of labor.
- An *Action Plan recording the work to be done* will be a standing agenda item for information and updated at each monthly leadership meeting to ensure the sustainability of the network.
- *MoE is acknowledging and supporting the changes that are required* to make this happen.

Discussion

The Youth Guarantee Community Partnership policy implemented nationwide by the New Zealand MoE aims to promote the sharing of knowledge, student data, and resources across local communities to improve student retention, progression, and achievement for priority learners (Ministry of Education, 2015a). For CPs to become effective they require a strengths-based leadership approach, which seeks high expectations for all students (Bryan & Henry, 2012; Santamaría & Santamaría, 2012). In turn, the cornerstone for implementation of policy in educational change to rebalance the power appears to be more successful when there is evidence of transformational, systemic change within schools at the local level (Hopkins, 2007; Levin, 2012). It is therefore imperative that we continue to find new and different ways to lead our youth through their transition from school to further education and into gainful employment. This research employed a comparative analysis methodology to search for evidence of the characteristics of the ACL approach when using secondary data from a process evaluation of six CPs and will be discussed using this lens.

Honor All Members of the Community

Having an inclusive approach to CP membership selection ensures that the diverse groups in a local community have representation from leaders within the following areas: schools, tertiary providers, support organizations, and employers (Bryan & Henry, 2012; McKinsey Center for Government, 2013; Obeidat & Al-Hassan, 2009; Semke & Sheridan, 2012; Santamaría & Santamaría, 2012). Table 15.1 also demonstrates evidence developed through this secondary data analysis that the MoE key stakeholders and the CP members also understood the significance of having the *right* stakeholders at the table who also had the *power* to implement the CP decisions made within their own organization and beyond.

Building Trust

Any sustainable relationship with others requires mutual respect. For CPs to experience success, the leader(s) need to ensure there is an underlying culture of instilling trust and building trustworthy relationships with each other (Billett et al., 2007). This is particularly important as the key stakeholders are volunteering their time, expertise, and skills, which sometimes bring with it "competing interests of individuals and institutions" (Billett et al., 2007, p. 648). In this study, all three data sources illustrated evidence of the need to build trusting relationships with one another and this is also reflected in Table 15.1.

Leading by Example to Solve an Unresolved Educational Need

To lead by example requires the CP leaders to govern by ensuring that there are "transparent and workable guidelines and procedures, . . . and strategic plans which are realistic . . . and communicated freely and fairly within the constituent community" (Billett et al., 2007, p. 651). In this comparative analysis, it was evident that the MoE key stakeholders were not just 'leading by example' but they were pioneering. They appeared to understand the complexity of the multiple challenges CP leaders faced during the initial establishment of CPs across such diverse community groups ranging from school leaders to tertiary leaders, through to employers and other supporting organizations, including Māori and Pasifika representatives. Therefore, the evidence in this study highlights the need for leaders implementing the policies to have an understanding of what it means to *facilitate* rather than *tell* communities what to do. This is reflected in the ACL approach to lead by example, and the common themes from the findings in this chapter are illustrated in Table 15.1.

Engaging Critical Conversations

Billett and associates (2007) outlined the importance of community partnership leaders to engage in the critical conversations in alignment with Santamaría &

Santamaría's (2012) ACL approach by asking key questions associated with ways in which we build capacity and shared goals to ensure improved student transitions from school to further education and into work. Similarly, there is evidence through this comparative analysis that the leaders within the MoE and the CPs are willing to engage critical conversations covering a range of issues. Table 15.1 identifies some of these topics, such as CP representation, gaining evidence over time through tracking and sharing student data, continuing to work on a transparent secondary–tertiary funding model, having a shared vision and shared goals, signing of MOU agreements by CPs, and, finally, breaking down the stigma between a vocational pathway and an academic pathway. In addition, the documentation enabled a triangulation to be completed to validate the critical conversations being undertaken within the CPs in this study.

Conclusion and Areas for Future Research

This chapter explored ways in which the ACL characteristics resonated with findings from an earlier process evaluation report for the Ministry of Education on six Auckland-based Youth Guarantee CPs in New Zealand. The ACL approach incorporates a strengths-based culturally responsive model to enhance educational leadership strategies implemented in schools and other educational settings to improve social justice and educational equity for underserved students. So, too, the New Zealand MoE Youth Guarantee Networks policy endeavors to serve a similar goal in which educational and other leaders within a local community setting share resources and assist students who are underserved to succeed, have self-confidence, and be able to choose whatever pathway they are interested in.

Unsurprisingly, the findings from the process evaluation when overlaid with the ACL approach confirmed seven ACL characteristics as illustrated in Table 15.1. It is essential that emerging and existing educational leaders working in diverse communities learn to acknowledge others by considering others' perspectives. The ACL approach gives leaders much to reflect upon within their own leadership context and this has been reflected in the findings within this chapter. Future research in this area from a 2015 MoE evaluation of CPs nationwide could further enhance and add to the findings in this chapter. In addition, the MoE key stakeholders could work on ways in which the ACL approach could be shared and discussed among the CP membership nationwide to enhance and strengthen local community leadership practice.

On a final note, it is my firm belief that educational leaders working in multicultural and diverse settings need to develop the habit of continuing to reflect upon their leadership strategies and to search for alternative approaches such as the ACL approach to further enhance their practice and in turn improve underserved students' education and employment opportunities.

References

Andrews, L., Higgins, A., Waring, M., & Lalor, J. (2012). Using classic grounded theory to analyse secondary data: Reality and reflections. *Grounded Theory Review, 11*(1), 12–26.

Billett, S., Ovens, C., Clemans, A., & Seddon, T. (2007). Collaborative working and contested practices: Forming, developing and sustaining social partnerships in education. *Journal of Education Policy, 22*(6), 637–665.

Bridgeland, J. M., Dilulio, J. J., & Morison, K. B. (2006). *The silent epidemic: Perspectives of high school dropouts* (pp. 1–31). Washington, DC: Civic Enterprises.

Bryan, J., & Henry, L. (2008). Strengths-based partnerships: A school-family-community partnership approach to empowering students. *Professional School Counseling, 12*(2), 149–156.

Bryan, J., & Henry, L. (2012). A model for building school-family-community partnerships: Principles and process. *Journal of Counseling and Development, 90*(4), 408–420.

Burrus J., & Roberts, R. D. (2012, February). Dropping out of high school: Prevalence, risk factors, and remediation strategies. *No. 18, R & D Connections*, 1–9. Princeton, NJ: ETS Research & Development Educational Testing Service.

Carnevale, A. P., & Desrochers, D. M. (2002). The missing middle: Aligning education and the knowledge economy. *Journal of Vocational Needs Education, 25*(1), 1–22.

DuFour, R. P., & Marzano, R. J. (2011). *Leaders of learning: How district, school, and classroom leaders improve student achievement.* Bloomington, IN: Solution Tree.

Education Counts. (2013). Retrieved from http://www.educationcounts.govt.nz/indicators/main/student-engagement-participation/1955

Glaser, B. (1963). The use of secondary analysis by the independent researcher. *American Behavioral Scientist, 6*, 11–14.

Glaser, B. G., & Holton, J. (2004). Remodeling grounded theory. In *Forum Qualitative Sozialforschung/Forum: Qualitative Social Research.* Retrieved from http://nbn-resolving.de/urn:nbn:de:0114-fqs040245

Hopkins, D. (2007). *Every school a great school.* Maidenhead, UK: Open University Press, McGraw Hill Education.

International Labour Organisation. (2015). Retrieved from http://www.ilo.org/global/topics/youth-employment/lang—de/index.htm

Levin, B. (2012). *System-wide improvement in education.* Geneva, Switzerland: International Academy of Education/International Bureau of Education. Retrieved from www.ibe.unesco.org

McKinsey Center for Government. (2013). *Education to employment: Designing a system that works.* McKinsey Center for Government. Retrieved from http://mckinseyonsociety.com/downloads/reports/Education/Education-to-Employment_FINAL.pdf

Ministry of Education. (2015a). *Focus on priority learners.* Retrieved from http://www.minedu.govt.nz/theMinistry/EducationInitiatives/InvestingInEducationalSuccess/Report/Part2/FoundationElements/Focus.aspx

Ministry of Education. (2015b). *Target 5: Better public service goals.* Retrieved from http://www.minedu.govt.nz/theMinistry/BetterPublicServices.aspx

Obeidat, O., & Al-Hassan, S. (2009). School-parent-community partnerships: The experience of teachers who received the Queen Rania award for excellence in education in the Hashemite Kingdom of Jordan. *School Community Journal, 19*(1), 119–136.

OECD. (2012). *Equity and quality in education: Supporting disadvantaged students in schools.* OECD. Retrieved from http://www.oecd.org/edu/school/50293148.pdf

Santamaría, L. J. (2014). Critical change for the greater good: Multicultural dimensions of educational leadership toward social justice and educational equity. *Education Administration Quarterly (EAQ), 50*(3), 347–391.

Santamaría, L. J., & Santamaría, A. P. (2012). *Applied critical leadership: Choosing change.* New York, NY: Routledge.

Semke, C. A., & Sheridan, S. M. (2012). Family-school connections in rural educational settings: A systematic review of the empirical literature. *School Community Journal, 22,* 21–46.

Statistics New Zealand. (2013). Retrieved from http://www.stats.govt.nz/Census/2013-census.aspx

Statistics New Zealand. (2014). Retrieved from http://www.stats.govt.nz/browse_for_stats/income-and-work/employment_and_unemployment/new-labour-market-data.aspx

Young, C., & Clinton, J. C. (2014). Process evaluation: Youth guarantee networks—Auckland. Unpublished, Ministry of Education Report.

Youth Guarantee. (2015). Retrieved from http://youthguarantee.net.nz/

EPILOGUE

Privileging Student Voice: Establishing Sustainable Pathways toward Culturally Responsive Leadership in Academe

Nelly A. Cruz

Educational inequity is present at all levels of our education system from Pre-Kindergarten to higher education. Unfortunately, these systems have created unequal access, disparities, and exclusion among other dire issues for systemically underserved communities. However, individuals in leadership roles play a critical function in genuinely promoting more opportunities for greater equitable outcomes. As leaders, we provide agency for historically oppressed communities who are underrepresented in administrative and policy-making positions. We can choose to serve as a catalyst for social justice by challenging the status quo of power systems, racial systems, and other systems of oppression that do not serve the needs of a diverse student populace. The Applied Critical Leadership (ACL) model encourages leaders to examine the social contexts of their communities and to empower community members by acknowledging how one's identity affects leadership through a critical lens (Santamaría & Santamaría, 2012).

In order to serve the needs of a growing diverse student population, we need to have more culturally responsive leaders who continue to move in a direction toward social change. It is essential for leaders to become aware of their values, goals, and assumptions by engaging in self-reflection. Moreover, the process of self-reflection allows an individual to become grounded in her/his purpose to espouse change, challenge her/his own assumptions, and create vision. ACL probes the following question: *In what ways does my identity enhance my ability to see alternate perspectives and practice effective leadership?* (Santamaría & Santamaría, 2012). This question provides a good starting point to reflect on one's privileges and unearned advantages that can bring self-awareness to change-leadership practices. Finally, the beauty of choice is that we have the power to take an active role inciting institutional change and resisting systemic oppression so that we may emancipate ourselves and future generations.

Diverse students are affected by the environments in which they are placed, which at times can be immersed with harsh conditions that make it difficult for students to thrive academically, socially, and economically. Student diversity is typically not reflected in the administrative positions of educational institutions. Consequently, the lack of multicultural competency can lead to unmet needs for students of color. For example, students of color may face issues of hostile campus climates (Solórzano, Ceja, & Yosso, 2000), lack of cultural and social capital, and cultural dissonance that impede their path to success (Gordon & Yowell, 1992). Moreover, our awareness of how we impact campus environments and student outcomes can enable us to find innovative ways to engage students through our leadership practices.

Transformative leadership recognizes the position of educational institutions within socio-political and socio-historical contexts to advance social justice. This form of leadership allows us to utilize a critical lens to break the legacy of institutional racism enshrouded behind rhetoric of meritocracy, color-blindness, and equal opportunity within educational institutions (Brayboy, 2005; Castagno & Lee, 2007). Throughout this book, we learned about courageous and inspirational leaders who chose to enact solutions to overcome institutional barriers and move us one step closer to achieving equitable outcomes. Additionally, at the micro level we make a difference in the lives of our students by believing in them and motivating them to pursue their goals.

As a first-generation Mexican American woman of Mixtec (Indigenous to Oaxaca) descent, I was charged to find my own means of navigating through educational institutions at an early age. My familial support at home was limited because my parents did not receive an American education; nonetheless they were fluent in English. However, I am beyond grateful to all the individuals with whom I crossed paths throughout my educational journey because they played a role in my success. These individuals were able to see beyond my physical appearance before judging me and created pathways to access, information, and opportunities.

My experiences and journey in higher education have impacted my life and encouraged me to become an agent of change both in my field of study and my community. I was blessed to encounter administrators, faculty, and staff who serve as role models through their leadership and scholarship by impacting the lives of students on campus. As an undergraduate student, I was surprised to find individuals who were willing to mentor me, provide me with internship opportunities, and engage me in intellectual activities, among other things. Furthermore, I felt empowered by these individuals to make a change in the world by using my talents and strengths as a Mixtec woman.

Individual efforts can be brought together collectively to give impetus to the advancement of access, equity, and disparities. The change begins within us to choose to develop into transformational and critical leaders who can serve the needs of a diverse populace by serving as a voice for historically underserved communities. As we become aware of our values and goals, we can seek to create collaborations and partnerships that will advance action-based plans. Whether we impact one life at a time or progress community goals, we leave a mark of hope, love, and inspiration for others to continue the effort to truly make the world a better place for every human being.

References

Brayboy, B. (2005). Transformational resistance and social justice: American Indians in Ivy League universities. *Anthropology and Education Quarterly, 36*(3), 191–211.

Castagno, A., & Lee, S. (2007). Native mascots and ethnic fraud. *Equity and Excellence in Education, 40*(3), 3–13.

Gordon, E. W., & Yowell, C. (1992). Cultural dissonance as a risk factor in the development of students. In R. J. Rossi (Ed.), *Schools and students at risk: Context and framework for positive change.* New York, NY: Teachers College Press.

Santamaría, L. J., & Santamaría, A. P. (2012). *Applied critical leadership in education: Choosing change.* New York, NY: Routledge.

Solórzano, D., Ceja, M., & Yosso, T. (2000). Critical race theory, racial microaggressions, and campus racial climate: The experiences of African American college students. *Journal of Negro Education, 69*(1/2), 60–73.

EDITOR BIOGRAPHIES AND CONTRIBUTOR BIOGRAPHIES

Editor Biographies

Lorri J. Santamaría, Ph.D., is an Associate Professor of Educational Leadership and Head of the School of Learning, Development and Professional Practice in the Faculty of Education and Social Work at the University of Auckland, New Zealand. Prior to this appointment she was Professor of Multicultural Multilingual Education at California State University San Marcos and the Director of the Educational Leadership Joint Doctoral Program with the University of California San Diego. Dr. Santamaría engages scholarly writing and research in the areas of Pre-K–HE leadership for social justice and educational equity including diversity for educational improvement. In her research she interrogates the roles and intersectionalities of race, sexuality, language, gender, and exceptionality in leadership and learning. Dr. Santamaría's collaborative cross-cultural research platform addresses the needs of systemically underserved peoples in the U.S. as well as Māori and Pasifika communities in the Auckland Metro area (e.g., as researcher for the Māori Achievement Collaborative [MAC]). Her scholarly work is focused on community-based successful actions associated with educational improvement for systemically underserved and excluded learners (e.g., two funded International Research Networks [IRNs]) with colleagues investigating similar issues in the U.S., South Africa, Spain, Brazil, Hungary, Australia, and Canada. Lorri is the author of *Applied Critical Leadership in Education: Choosing Change* with Dr. A. P. Santamaría (Routledge, 2012) and editor of *Cross Cultural Women Scholars in Academe: Intergenerational Voices* with G. Jean-Marie and C. Grant (Routledge, 2014). Dr. Santamaría received her B.A. in Multiple-Subject Teacher Education (bilingual Spanish-English endorsement), her M.A. in Bilingual Special Education, Rehabilitation and School Psychology, and her Ph.D. in

Multicultural Multilingual Special Education, Rehabilitation and School Psychology from the University of Arizona.

Andrés P. Santamaría, Ed.D., is a Lecturer in Educational Leadership for the School of Education at Auckland University of Technology, New Zealand. His area of expertise is leadership for diversity and his research interests range from leadership for social justice and educational equity to principal efficacy in underperforming schools. Dr. Santamaría currently serves on an interdisciplinary, cross-cultural team of scholars in partnership with the Māori Achievement Collaborative (MAC), a network of approximately 60 Māori and non-Māori mainstream school principals throughout Aotearoa New Zealand. The focus of this research project is to support, engage, improve, and promote culturally responsive leadership practices for improving 'Māori student success as Māori' via *Kaupapa Māori* (Treaty responsiveness) and critical race theory research methodologies. While at the University of Auckland, Dr. Santamaría was involved with the Starpath Project, which focused on increasing NCEA achievement outcomes and postsecondary pathway attainment for Māori and Pasifika students. Prior to his academic appointment, Dr. Santamaría was a primary school principal in Southern California serving schools with high populations of culturally and linguistic diverse learners as well as learners from low socioeconomic backgrounds. He is the author of *Applied Critical Leadership in Education: Choosing Change* with Dr. L. J. Santamaría (Routledge, 2012). Dr. Santamaría received his B.S. in Ecology, Behavior and Evolution from the University of California San Diego, his M.A. in Bilingual Special Education, Rehabilitation and School Psychology from the University of Arizona, and his Ed.D. in Educational Leadership from the regional Joint Doctoral Program between UC San Diego, San Diego State University, and California State University San Marcos.

Contributor Biographies

Airini, Ph.D., specializes in research into equity in higher education, with a particular focus on Indigenous and underserved students. She is Dean, Faculty of Human, Social and Educational Development, at Thompson Rivers University, Canada. Current research includes how universities can support success by first-generation university students. As a Fulbright Scholar in Washington, DC, Airini investigated how to convert education policy into better results for underserved students. (webpage: http://kamino.tru.ca/experts/home/main/bio.html?id=airini)

Amani Bell, Ph.D., is an academic in the Institute for Teaching and Learning at the University of Sydney. Amani's teaching and learning development work includes leadership of sessional staff development and the #edtech Network. Amani's primary research focus is how academics, particularly those early in their career, develop their teaching via critical reflection, peer observation, and engagement with students.

Nelly A. Cruz is a first-generation college graduate who received baccalaureate degrees in public policy and sociology from the University of California Riverside. She is currently pursuing her Master's in Education with an emphasis in Higher Education Administration and Policy. She currently works at a Hispanic-Serving Institution serving predominantly first-year students through learning community programs and other programming. Additionally, she enjoys establishing campus partnerships to promote academic success, persistence, retention, and building community. Nelly was born in Oceanside, California. Her parents migrated from Oaxaca, Mexico, to the United States. She is from Mixtec descent and the eldest of four children. The lack of educational access in her family's *pueblo* motivated Nelly to seek educational opportunities that would allow her to satisfy her hunger for knowledge and intellectual growth.

Annette Daoud, Ph.D., is a Professor at California State University San Marcos where she teaches courses in multicultural and multilingual education. Throughout her career in higher education, Dr. Daoud has focused her teaching, research, and service on issues of educational equity and social justice. Dr. Daoud served as the founding director of the Social Justice and Equity Project at California State University San Marcos. Currently, her teaching focuses on teaching credential candidates how to equitably teach their English-learner students. She is the author of *Middle and High School English Learners and the Common Core Standards: Equitable Instruction in Content Area Classrooms* (Pearson, 2014). Dr. Daoud is currently the principal investigator for a National Professional Development grant funded by the U.S. Department of Education's Office of English Language Acquisition titled *Leading and Learning: Supporting English Learners with Effective Teacher Preparation and Professional Development*.

Emelyn A. dela Peña, Ed.D., is Assistant Dean for Equity, Diversity and Inclusion at Harvard College, where she oversees the Women's Center, Office of BGLTQ Student Life, and initiatives for undocumented students, first-generation college students, and foster youth. Prior to Harvard she was a campus diversity officer and Director of the Women's Center at the University of California San Diego. She holds a Bachelor of Arts in Ethnic Studies from the University of California San Diego, a Master of Arts in Postsecondary Educational Leadership from San Diego State University, and a Doctor of Education from a joint program between UC San Diego, San Diego State, and CSU San Marcos. Emelyn specializes in gender and violence, and the intersections of such issues to broader social justice movements. She brings an intersectional approach to her scholarship and practice and is particularly influenced by the third space theory and practice of queer women of color.

Katie Fitzpatrick, Ph.D., is an Associate Professor of Health and Physical Education at the University of Auckland. She has a background teaching, and as a curriculum leader, in diverse schools in New Zealand, and is passionate about critical approaches to education. Since 2004 she has worked in teacher education programs and has conducted research into young people's perspectives of health, physical education, and schooling. She has also worked on policy documents including the New Zealand Curriculum and, most recently, as the lead writer on the revised Sexuality Education Guidelines (released in 2015). She is the author of *Critical Pedagogy, Physical Education and Urban Schooling* (Peter Lang, 2013) and co-editor of *Health Education: Critical Perspectives* (Routledge, 2014).

Cosette M. Grant, Ph.D., is an Assistant Professor of Educational Leadership and Policy at University of Cincinnati. In 2011, she co-founded Advancing Women of Color in the Academy (AWOCA) as a scholarly network of women of color who are connected through research in the field of education and their affiliation in higher education. AWOCA is an inter-ethnic, trans-disciplinary and cross-institutional collaborative group dedicated to the advancement of women of color in the academy. Her research focuses on culturally relevant pedagogy in leadership-preparation programs that might inform equity and access to enhance learning outcomes for underrepresented populations in U.S. schools. Her work also includes emergent work on effective leadership for educational equity in P–12 schools and for enhanced student learning outcomes.

Gaëtane Jean-Marie, Ph.D., is Professor of Educational Leadership and Department Chair of Leadership, Foundations and Human Resource Education in the College of Education and Human Development at the University of Louisville, Kentucky. Her research focuses on leadership development and preparation in a global context, educational equity in K–12 schools, and women and leadership in the P–20 system. To date, she has over 70 publications, which include books, book chapters, and academic articles in numerous peer-reviewed journals. Her recent publications include two co-edited books, *The Duality of Women Scholars of Color: Transforming and Being Transformed in the Academy* (Information Age, 2014) and *Cross Cultural Women Scholars in Academe: Intergenerational Voices* (Routledge, 2014). Actively involved nationally, she is the editor of the *Journal of School Leadership*, and serves on the editorial board of the *Journal of Research on Leadership Education* and *Journal of Educational Administration*, and is a reviewer for several journals.

Jennifer Jeffries, Ed.D., earned her Doctor of Education from the University of San Diego in Leadership Studies. She earned her B.A. in English and her M.A. in Educational Administration from San Diego State University. She has served as a middle school teacher, high school assistant principal, elementary school principal, assistant superintendent, and superintendent. After 25 years in K–12 educational settings, she joined the faculty at California State University San Marcos where she served as the founding director of the Educational Leadership Doctoral Program and as Associate Vice President for Planning, Accreditation and Assessment. She takes great joy in assisting individuals and organizations in taking action in pursuit of greater effectiveness and fulfillment of organizational vision. She is a firm believer that leaders are not born, but develop through intellectual growth, emotional maturity, experience in politically charged environments, and engagement in personally meaningful endeavors.

Roisin Kelly-Laubscher, M.A., is a Lecturer at the University of Cape Town. She has been involved in academic development at the University since 2009. From 2009–2013 she was a lecturer in the Department of Human Biology at the University of Cape Town where she convened the Anatomy and Physiology courses for the School of Health and Rehabilitation Studies Intervention program. Since then she has joined the Academic Development Programme and Department of Biological Sciences where she currently runs the first-year biology course for the extended science degree program. She has a Ph.D. in Physiology and is currently completing a Master's in Higher Education. Her main education research foci include student access to knowledge within the Biological Sciences and the experience of students who are first in the family at university.

Vanessa Langi is a recent graduate of the University of Auckland and is currently teaching at Otahuhu College—a diverse and low socioeconomic urban high school in South Auckland, New Zealand. Her academic interests are in critical and multicultural pedagogies, sociology, culture and curriculum, and Indigenous concepts of teaching and learning. She has developed a critical awareness of social issues and her positioning within them, and is passionate about bringing these perspectives to her high school teaching.

Brenda Lloyd-Jones, Ph.D., is Associate Professor and Associate Chair of the Department of Human Relations in the College of Arts and Sciences at the University of Oklahoma. Her research focuses on higher education leadership, human diversity, and community engagement, She is co-editor of a two-volume book: *Women of Color in Higher Education: Turbulent Past, Promising Future* and *Women of Color in Higher Education: Changing Directions and New Perspectives* (Emerald Group, 2011). Her research has been published in scholarly journals, books, and edited volumes. She has received the University of Oklahoma President's Award for Outstanding Leadership Contributions.

Hollie Mackey, Ph.D., (Northern Cheyenne) is an Assistant Professor of Education at the University of Oklahoma. Her research includes K–12 educational leadership for equitable schools, American Indian education, education law and ethics, Indigenous research paradigms, and leadership for social justice. She currently serves on the advisory board for the South Central Comprehensive Center (SC3) focusing on American Indian education, and is a current nominee for the National Advisory Council for Indian Education (NACIE). Awards include the 2009 Harold F. Martin Outstanding Graduate Teaching Award, the 2013 International Willower Award for Excellence, and the 2014 Jack A. Culbertson Award for outstanding accomplishments as a junior professor of educational leadership. Dr. Mackey's publications can be found in Information Age, Emerald, Rowman and Littlefield, and Routledge publishers and in the *International Journal for Qualitative Studies in Education, Mentoring and Tutoring*, the *Journal of Educational Administration*, and the *Journal for Critical Thought and Praxis*.

Elizabeth T. Murakami, Ph.D., is a Professor and Director of Programs in Educational Leadership in the College of Education and Human Development at Texas A&M San Antonio. She earned her Master's and Doctorate at Michigan State University. Her research focuses on successful school leadership and social justice at national and international levels, including research on leadership dynamics and identity, gender, race, and the academic success of Latin@ populations from P–20 to advanced professions in education. She is published in prestigious journals such as *Journal of School Leadership, Educational Management Administration and Leadership (EMAL), Journal of School Administration, Academe, Journal of Studies in Higher Education*, and the *International Journal of Qualitative Studies in Education*. Her latest co-edited book focuses on a social justice leadership agenda for P–20 professionals and is entitled *Educational Leaders Encouraging the Intellectual and Professional Capacity of Others: A Social Justice Agenda*. Email: Elizabeth.Murakami@tamusa.tamus.edu.

Anthony "Tony" H. Normore, Ph.D., holds a Doctorate in Educational Leadership and Policy Studies from the University of Toronto and is currently a Professor and Department Chair of Graduate Education at California State University Dominguez Hills. Other leadership experiences include Chair of Special Education; Co-Chair of Teacher Education; visiting professor at Seoul National University; Director of Doctoral Programs at California Lutheran University; visiting professor at Guelph/Humber; and a graduate professor for the Summer Leadership Academy at Teachers College–Columbia University. His 30-plus years of professional experiences have taken him throughout the world. His research focuses on urban school leadership development in the context of ethics and social justice, in which he has authored and edited numerous books, including *Inclusive Practices and Social Justice Leadership for Special Populations in Urban Settings* (Information Age, 2015); and *Cross-Cultural Collaboration and Leadership in Modern Organizations* (IGI Global, 2015). He has published a litany of book chapters and articles, and was the 2013 recipient of the Bridge People Award with the American Educational Research Association. He was recently appointed Chairman of the Criminal Justice Commission for the International Academy of Public Safety.

Anne-Marie Núñez, Ph.D., is an Associate Professor in the Educational Leadership and Policy Studies Department at the University of Texas at San Antonio (UTSA). Her award-winning research focuses on how to promote equity in postsecondary access and success, particularly for members of historically underserved groups, particularly Latino students. In 2014, she served as Program Chair for the Association for the Study of Higher Education (ASHE) annual conference. Her research has been published in several journals, including *Educational Researcher, Harvard Educational Review*, and the *American Educational Research Journal*. She is also the lead author of the book *Latinos in Higher Education and Hispanic-Serving Institutions: Creating Conditions for Success* (Jossey-Bass, 2013) and the lead editor of the book *Hispanic-Serving Institutions: Advancing Research and Transformative Practice* (Routledge, 2015). She holds a Ph.D. in Education from University of California Los Angeles, an M.Ed. in Education from Stanford University, and a B.A. in Social Studies from Harvard University.

Moragh Paxton, Ph.D., is Associate Professor in the Centre for Higher Education Development at the University of Cape Town. She has worked in the area of language and literacy development in institutions of higher education in South Africa, Australia, and Canada for the past 40 years. She was coordinator of the Language Development at UCT from 2004–2010. Her main research area is writing and she has used text-oriented ethnographic approaches to gain insights into the experiences and practices of a very diverse group of students at both undergraduate and postgraduate levels. In addition to being a member of the *First in the Family at University* project team, she currently leads the *Integrated Literacies for Learning in Science* project, which explores the teaching and learning of multimodal literacies in the earth and life sciences.

Tepora Pukepuke is undertaking doctoral studies at the University of Auckland. Her research tracks the pathways of Māori students from their first tertiary experience through to doctoral success. Her participant narratives capture the sparkling moments and academic milestones of student life that sustain and nurture their studies. Tepora brings together her work in Māori tertiary student support and her social work profession to identify exemplars of academic and pastoral doctoral support. She also hosts a range of e-learning forums under the branding @TeporaTeach. She sits comfortably in the embrace of her family with tribal affiliation to NgaiTuhoe and Whakatohea.

Sonia Rosado, Ed.D., is an Assistant Director of Residence Life at the University of California San Diego. She has trained her community on social justice topics, equity-mindedness, and diversity issues through workshops promoting the use of inclusive language and the understanding of LGBT, racial/ethnic, and multicultural identities. Rosado has taught a course on the role of cultural diversity in schools concentrating on achieving educational equity for all students. She continues to build communities through active participation in local and national conferences. Rosado is a Los Angeles native who attended the University of California Santa Cruz and graduated with a B.A. in Sociology. She later received an M.S. in Higher Education and Student Affairs highlighting Mentor and Protégé Relationships at Indiana University Bloomington. Recent publications include Dr. Rosado's dissertation (2011) titled *Browning the Rainbow: The Academic Persistence and Multiple Identities of Lesbian, Gay, Bisexual Latino/a Students.*

Kimberley Stiemke, Ed.D., currently serves as an academic faculty member in the Department of Academic Affairs at the University of Phoenix where she is transforming lives one student at a time. She holds membership in the prestigious Yale University Edward Alexander Bouchet Graduate Honor Society, and the esteemed University Council for Educational Administration Barbara L. Jackson Scholars Network. Dr. Stiemke earned her Ed.D. in Educational Leadership from the University of California San Diego and California State University San Marcos. She completed her B.S. and M.S.T. degrees at Clark Atlanta University. Her research interests include leadership in higher education, equity and access in education, and the relevance of program curricula as it pertains to student (dis) engagement. Through her leadership and advocacy in local nonprofit organizations, Dr. Stiemke supports the growth and development of San Diego County's youth. She is the proud mother of Kevin, Khalil, and Kaycee, and wife of Kevin.

Gregory J. Toya, Ed.D., currently is the Director of Student Development at El Camino College. Greg previously served as the Associate Dean of Students and Interim Associate Dean of Student Life and Leadership at California State University San Marcos (CSUSM), the inaugural Coordinator of the Cross-Cultural Center at San Diego State University and the Interim Director and Assistant Director for the Cross-Cultural Center and Lesbian, Gay, Bisexual and Transgender Resource Center (LGBTRC) at the University of California Davis. Greg's student affairs career commenced in residential life at the University of California Irvine, University of California Berkeley, and the University of Maryland. Greg earned a bachelor's degree in Social Ecology from the University of California Irvine, a Master's degree in Counseling and Student Development from the University of Maryland, and a Doctorate in Educational Leadership from the University of California San Diego and CSUSM.

Natalie A. Tran, Ph.D., holds a Doctorate in Educational Leadership and Policy Analysis from the University of Wisconsin and is currently Associate Professor in the College of Education at California State University Fullerton. Dr.

Tran's research focuses on evaluating the effectiveness of curriculum and services related to science, technology, engineering, and mathematics (STEM) education and examining factors that affect students' learning experiences both in the classroom and out-of-school settings. Her other research interests include integrating the practice of mindfulness in K–12 classrooms and exploring issues related to diversity in higher education. These areas align with her methodological research interests, which include hierarchical linear modeling, experimental design, quasi-experimental design, and survey studies. Natalie received her Master of Education in Education and her Bachelor of Science in Psychobiology from the University of California Los Angeles.

Shaun Travers, Ed.D., is a Campus Diversity Officer and Director of the Lesbian Gay Bisexual Transgender Resource Center at the University of California San Diego. His current practice and leadership involves a deep understanding of intersectionality, power, privilege, oppression, and the dynamic tension inherent in university environments. Dr. Travers currently serves on the Board of Directors for the San Diego LGBT Community Center, the Executive Committee of the National Consortium of Lesbian Gay Bisexual Transgender Resource Professionals in Higher Education, and chairs the San Diego LGBT Community Leadership Council. He received a Psychology and Theatre degree from California Lutheran University, a Master of Science in Education from Indiana University, and a Doctorate in Education from a joint program between the University of California San Diego, San Diego State University, and California State University San Marcos.

Edwina F. Welch, Ed.D., serves as a Campus Diversity Officer and Director of the University of California San Diego Cross-Cultural Center. Dr. Welch works with students, staff, and faculty on issues of social justice, diversity, and campus climate for the campus and the surrounding San Diego community. Her current research areas include social justice, leadership, organizational capacity building, and cultural competence. Edwina has been involved in training, speaking, and evaluating diversity and social justice programs at other campuses and universities. She has been an adjunct professor at California State University San Marcos, teaching courses on research methodology, as well as diversity in K–12 education. Edwina received her B.A. in Communication Studies and Business Administration from California State University Sacramento, her Master of Science in Higher Education Administration from the University of Oregon, and her Doctorate in Educational Leadership from the Joint Doctoral Program between the University of California San Diego, San Diego State University, and California State University San Marcos.

'Ema Wolfgramm-Foliaki, Ph.D., is currently a Lecturer at the Centre for Learning and Research in Higher Education (CLeaR) at the University of Auckland,

New Zealand, where her main role is to work with staff to develop inclusive teaching pedagogies to meet the needs of the diverse student population. She is of Tongan descent and her current research work includes examining the educational journey of First in the Family students in higher education and how Pacific Island students experience graduate supervision. Like the students whose personal narratives are represented in Chapter 9 of this volume, she too was the first in her family to study at university. Since gaining her Doctorate from the University of Auckland, 'Ema has worked as a learning academic adviser within the Library and Learning Services at the University of Auckland.

Colleen Young, Ph.D., is a research assistant and Lecturer at the University of Auckland. Colleen's academic interests are in mixed-methods research, including evaluation utilizing the program logic conceptual framework, student success initiatives leading to seamless transitions from secondary school to postsecondary institutions and finally into gainful employment, community partnerships, and access and equity for underserved youth.

Miguel Zavala, Ph.D., is Associate Professor in the College of Educational Studies (CES) at Chapman University. He has been engaged in grassroots organizing since 2005 and is current Chair of the Los Angeles Regional Network of the California chapter of the National Association for Multicultural Education (CA-NAME). His research interests center on youth participatory action-research and learning in grassroots spaces. He uses a Chicana/o standpoint theory rooted in Indigenous epistemologies together with decolonizing frameworks in the study and generation of pedagogical and community projects.

INDEX